# Jane Austen
## Inside Her Novels

Matthew Coniam

# Important Dates

**1775** Jane Austen is born in Steventon, Hampshire (16 December).

**1785–86** Jane and her sister Cassandra attend the Abbey School, Reading.

**1787** Jane begins writing her *Juvenilia* (completed in 1793).

**1794** Writes *Lady Susan*.

**1795** Writes *Elinor and Marianne* (the first version of *Sense and Sensibility*). Jane begins aborted flirtation with Tom Lefroy in December; he leaves for London the following January and never sees Jane again.

**1796** Begins writing *First Impressions* (the first version of *Pride and Prejudice*).

**1797** Completes *First Impressions* and begins converting *Elinor and Marianne* into *Sense and Sensibility*. Jane's father attempts unsuccessfully to place *First Impressions* with publisher Cadell.

**1798** Begins writing *Susan* (later retitled *Northanger Abbey*).

**1801** Jane's father retires; the Austens leave Steventon and move to Bath.

**1802** Harris Bigg-Wither proposes marriage to Jane; she accepts but then changes her mind the following day.

**1803** Jane sells *Susan* to publisher Crosby of London, but it is never published.

**1805** Jane's father dies in Bath.

**1806** Jane, her mother and sister leave Bath for Hampshire.

**1809** Jane, her mother and sister move into Chawton Cottage. Jane begins to write again.

**1811** *Sense and Sensibility* is published. Jane starts writing *Mansfield Park* and begins revising *First Impressions* into *Pride and Prejudice*.

**1813** *Pride and Prejudice* is published. *Mansfield Park* is completed.

**1814** Begins writing *Emma*. *Mansfield Park* is published.

**1815** Begins writing *Persuasion*. *Emma* is published.

**1816** Jane's brother Henry, acting as her literary manager, buys back copyright of *Susan* and Jane begins revising it into what will become *Northanger Abbey*. *Persuasion* is completed. The first signs of Jane's illness become apparent.

**1817** Now seriously unwell, Jane begins work on what will become *Sanditon*. It is never completed. Jane dies, probably of Addison's disease, on 18 July and is buried in Winchester Cathedral. *Persuasion* and *Northanger Abbey* are published in December.

# ❧ Introduction ☙

When the BBC mounted a poll in 2003 to discover Britain's most popular novel, Jane Austen's Pride and Prejudice reached second place. In a similar survey conducted in 2007, it came first. In lists dominated by works from the 20th century and later, these results underlined the unique status Jane continues to enjoy as a writer, some two centuries after her death.

More than merely secure in her critical reputation, she is also truly popular with readers, to a degree comparable with no other author of her era. Aided by a seemingly endless series of profitable sequels, spin-offs and TV and cinema adaptations of her works, her wit, wisdom and sparkling characterisation recruit legions of admirers from every successive generation.

She lived quietly, drawing her study of human nature and emotion from her own experiences, and those of the people she knew and interacted with. Her six major novels, two of them published posthumously, were at most providers of only modest reward and acclaim. But as all her fans know, they remain among the acutest sources of psychological perception in all literature.

*A 2016 portrait of Jane Austen, commissioned by the Jane Austen Centre in Bath. Its inspiration was a waxwork of Jane, itself created from the forensic portrait seen on p31.*

# ꙅ A Writer's Life ꙅ

Jane Austen was born in Steventon, Hampshire, on 16 December 1775, the seventh child of the Reverend George Austen and his wife Cassandra. Cassandra was also the name of the family's other daughter, two years Jane's senior, who would be Jane's closest friend and companion throughout her life.

Georgian society was ill-provisioned for the education of girls, whose natural role was, it was presumed, to become wives, mothers and housekeepers. As such, the teaching they received placed priority on needlework, music, drawing and the social graces. Jane's enlightened father, however, believed that she was entitled to as complete an education as his sons, and tutored her personally.

Jane was already beginning to write by the age of ten, and thanks to her father's excellent library, reading and learning became two of her biggest passions. These preoccupations are reflected in her novels, which centre their drama on the limited choices available to women in Georgian society. Education, therefore, is not a mere acquisition, to be displayed like excellent manners or a beautiful singing voice, but rather a means of independence, the source of discernment, and an invaluable guide to the moral and personal choices that every individual has to make.

At first, Jane wrote pastiches and parodies of the works of the other writers to whom she was being introduced, but it wasn't long before she settled upon the unique style in which she would achieve greatness as a writer. In this she was aided by her own circumstances and social station. Despite a number of flirtations, and one serious proposal,

*A portrait of Jane's father, the Rev. George Austen.*

*The Church of St Nicholas in Steventon, where Jane's father was the rector.*

*A Regency-era family.*

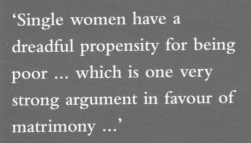

*The only contemporary portrait in existence of Jane Austen, adapted from a pencil and watercolour drawing by Jane's sister, Cassandra, in 1810.*

Jane never married. Though left at considerable financial risk as a consequence, she was nonetheless freed from the burden of running a household and tending to the needs of a husband and family, giving her more time to write.

Further, as an unattached person, she was better able to mix freely in society and cultivate those habits of keen and subtle observation of human behaviour that informed the penetrating psychological insight of her mature writings.

Due to her father's role as rector, Jane encountered both the upper classes – at glittering balls and social functions – and the lower. She was therefore able to study the full panorama of 18th-century society, and this, combined with her wit, intelligence and literary style, set her on her future course.

# The Juvenilia

I n his 'Biographical Notice' that appeared with the first posthumous edition of *Persuasion* and *Northanger Abbey*, Jane's brother Henry wrote that 'Neither the hope of fame nor profit mixed with her early motives'. Intentionally or not, this sense of Austen as one who wrote for the amusement of herself and her family and friends – a spinster whose writing was essentially a pastime – took root thereafter and remains widely held.

The reality is that Jane took her work very seriously, was in no doubt as to its merit, and almost from the first set her sights upon publication. In that sense, the works she created between 1787 and 1793, now known as her Juvenilia, were not frivolities, but a conscious training for the writer's life. She collected them in three notebooks labelled Volume the First, Second and Third, in deliberate emulation of a published work.

Not yet informed by her gift for subtle characterisation, these 'childish effusions' (as her nephew Edward later described them in his Memoir of Jane Austen) are exercises in manner and form, and as Edward also noted, 'quite free from the over-ornamental style which might be expected from so young a writer'. They are energetic and wide-ranging, and clearly display an already keen intelligence and awareness of life and custom.

*Fanny Burney (b.1752) paved the way for Jane Austen. Like Jane she observed and wrote about society and had a sharp wit. She had two novels published, the first anonymously, again like Jane.*

*Jane sat at this writing table to pen her novels and other stories.*

Her History of England ('By a Partial, Prejudiced and Ignorant Historian') was dedicated to and illustrated by Cassandra, and filled with in-jokes designed to amuse her family. Jane describes one of the volumes as 'Effusions of Fancy by a very Young Lady Consisting of Tales in a Style entirely new'. Cassandra's illustrations depict figures from all eras of history in contemporary dress, and Jane's text makes overt the personal prejudices that other historians might attempt to obscure: 'my principal reason in undertaking this History of England,' she wrote, was 'to prove the innocence of the Queen of Scotland, which I flatter myself with having eventually done, and to abuse Elizabeth.'

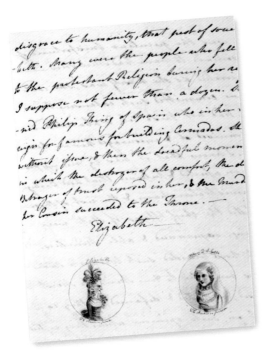

Cassandra's original medallion portraits of Queen Elizabeth and Mary, Queen of Scots in Jane's History of England (Volume the Second), c.1790–93.

'Ah! What could we do but what we did! We sighed and fainted on the sofa.'

Laura, *Love and Freindship*

There is a great deal of parody and broad humour in these early pieces, but also some clear signs of the writer Jane would eventually become. Lesley Castle, The Three Sisters and Love and Freindship – all written in the fashionable epistolary style in which the later Lady Susan and Elinor and Marianne, her original version of Sense and Sensibility, were also composed – are social satires that reveal a keen eye for human foibles and frailties. Despite their broad humour and obvious parody, they anticipate her mature novels with their intimate settings and emphasis on the rituals of courtship and conduct.

Jane liked to write about romance and courtship.

# *Northanger Abbey*

What should have been Jane's first published novel was in fact her last (issued jointly with *Persuasion* after her death in 1817). Originally titled *Susan*, it was begun in 1798, completed some time after, and then revised in the winter of 1802 and 1803. That same year it became the first of her novels to be accepted for publication. Copyright was sold to the publisher Richard Crosby for the sum of £10, and the book was advertised as forthcoming. For no clear reason, however, it never appeared, and Jane's enquiries as to its fate were met only with the surly assurance that she could reassert her copyright over

*In a letter to her sister Cassandra, dated 24 January 1813, Jane discusses what she and her mother are reading.*

*An original sketch of Jane's heroine, Catherine Morland, in* Northanger Abbey. *(Austen-Leigh Archive: 23M93/64/6/1)*

'The person, gentleman or lady who has not pleasure in a good novel must be intolerably stupid.'

*Henry Tilney,* Northanger Abbey

it for the return of the originally paid sum. This her brother Henry eventually did on her behalf in 1816, after her later novels had achieved significant success. Crosby had failed to realise the value of the property he had owned all that time.

There is a double irony in the book's late appearance in that not only was it chronologically the first of the six main novels, it is also clearly the first in spirit and style: lighter, more mischievous, and very much the work of a young woman announcing herself and finding her feet as a novelist. It is a book about books, and it shares with the *Juvenilia* a desire to spoof the fashionable literature of the age, in this case the Gothic novel.

The book's heroine, Catherine Morland, is a naive, idealistic young woman, addicted to the pleasures of reading romances. One of several children of a rural clergyman (like her creator), she is 'noisy and wild', neither beautiful nor accomplished, and little diverted by the genteel pursuits commonly reserved for young ladies. We are told that she 'greatly preferred cricket' to 'the more heroic enjoyments of infancy, nursing a dormouse, feeding a canary-bird, or watering a rose-bush'.

The novel follows Catherine's first immersion into the social world of fashionable Bath, her head filled with the dramatic episodes of Matthew Lewis's *The Monk* and Ann Radcliffe's *Mysteries of Udolpho*.

'The mess-room will drink Isabella Thorpe for a fortnight': an original illustration in Northanger Abbey by Hugh Thomson.

She soon believes herself to be in the middle of her own Gothic adventure, fashioning a sinister mystery from the ultimately explicable events she experiences as a guest of Henry Tilney – the man she will eventually marry – and his volatile father at their imposing ancestral home. At the end, a chastened Catherine concedes that romantic fiction may not be the best training for the experiences of real life.

As well as being a good-natured spoof of the Gothic novel, the book is also a defence of fiction and the fiction-reading habit. And such a defence was very much needed: novels were commonly demonised as a trivialising or even corrupting force, encouraging slovenliness and idle fantasy. (Jane once described her family in a letter as 'great novel-readers, and not ashamed of being so'.) In particular, as a female reader and a female author, Jane felt compelled to make a case for her art, and so interlaced within the novel's broader narrative is a wealth of subtle detail in what may now be seen as the pure Austen style.

The story of Catherine's growth as a young woman – as she learns who can and cannot be trusted, and determines which considerations are important and which trivial – displays for the first time Jane's gift for the ironic observation of social convention and personal interaction, along with a fully developed epigrammatic wit. We discover Jane's views on love and marriage, vanity and hypocrisy, a person's obligations to others, and the vagaries of the human heart. In this respect, the book reads as her calling card as a novelist, an announcement of the more serious works to follow.

*Bath was the setting for* Northanger Abbey.

Northanger Abbey *revolves around books.*

# Sense and Sensibility

*S*ense and Sensibility was the first of Jane's novels to be published. Her name did not appear on the title page (the credit read simply 'by a lady') and she was so sure that it would not be a success that she set aside funds from her small income to cover the loss. (The book was published at the author's expense, which was common practice at that time.) 'I can no more forget it than a mother can forget her sucking child,' Jane wrote to Cassandra as the book was being prepared for printing.

The first draft had been completed in 1795 under the title *Elinor and Marianne*, but it had been completely revised by the time it finally appeared under its more familiar title in 1811. The gap between the two dates encompassed many of the most important events of Jane's life: a possibly significant flirtation with a young man and a disastrous proposal of marriage; the momentary excitement of having *Susan* accepted for publication followed swiftly by the disappointment of its non-appearance; her move to Bath and the subsequent death of her father there, precipitating the family's return to Hampshire. In the quiet and simplicity of Chawton Cottage, Jane again found the creative inspiration that had been stifled in the bustle and distraction of Bath. The publication of *Sense and Sensibility*, therefore, was vindication as well as triumph and it heralded the busiest years of Jane's professional life.

The book swaps the literary satire of *Northanger Abbey* for social satire, and in sisters Elinor and Marianne Dashwood introduces the first of Austen's great heroines. Marianne, the younger of the two, is naive, impulsive and allows her heart to rule her head; in consequence, her infatuation with the dashing but unreliable Mr Willoughby ends in profound disappointment. Elinor, the elder, is restrained, pragmatic and tactful, and we begin the novel – guided by Jane's voice as

> 'What have wealth or grandeur to do with happiness?'
>
> *Marianne Dashwood,*
> *Sense and Sensibility*

*A 19th-century edition of* Sense and Sensibility.

*Chawton Cottage in Hampshire, where Jane wrote most of her novels.*

narrator – assuming that her outlook and conduct are to be preferred, while Marianne's experiences warn of the dangers of unfettered honesty.

As the novel progresses, however, a note of ambiguity creeps in; we come to see value in Marianne's intuitiveness and watch Elinor's reticence lead her just as surely towards romantic disappointment. As the two sisters arrive at the recognition of their own errors and the other's strengths, the reader comes likewise to a compromise between the two, recognising them almost as the two essential halves of a single personality.

In this we see how Jane was intent on advancing her art with each new work. The basic plot of *Sense and Sensibility*, with its wicked mothers, caddish seducers and designing women, may seem as formulaic as that of its predecessor, but the book's emotional power is vastly the greater. This time Austen is using such elements not as ends in themselves, but as the means to make potent universal observations about human nature, frailty, pretension and self-deception. In this sense, it makes fully the argument on behalf of the novel as a true art form that *Northanger Abbey* could only call out for.

*A sketch of Marianne Dashwood by Laurie C. Conley.*

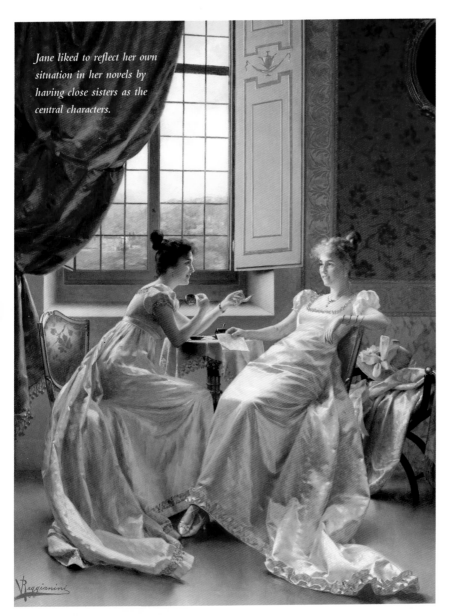

*Jane liked to reflect her own situation in her novels by having close sisters as the central characters.*

Today, it is easy to forget the radical importance of the novel in terms of its potential for psychological description. Even the subtlest and profoundest works written for the theatre can only hint at the inner lives of their characters, just as in life the only people we know completely are ourselves. The novelist, however, has a unique licence to provide a true psychological portrait of all their characters, and to show the extent to which

*The fireplace at Chawton Cottage.*

our internal self is at odds with the external – with the choices we make and the version of ourselves we present to others. In *Sense and Sensibility* Austen shows herself to be a true genius of the art, leaving far behind the sensation novels that *Northanger Abbey* had so amusingly parodied and establishing instead the notion of the novel as scalpel – a precision tool for the cutting away of artifice and deception, and the revelation of our interior reality.

Jane had confessed the secret of her authorship to few; even some members of her extended family were kept in the dark. However, the book sold well from the first, aided by two positive reviews and notices in the London press, and quickly went into profit. Her brother Henry later recalled: 'She could scarcely believe what she termed her great good fortune, when *Sense and Sensibility* produced a clear profit of about £150. Few so gifted were so truly unpretending.'

It is unnerving to speculate what might, or might not, have happened had it proved a failure. More than just financial reward, the success of the novel gave Jane reassurance that she had indeed found her calling. Though she had but six years remaining to live, an almost unceasing stream of great work would now flow from her pen.

*Emma Thompson played Elinor Dashwood and Hugh Grant played Edward Ferrars in the 1995 film adaptation of* Sense and Sensibility.

*The ballroom scenes in the 1995 film adaptation were filmed at Wilton House in Wiltshire.*

# Pride and Prejudice

In August 1797, Jane completed a new novel that she had titled *First Impressions*. As was her custom, she read it aloud to her family, who all agreed it was her best work yet. Consequently, her father took it upon himself to offer it to London publisher Thomas Cadell. 'As I am well aware of what consequence it is that a work of this sort should make its first appearance under a respectable name,' he wrote, 'I apply to you.' But Cadell declined the offer. Finally published in 1813 in a revised form and under the new title *Pride and Prejudice*, the book that Jane called 'my own darling child' immediately found favour. It remains her most popular work, and one of the most acclaimed and beloved novels ever written.

Again, the drama revolves around two sisters – Elizabeth and Jane Bennet – though this time, like Jane and Cassandra, they have a large number of other siblings, all of whom we are allowed to get to know as the novel progresses. (Unlike the Austens, however, the Bennet siblings are all girls.) For many,

Lizzy Bennet is Jane's most delightful heroine, and in the character of Fitzwilliam Darcy she created her most enduring romantic hero.

At the heart of *Pride and Prejudice* is a very simple love story of the 'I hated him but now I love him' school, as can be found in countless romantic novels then and since.

What distinguishes this one, and marks it as truly great, is the detail, the depth of its insight and the

*An original pencil sketch of Jane's heroine, Elizabeth Bennet. (Austen-Leigh Archive: 23M93/64/6/1)*

*An 1894 cover of* Pride and Prejudice.

*Balls often feature in Jane Austen's novels and indeed, it is at a ball that Jane and Elizabeth Bennet meet their future husbands.*

breadth of its observation. There is a large cast of characters, none of whom is merely there to take up space or to advance the plot without first making some kind of mark upon the reader. Each is invested with characteristics that the reader immediately recognises – either in themselves or in others – and the dialogue is witty and convincing.

The novel's guiding sentiment seems to be that which Jane herself expressed in an 1814 letter to her niece Fanny: 'Anything is to be preferred or endured rather than marrying without affection.' Recurring throughout Austen's work is this theme of the choices we make; she contrasts the satisfaction of a good match with the torment of one entered

*Jennifer Ehle and Colin Firth starred in the ultimate TV adaptation of* Pride and Prejudice *in 1995.*

burgeoning affection was cut short by Lefroy's family, who were concerned by Jane's unsuitability as a match. The popular book and film *Becoming Jane* elaborates upon the known facts to portray it as a serious romance, the unhappy ending of which directly informed much of Jane's later work. 'At length the day is come when I am to flirt my last with Tom Lefroy, and when you receive this it will be over,' Jane wrote to Cassandra in 1796. 'My tears flow as I write, at the melancholy idea.'

Whatever really happened on that occasion, there is no doubt as to the consequence of the

*Jane Bennet wins over Mr Bingley.*

*A gentleman whose eyes looked as if they saw no one else*

*Burghley House in Lincolnshire was the stunning setting for the much-acclaimed Rosings, residence of the haughty Lady Catherine de Bourgh, in the 2005 film adaptation.*

proposal of marriage she received in November 1802 from Harris Bigg-Wither, the brother of three of her childhood friends. Jane rashly accepted the offer and then, after a night of intense deliberation, declined in the morning. Bigg-Wither was heir to a substantial estate, and had Jane married him she would have been financially secure for the rest of her days – but it is unlikely she would have written another novel. That, perhaps, was the dilemma, as much as the simple fact that there was no bond of love between them.

*Pride and Prejudice* abounds with bad matches eagerly sought, narrowly avoided and stoically endured, as well as good ones impeded by the objections of others. Lizzy's sister Lydia elopes with the disreputable Mr Wickham, to whom Lizzy is also briefly attracted. Mr Darcy intervenes to curtail the pairing of Jane Bennet and his friend Mr Bingley; and

'Vanity and pride are different things, though the words are often used synonymously. A person may be proud without being vain. Pride relates more to our opinion of ourselves; vanity to what we would have others think of us.'

*Mary Bennet, Pride and Prejudice*

PRIDE AND PREJUDICE.

*She then told him what Mr Darcy had voluntarily done for Lydia. He heard her with astonishment*

London Published by Richard Bentley 1833.

Lizzy herself rejects two proposals in the book, the first from the buffoonish Mr Collins. We can perhaps see something of Jane's musing on the fate she herself avoided when Lizzy's friend Charlotte accepts Mr Collins in a loveless marriage of convenience: 'I am not a romantic you know,' Charlotte explains, 'I ask only for a comfortable home.'

Lizzy's second proposal, of course, comes from the arrogant and objectionable Darcy himself, though as all readers know, the consequence of that is altogether different, and happier, when he swallows his pride and asks again.

*An 1833 illustration depicting the moment Elizabeth Bennet tells her father of the truth about Fitzwilliam Darcy.*

# Mansfield Park

For many, *Mansfield Park* is Jane Austen's most perfectly accomplished novel, but there is no question that its seriousness of tone, and the pious respectability of its heroine, can surprise those readers expecting the lightness, wit and romance of *Pride and Prejudice* or *Emma*. Among Jane's immediate family, and the friends upon whom she relied for a frank and honest opinion, it was generally felt that the book, though excellent, was not quite up to the standard of its predecessor. Most of the usual ingredients are there, but there are fewer broad comic strokes, and a more concerted effort to draw moral distinctions between the attitudes and behaviour of her characters.

Fanny – perhaps named for the daughter of her brother Edward, the favourite of her many nieces – is easily the most uncompromising and least flawed of Austen's lead characters, whose integrity and rightness of attitude never falter. With the earlier heroines, we tend to see personalities that journey through experience from naivety, impulsiveness or triviality towards maturity. But Fanny is *Mansfield Park*'s fixed point, and it is those around her that change and reach maturity under her subtle but pervasive influence (or are undone for the want of it).

She is also timid, her strength of character being, as it were, held in reserve for most of the novel and confided only to the reader, who is thus put in the pleasant position of being able to chide the

*'She watched them till they had turned a corner.' Jane's heroine, Fanny Price, gets left behind by Edmund, the man she loves, and the bewitching Mary Crawford.*

> 'Selfishness must always be forgiven you know, because there is no hope of a cure.'
>
> Mary Crawford, *Mansfield Park*

other characters for not observing in her what is so obvious to us. Unlike Jane's other heroines, she does not speak fluently, wittily, or even very often. As a consequence, while many readers adore Fanny, others can find her rigid, dull and overbearing.

By contrast, it is in the generally disruptive character of Mary Crawford, who almost comes between Fanny and her true love Edmund, that we find much of the wit, imagination and audacity that Jane usually places centre stage (and which we find in many of her own letters and observations). We arrive at the curious conclusion that, while Fanny herself thoroughly disapproves of Mary, Jane's own feelings are more ambivalent. As in *Sense and*

*The heroine Fanny Price writes a letter, in an illustration by H.M. Brock in 1898. Henry Brock also illustrated works by Charles Dickens and Arthur Conan Doyle; his elder brother Charles illustrated Austen's books as well and is the better-known artist.*

*The Knight family lands in Hampshire that Jane's brother Edward was to inherit. The map, compiled in 1771, shows Chawton House and church, and, on the road to Alton, the cottage that was to become Jane Austen's house. At this date the cottage was an inn. (Knight Archive: 39M89/E/B384/1, courtesy of Richard Knight)*

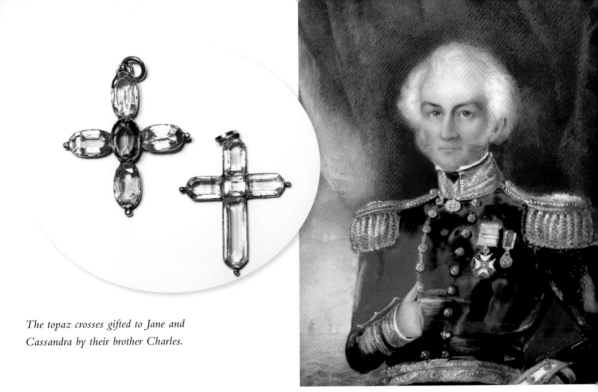

The topaz crosses gifted to Jane and Cassandra by their brother Charles.

Jane's brother Charles, an officer in the Royal Navy.

*Sensibility*, we get the feeling that maybe in the two women we are in fact seeing two halves of a single whole, and this time, perhaps, of Jane herself.

As if to confirm such notions, the book incorporates several echoes of Jane's own life and childhood. Fanny being uprooted at the age of ten from her modest surroundings, and sent to live at Mansfield Park among the family of her rich relative Sir Thomas Bertram, seems to evoke the fate of Jane's brother Edward, who at the age of 16 was adopted by the wealthy Thomas Knight – who lacked an heir – and came in line to inherit his estates in Hampshire and Kent.

A scene in which the family enact a play for their own amusement, only to be sternly rebuked by Sir Thomas, recalls the theatricals Jane's brothers would stage in the barn opposite the rectory. Also, the moment in which Fanny's brother returns from the Navy with a gift of a cross necklace for her is inspired by an identical gesture made to Jane and Cassandra by their brother Charles. Purchased with part of his reward for capturing an enemy privateer, Charles's gesture

prompted Jane to write to Cassandra: 'He must be well scolded.'

*Mansfield Park* was published in May 1814 and, despite receiving no reviews in contemporary newspapers or journals, proved popular. By November the first edition had entirely sold out, yielding Jane £350 in royalties – her largest profit from a single work.

Though Jane could never in her dreams have imagined the full and ultimate extent of her popularity and acclaim, she was nonetheless by now finding herself, in a modest way, something of a celebrity. One might imagine her rising to the moment and deriving both pleasure and a store of new material from the situation. Part of her no doubt would have relished it – the part we see reflected in the character of Mary Crawford, perhaps.

However, when confronted with the reality of literary fame, it was the impulses we would more associate with Fanny that asserted themselves. Her brother Henry recalled an encounter 'on a visit to London soon after the publication of Mansfield Park', in which 'a nobleman, personally unknown to her, but who had good reasons for considering her to be the authoress of that work, was desirous of her joining a literary circle at his house'. Even though he 'communicated his wish in the politest manner', Jane 'immediately declined' his overtures. 'To her truly delicate mind,' Henry concluded, 'such a display would have given pain instead of pleasure.'

*A theatre playbill for* Lovers Vows, *which was performed at Winchester's theatre in 1809 and was included in the plot of* Mansfield Park. *Jane may very well have seen this production. (Hampshire Chronicle Archive: 3A00W/E14)*

### WINCHESTER THEATRE.

By Desire and under the Patronage of several LADIES and GENTLEMEN.

FOR THE BENEFIT OF

## Mrs. SMITH, Mr. GILBERT, and Mrs. BARRE.

On Friday Evening, *August* 11, 1809,

Will be presented the favourite Comedy, called

# LOVERS VOWS.

| Baron Wildenheim, Mr. TAYLOR. | Anhalt, Mr. KELLY. |
| Count Cassell, - Mr. HORTON. | Frederick, Mr. MAXFIELD. |
| Landlord, - Mr. MORGAN. | Cottager, - Mr. GILL. |
| Farmer, - Mr. YOUNG. | Countryman, - Mr. MARDIN. |
| Verdun, (the Rhiming Butler) Mr. GILBERT. | |

Agatha Friburg, Mrs. BRERETON.—Amelia Wildenhaim, Mrs BARRE.
Cottager's Wife, Miss DOWNER—Country Girl, Mrs. MAXFIELD.
End of the Play, (for this night only;) Mrs. BARRE will recite Collins's celebrated

"ODE ON THE PASSIONS,"

With appropriate Music.

After the Play, the following Entertainments.

Two entire New Comic Songs by Mr. GILBERT,
"John Bull in Town." or " British Wool for Ever."
"What a Beauty I did grow."

The three following Songs, by Mrs. SMITH,
"The Poor Baby's Hush-a-bye,"
" Remember when we walked alone,"
" White Man never go away."
" Jemmy Linkum Feedie," by Mr. FLOYER.

To conclude with, by Desire the favourite Comic Opera, called

# Inkle and Yarico.

| Inkle, Mr. HORTON.—Trudge, Mr. FLOYER.—Sir Christopher, Mr. GILBERT. |
| Captain Campley, Mr. MARDIN.—Mate, Mr. Maxfield.—Medium, Mr. GILL. |
| Sailors, Messrs. Kerr and Morgan. |
| Wouski, Mrs. SMITH. | Narcissa, Miss DOWNER. | Patty, Mrs. MAXFIELD. |
| Yarico, Mrs. BARRE. |

Tickets to be had of Mrs. SMITH, at Mr. KERBOY's, near the Black Swan—Mrs. BARRE, at Mr. Bruce's,
Upper-brook-street ;—Mr. GILBERT, Mr. DEACON's, Grocer, near the Market ; and at the Libraries.

JAMES ROBBINS, Printer, Winchester.

'The Great House and Park at Chawton', painted by Adam Callander, c.1780. Chawton House was built c.1583–91, was owned by the Knight family and was lived in by Jane Austen.

# Emma

In stark contrast to the prim and precise Fanny, Austen's next novel showcased what she described as 'a heroine whom no one but myself will much like'. Emma Woodhouse – 'handsome, clever, and rich' – is alternately (and even simultaneously) likeable and infuriating, and is the first of Jane's leading female characters to possess all she requires in terms of social and financial advantage. As a result of this, she spends much of her time meddling in the affairs of others, using her own entirely unrealistic standards to advise disastrously on the romantic lives of her friends and acquaintants.

Though whimsical, Emma's behaviour almost leads to serious distress, as when, in one of the novel's most famous scenes, her glib wit causes pain to both the reader and the characters when she offhandedly insults the poor and hopeless Miss Bates. But she is also sincere and intelligent, a loving daughter, and solicitous to the sick and needy. It is almost as if Jane had finally set her mind to focusing, in one complex personality, the attributes she had often shared among contrasting pairs, such as Elinor and Marianne or Fanny and Mary Crawford.

Amusingly, Emma is fully as resolute, and concerned with always doing and being seen to be doing the right thing, as Fanny had been, but with the difference that her certainties tend to be proved wrong. The result is a novel that combines serious themes with some of Jane's most effortlessly fine comedy. Emma's slow journey towards the realisation that family friend

*An original pencil sketch of the heroine, Emma Woodhouse. (Austen-Leigh Archive: 23M93/64/6/1)*

*First edition copies of* Emma.

*Gwyneth Paltrow and Jeremy Northam star as Emma and Mr Knightley in the 1996 film adaptation.*

Mr Knightley is the man she loves, and furthermore is also very much in love with her, makes for one of the most satisfyingly developed romance plots in the entire Austen canon.

As ever there are autobiographical echoes: as the daughter of a country parson, Jane would have visited the poor and sick of the parish with donations of food and clothing, just as Emma does. Jane further drew on her experience of attending a girls' boarding school to describe the school in Highbury where Emma meets her friend Harriet, on whom she works her well-meant but destructive mischief. There is also an interesting twist on the now-recurring theme of the turned-down proposal: unlike Lizzy's rejection of the unctuous Mr Collins, and Fanny's of the frivolous Henry Crawford, Harriet's decision, under Emma's influence, to spurn

the hand of the farmer Robert Martin is shown to be ill-advised and is eventually corrected.

Completed in March 1815, the novel was published by the famous John Murray, but with a catch: the £450 he offered Jane was also to include the copyright of *Mansfield Park* and *Sense and Sensibility*. Jane's brother Henry, who oversaw her literary affairs, intervened on her behalf, telling Murray that his offer was 'so very inferior to what we had expected that I am apprehensive of having made some great error in my arithmetical calculation' – but without success.

A surprising development occurred before publication. Henry, having fallen ill with what seemed for a while to be a grave ailment, was being cared for by a physician who also tended the Prince Regent. The Prince was, he confided, a considerable

> 'Better be without sense than misapply it as you do.'
>
> *Mr Knightley, Emma*

*In the novel, Emma performs her duties by visiting the poor and sick.*

*It was at first a considerable shock to him*
*Chapter LIII*

*Emma tells her father the unexpected news that she is to marry Mr Knightley.*

fan of Miss Austen's work. As a result, she was invited to a private audience with Mr Clarke, the Prince's librarian, who told her she was 'at liberty' to dedicate her forthcoming work to the Prince. At first taking him at his word, Jane paid little heed to the suggestion, until it was explained to her that 'at liberty' essentially meant 'was obliged'.

Accordingly, the novel appeared with the note that it was 'most respectfully dedicated' to the Prince Regent, by 'his dutiful and obedient humble servant, the author'. To Mr Clarke's other suggestions, however, Jane was less amenable. Suggesting that she turn her attentions to a historical epic, she replied with a flattering refusal that doubled as a proud assertion of her true gifts and value:

'You are very, very kind in your hints as to the sort of composition which might recommend me at present, and I am fully sensible that an historical romance founded on the House of Saxe Cobourg might be much more to the purpose of profit or popularity than such pictures of domestic life in country villages that I deal in … No – I must keep to my own style and go in my own way, and though I may never succeed again in that, I am convinced that I should totally fail in any other.'

Jane could take reassurance from the fact that the book proved another success on publication, with readers on the whole taking her quixotic and often downright annoying heroine to their hearts. By that time, however, she had already embarked upon her next work, which would prove altogether more sombre and poignant in tone. It would also be her last.

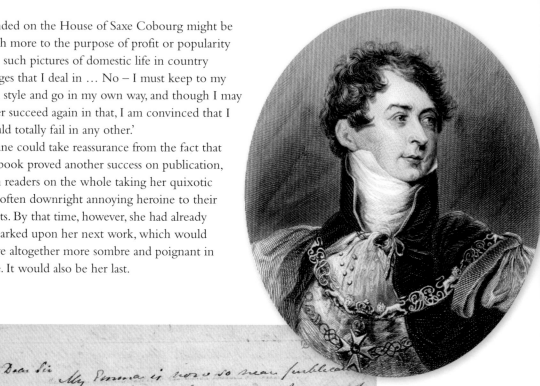

*Jane was compelled to dedicate* Emma *to the Prince Regent, the future George IV.*

*In a letter dated 11 December 1815 Jane talks about her latest novel,* Emma, *to Rev. James Stanier Clarke, the Prince Regent's librarian.*

# Persuasion

'I have a something ready for publication,' Jane wrote to her niece Fanny in March 1816. The 'something' was the story of Anne Elliot who, seven years before the novel begins, had accepted a proposal of marriage from Frederick Wentworth, a young naval officer. But Anne's family, mindful of his lack of fortune and connection, had persuaded her to break it off. A series of chance events bring Wentworth back into her life, and with them the prospect of putting right the wrong decision that has haunted her ever since.

*Persuasion* was a shift in direction after the playfulness of *Emma*. Gone are the flighty young girls and taciturn men upon whom the previous novels were focused, and in their place are two older, more deeply etched and potentially tragic figures. Unlike *Emma*, who wishes to impose herself upon all situations, Anne would be invisible; she wants to attract no notice and leave no mark. She is trapped in the past and unable to assert herself in the present, for to do so would be finally to admit that the chance of happiness she allowed others to deny her is gone forever.

Though it is far from lacking in comedy, these powerfully communicated feelings of loss, guilt, sadness and regret dominate the book and make it uniquely vivid and affecting. As Wentworth so memorably describes it in his famous letter to Anne, they live in a perpetual state of 'half agony, half hope', and their ultimate reconciliation (in Bath's Gravel Walk, a real location that can still be visited today) is among the most profoundly moving moments in all of Austen's work.

*A watercolour of Fanny Austen-Knight, niece of Jane and Cassandra Austen, painted by Cassandra.*

*Lyme Regis, one of the many real locations that feature in* Persuasion.

'*Sits at her elbow, reading verses.*'

*Captain Benwick sits with Louisa Musgrove following her fall from the Cobb, in* Persuasion.

It is also hopeful, because it announces that there are, after all, such things as second chances, and that happiness can indeed be reclaimed from the grip of despair. In that sense, the novel seems to absorb within it the circumstances of Jane's own life (and Cassandra's, whose own engagement had been cruelly ended by her fiancé's death; a tragedy that also befalls the novel's Captain Benwick) and those circumstances are transformed into poignantly optimistic fiction.

'Let other pens dwell on guilt and misery,' Jane had written in *Mansfield Park*. 'I quit such odious subjects as soon as I can, impatient to restore everybody, not greatly in fault themselves, to tolerable comfort, and to have done with all the rest.' Fiction, Jane almost seems to be saying, is the one thing in her life over which she has complete control, and she will use her power justly.

Tragically, however, reality chose this moment to reassert its authorial privilege. As Jane was about to prepare the novel for publication she noticed early signs of illness. As the year continued, she grew steadily worse. It is still not certain exactly what it was, though the most likely suggestion is

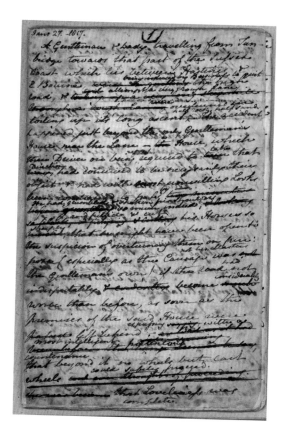

Addison's disease, an endocrine disorder that was not diagnosable at that time. Whatever their cause, her symptoms responded only briefly to the many and various efforts to relieve them, and the disease's inexorable march continued apace.

Jane began a new novel, eventually published as *Sanditon,* but was unable to find the strength to finish it. Eventually, even rising from the sofa became impossible without extreme effort. Then, early in the morning on 18 July 1817, when Cassandra asked if there was anything she wanted, she replied, 'Pray for me, oh pray for me.' Shortly afterwards Jane died in Cassandra's arms. She was 41. Two days later, a desolate Cassandra wrote to their niece Fanny to tell her of their loss. 'She was the sun of my life,' she wrote.

*Right: The first handwritten page of Jane's* Sanditon. *Jane did not give it this title, however; there is reason to believe she intended it to be called 'The Brothers'. The first complete transcription was published under the title* Fragment of a Novel *in 1925.*

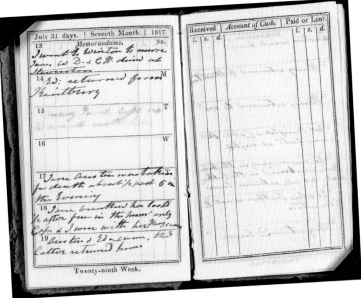

*Extract from the diary of Mary Austen (née Lloyd), for 17 and 18 July 1817. On the 17th she writes: 'Jane Austen was taken for death about ½ past 5 in the Evening.' And the next day: 'Jane breathed her last ½ after four in the morn; only Cass[andra] and I were with her …' (Austen-Leigh Archive: 23M93/62/1/8)*

# 200 Years Later

J ane was buried at Winchester Cathedral, the sparsely attended funeral held early in the morning so as not to disrupt the day's services. The inscription on the grave praises her character and temperament, but makes no mention of the fact that she was a writer. For while none who knew her work was in any doubt as to its quality, surely none would have countenanced for a second that on account of it, the name Jane Austen would be remembered forever.

Today, the picture is very different. After a brief dip in popularity in the Victorian era, Jane's novels grew steadily in acclaim and now occupy a position that seems permanently unassailable. The six main works seem to be constantly made and remade as film and TV adaptations, while sequels, spin-offs and retellings are almost beyond number. It is hard to imagine what Jane would have made of a novel like *Pride and Prejudice and Zombies* (adapted into a film in 2015), when even the fact that *Pride and Prejudice* itself is still remembered would surely have astounded her.

Of course, the main reason for her work's longevity is its excellence, both in the skill and precision of its writing and the timeless effectiveness of the plots and situations. Maybe a part of the appeal, too, is that Jane herself remains largely unknown to us. Everything we need to know is

The memorial brass to Jane Austen in Winchester Cathedral.

*Jane's sister Cassandra writes to their niece Fanny Knight on 30 July 1817 to discuss Jane's funeral arrangements.*

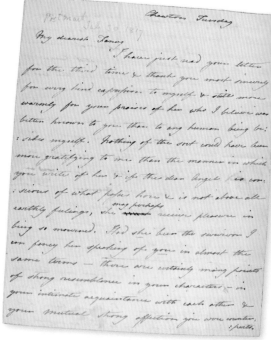

*Commissioned by the Jane Austen Centre in Bath, and on public display, this waxwork of Jane was developed from the forensic portrait that features opposite.*

*Melissa Dring researched every detail of her forensic portrait. Making use of her experience in facial reconstruction with the police, she also made sure such items as the dress, quill pen and even the cross around Jane's neck were authentic.*

there in her novels, she might have argued, and there is much to commend that. But still, it seems almost unjust that so compelling a personality should exist for us only in the recollections of others and in her letters, only a small fraction of which survive.

Even her appearance is not certain: the famous likeness of her by Cassandra – the only complete depiction of her from life – prompted her niece Caroline to note that 'the general resemblance is not strong'. The portrait on the cover of this book was

commissioned by the Jane Austen Centre in Bath in an effort to redress this deficiency; it was created by forensic artist Melissa Dring and based on the descriptions of those who knew her.

So Jane's novels succeed in fulfilling two functions: we not only develop an acquaintance with Jane herself, of whose company we never tire, but we also enjoy reading the novels for what they are – six of the most perfect works in the canon of English literature.

# Places to Visit

## Bath

Jane lived here between 1801 and 1806, and it served as the principal location of *Northanger Abbey* and *Persuasion*, as well as being mentioned in all her other major novels. Her homes in Gay Street and Sydney Place still stand: the former is now a dentist's surgery, while the latter is sectioned into rentable holiday apartments.

The Jane Austen Centre in Gay Street is an interactive visitors' centre, detailing Jane's life in the city (www.janeausten.co.uk). Many of the locations featured in Jane's novels, such as the Assembly Rooms, Pump Room and Gravel Walk, are a short distance from each other in the city's centre and are relatively unchanged since Jane's day. Jane's father, the Reverend George Austen, is buried at the Church of St Swithin, where he and Jane's mother Cassandra were married.

## Chawton

Jane found contentment here. It is where she spent her final years and completed her most important literary work. Her house is now the Jane Austen's House Museum (www.jane-austens-house-museum.org.uk). Chawton Great House, once owned by Jane's brother Edward, is now Chawton House Library, a research and learning centre for the study of women's writing from 1600 to 1830 (www.chawtonhouse.org). Jane's mother and sister are buried at nearby St Nicholas Church.

## Godmersham

This Kent village is the site of Godmersham Park House, once owned by Jane's brother Edward and to which Jane was a frequent visitor. The house is now home to the Association of British Dispensing Opticians College.

## Lyme Regis

This attractive seaside town was a holiday destination of the Austens and also features notably in *Persuasion*. Jane also holidayed at Sidmouth in Devon.

This page was intentionally left blank

Or was it?

# This is a story that starts with a blank page

# I was given one at birth

For a long time I was unaware of my blank page. But eventually questions began to float around my head.

As I grew older the questions didn't go away.
They just seemed to get bigger.

This book is about answering
those questions.

It's a book about authenticity.

Today when people say they are being authentic they normally mean that they are being honest and open.

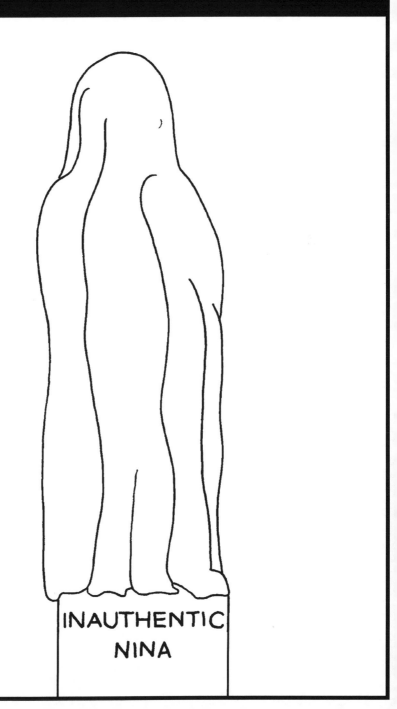

INAUTHENTIC
NINA

If I want to understand 'authenticity' I need to look beyond our present day use of the word

Authentic *adj.* **1** of undisputed origin or authorship; genuine. **2** accurate in representation of the facts; trustworthy; reliable

Being authentic isn't about *revealing* who I am. It's about being the *author* of my self

My authenticity is my response to the blank page I've been given.

I have the opportunity to be the author of my self. What will I write?

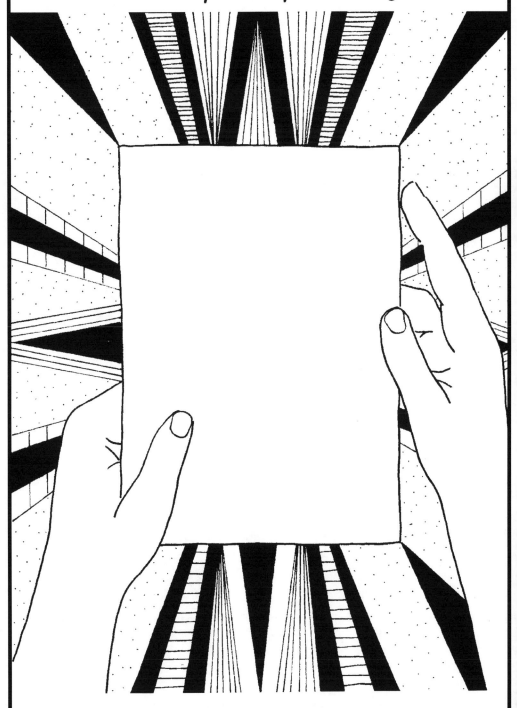

The freedom can feel overwhelming.

It can make the task feel too big.

And me too small.

No rules.

No way of answering the question that feels most important to me.

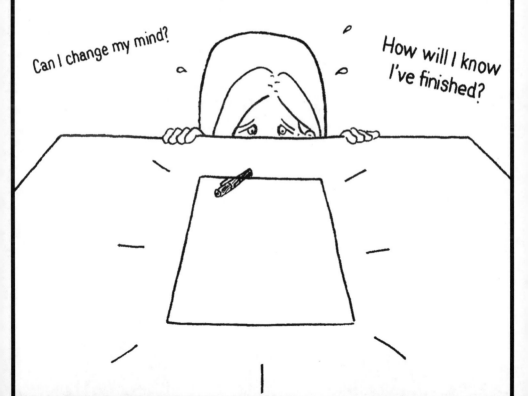

I'm not the only person with a blank page.
Everyone has one.

Maybe someone else has the answers.

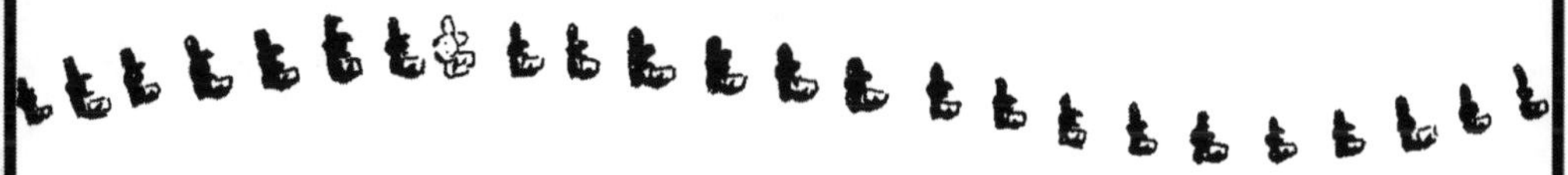

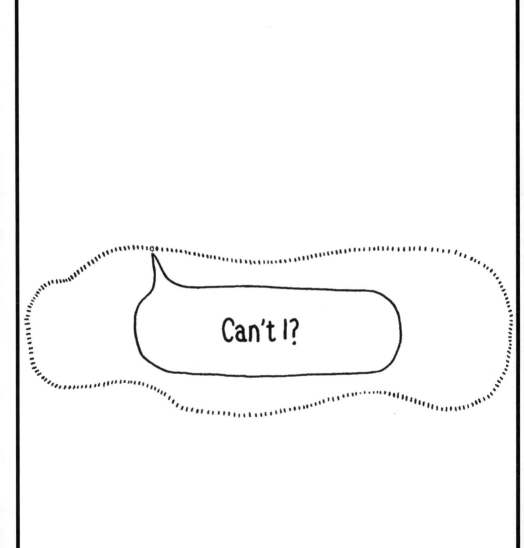

Instead of copying I can seek guidance.
I'll find no shortage of authorities on the
topic of 'Who I *should* be'

But they are not authorities.
They can't be.

The only person who can be an _authority_ on 'me' is me.

My authenticity can only happen when I sit alone with my blank page and choose what to put on it.

Why is this so hard?

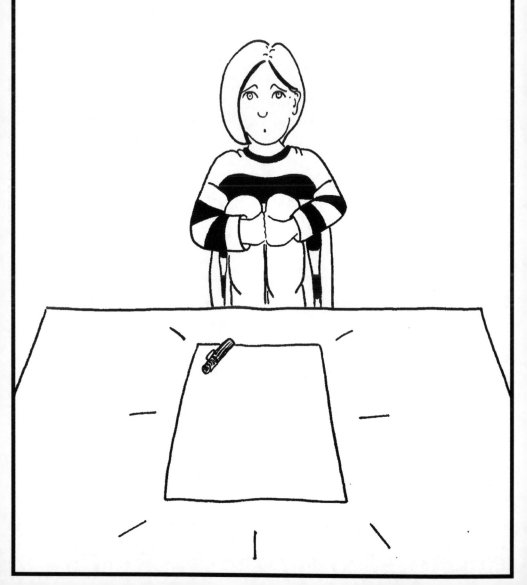

It's hard because my blank page reflects me in a way I find uncomfortable.

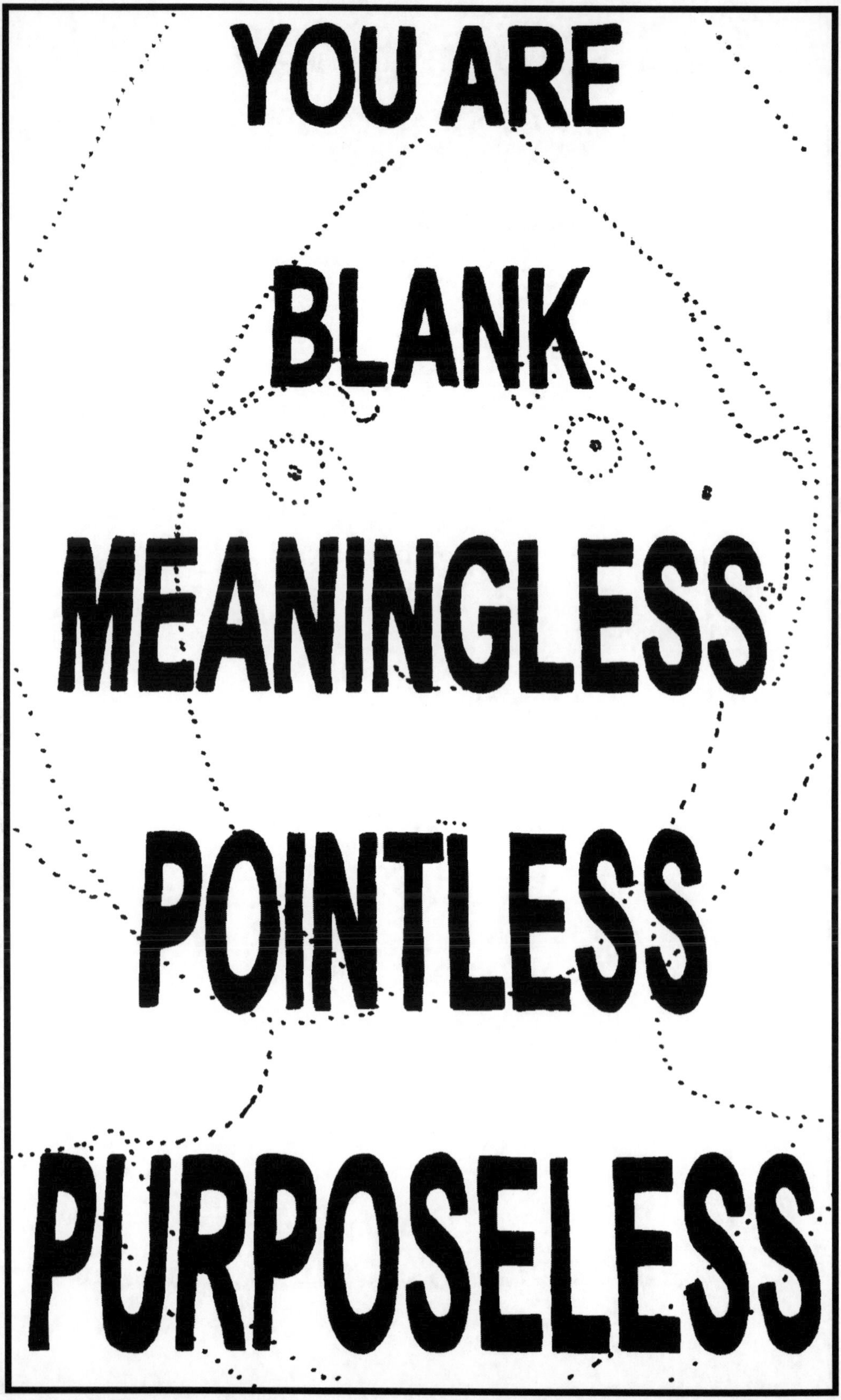
YOU ARE
BLANK
MEANINGLESS
POINTLESS
PURPOSELESS

Being authentic means having the
courage to recognise that this is true.

I have to be

so that I have the
freedom to make my mark

I have to be

# MEANINGLESS

so that I can create my own meaning.

I have to be

# POINTLESS

so that I can create the point of me.

I have to be

# PURPOSELESS

so that I can choose my own purpose.

These are intimidating ideas that I'm tempted to avoid.
YOU ARE MEANINGLESS
Gulp! Hmmm. I wonder what's on the telly?
But is it possible to avoid these ideas?

Facing my blank page is also hard because doing my own thing means risking rejection from others.

My blank page is also hard to face because the lack of boundaries or rules feels like facing chaos.

I like stability.

To face my blank page is to face meaninglessness, the risk of rejection and chaos.

I don't *have* to face these fears.

I could choose to go through life as a blank page.

I could choose to copy others
and win easy acceptance.

We're united by our nothingness.
It's a tight but empty bond.

I could choose to invite other
people to write on my page.

Please take the responsibility
away from me.

But whatever I do a nagging feeling is likely to remain.
Something is missing...
me
me
me
me
me
me
me
me
me
me
me
me
Until I have the courage to face my blank page I'll never experience my greatest gift.

My blank page is the only doorway to me.

It's the only way to become a full person.

A self.

Instead of a...

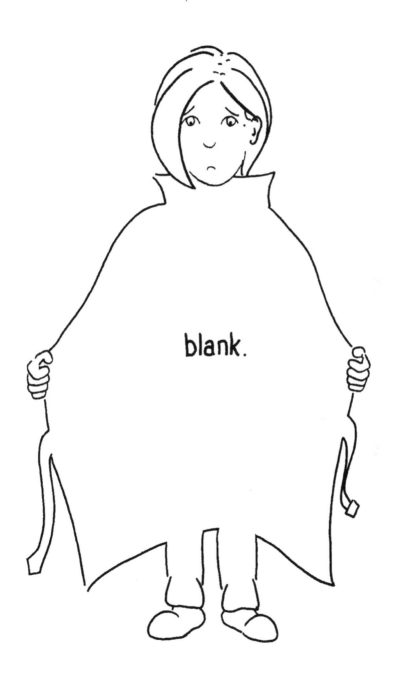

blank.

I choose not to be a blank page.
I try to see my blank page as the gift it is.

I feel all of the discomfort

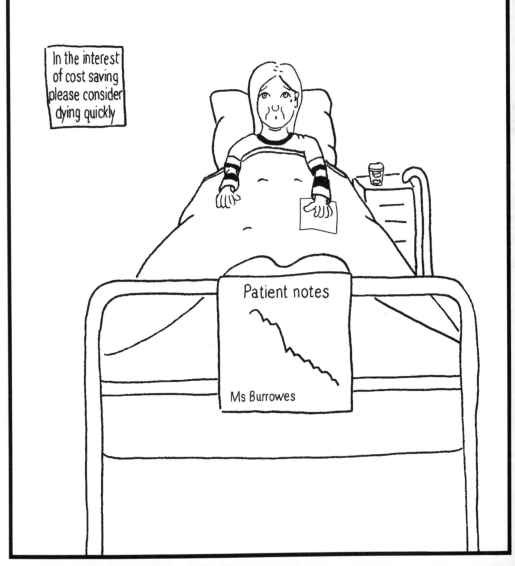

I've always been the person I thought
I was expected to be.

I lived my life as if I was waiting for permission to be me.

# Waiting to be invited to be me.

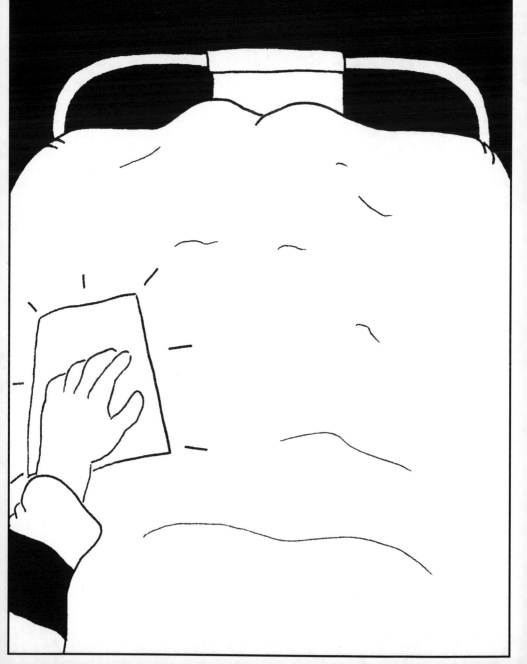

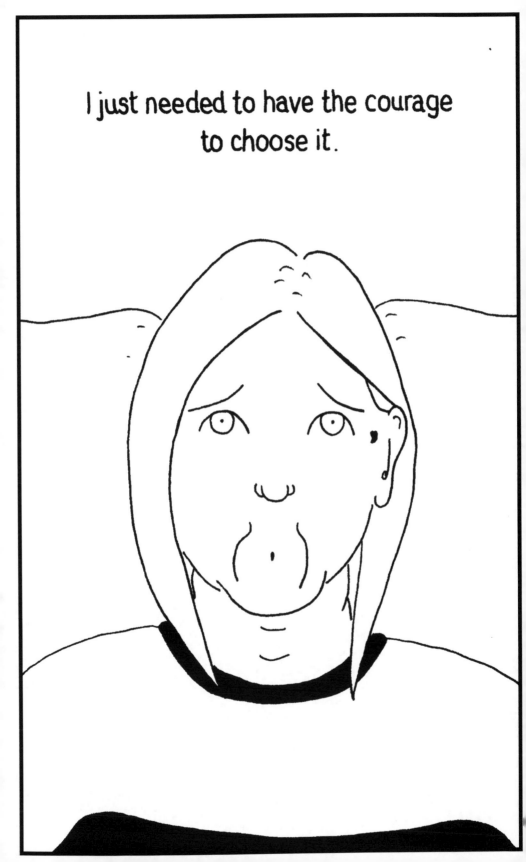

Bugger.

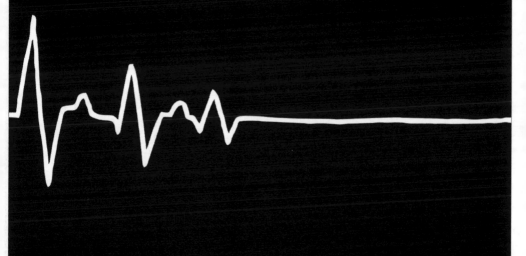

So despite my fears, doubts and anxiety
I choose to create something
on my blank page.

On my page I create a character.

I make her the type of person
I aspire to be.

On a page of meaninglessness
I give her meaning. These are her values.

I choose values that feel bigger than her.

I sew this meaning into the fabric of my character.

This is who she is.

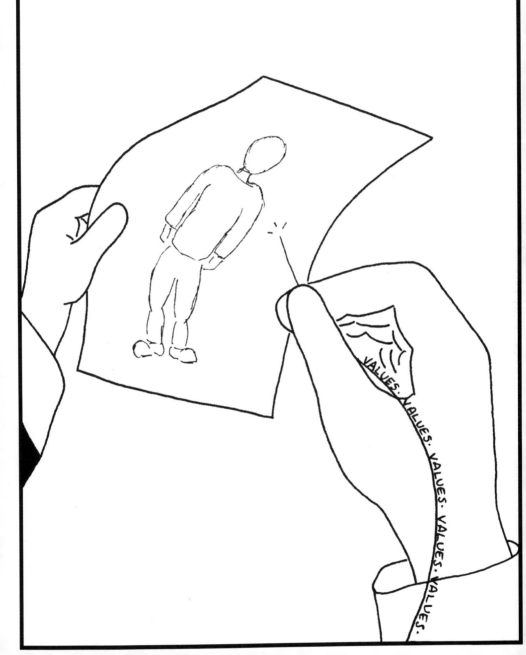

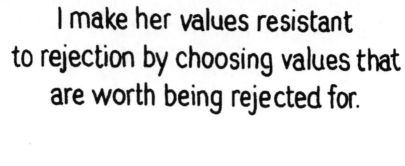

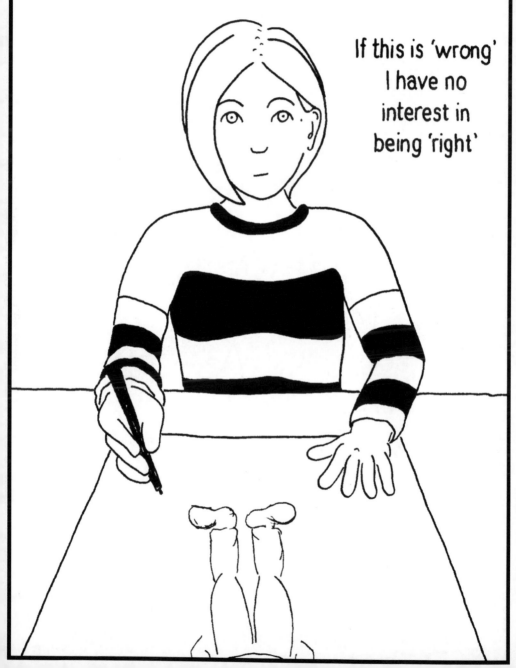

I give my character a sense of stability by choosing values that can transcend contexts.

Values that can be lived in any situation.

I help my character grow by choosing values that can never be fully achieved.

Only strived for.

By doing this I consciously choose the type of person I aspire to be.

By doing this I build the root of me.
My authenticity.

It's a root that gives me a sense
of stability, a sense of purpose,
a foundation from which to grow.

But the strength of this root lies in its flexibility.

AUTHENTICITY

My values are a choice. They are not the *right* way to be they are simply my *chosen* way to be.

# If I cling rigidly to my values the cracks will soon appear.

It's through my willingness to live with uncertainty that I find the security I seek.

Having chosen what kind of person I aspire to be the next step isn't to *reveal* my values.

It is to *become* them. To *live* them.

To live them so wholeheartedly that I won't need to tell anyone what my values are.

They will be able to see my values in the way I live my life.

To be fully authentic is to live my life as if I am the character I have chosen to create.

Which means that choosing what type of person I aspire to be is only the start of being me.

The beginning.

# About the author

Dr Nina Burrowes is a psychologist and researcher who specialises in the psychology of rape and sexual abuse.

Ha! I look nothing like that!

I originally began learning to draw as a way of relaxing from my day job.

Now I use my drawings to help people
understand the things they may
normally avoid...

VULNERABILITY

GUILT

DOUBT

ANXIETY

SHAME

...to celebrate the things about us humans
that are brilliant...

# AUTHENTICITY

# LOVE COURAGE

INTEGRITY

CREATIVITY

...and to tell the stories that don't normally get told.

# Whilst I write about lots of different topics all of my work is about one thing:

I help people understand people.

Find out more at
www.ninaburrowes.com

*Other titles by Nina Burrowes*

The courage to be me.

*Coming soon*

The little book on choice.
The little book on courage.

14889101R00054

Printed in Great Britain
by Amazon.co.uk, Ltd.,
Marston Gate.

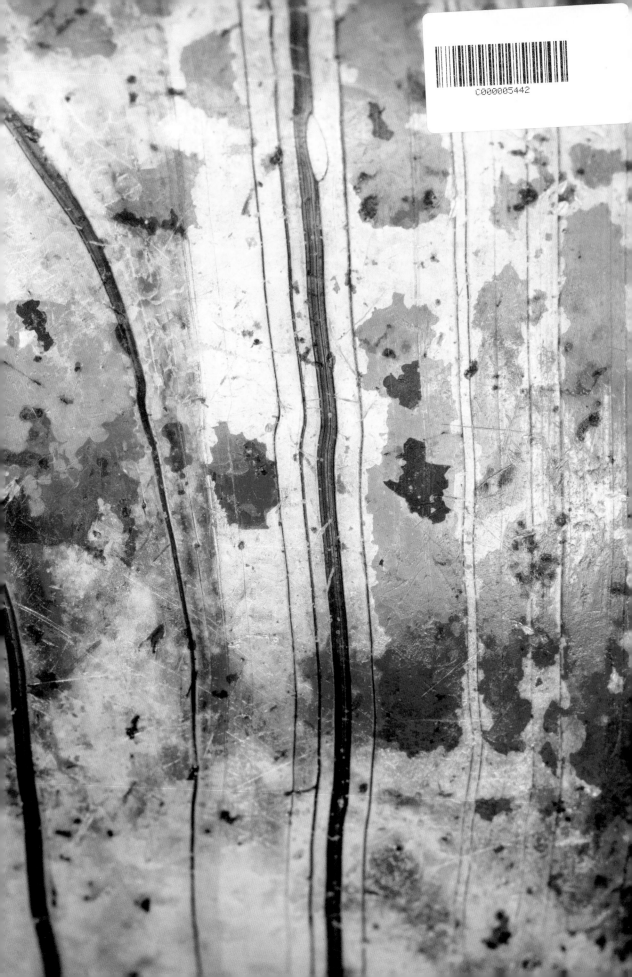

# Mudlark'd.

# MUDLARK'D.

HIDDEN HISTORIES

*from*

THE RIVER THAMES

—

MALCOLM RUSSELL

—

*foreshore photography*
MATTHEW WILLIAMS-ELLIS

PRINCETON UNIVERSITY PRESS
Princeton and Oxford

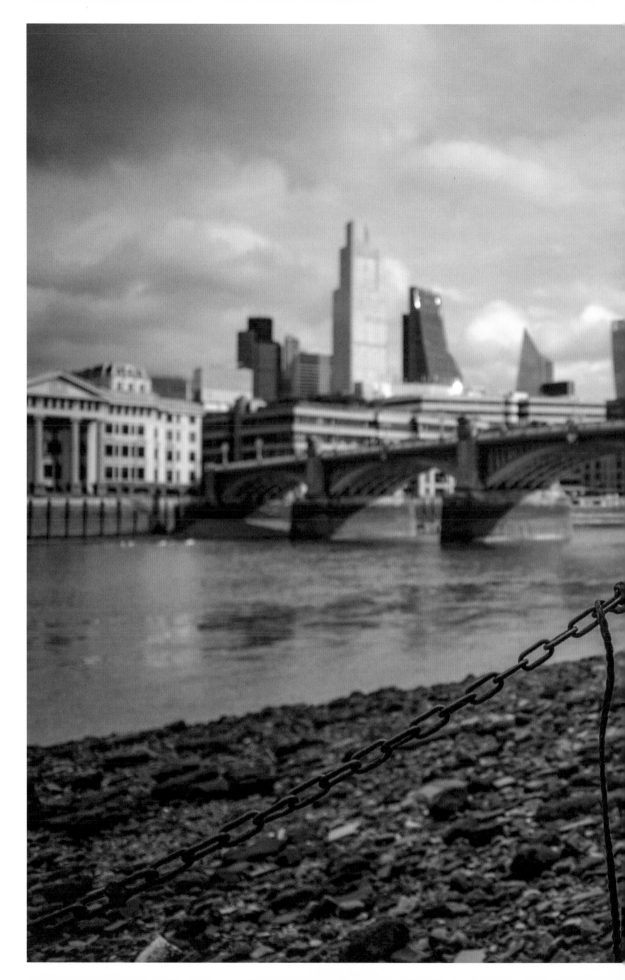

# CONTENTS.

# MUDLARKING.

*THE LIFE OF TRADE UNIONIST* and Liberal MP John Burns had been intimately entwined with the River Thames. He had spent seven years as an engineer's apprentice working alongside it, led one hundred thousand of its striking dockers to victory in 1889 and married the daughter of a Battersea shipwright. When, in 1929, an American visitor compared the Thames unfavourably to the rivers of his home country, Burns retorted: 'The St Lawrence is mere water. The Missouri muddy water. The Thames is liquid history.'[1] He was right. The Thames has been witness to much momentous history in the making: Roman invasion, Viking incursion, the signing of the Magna Carta, Elizabeth I spurring on her sailors before they set sail to face the Spanish Armada, the building of an empire, the devastation of the Blitz and the docking of the *Empire Windrush*.

But beyond these transformational episodes, the Thames has also been witness to the day-to-day lives of millions of London's ordinary citizens: sailors, traders, craftsmen, dockers, criminals, gamblers, sex workers, drinkers, shipbuilders, entertainers and immigrants, who lived and worked alongside it or who traversed it every day. Throughout the city's past, objects that belonged to them have found their way into its waters. Rings slipped from fingers, buttons became snagged on ropes, pins fell from hair, coins were tossed from bridges for luck, cargoes were spilt, broken pottery and other household rubbish was dumped over river walls – packed behind revetments or used to build barge beds – and incriminating evidence was disposed of hastily.

The Victorians were the first to recognize that the Thames provided a rich source of objects from London's past. Antiquarians enthusiastically acquired spectacular artefacts found by dredgermen, bridge builders and dock diggers. Newsworthy finds included Bronze Age shields, an Iron Age horned helmet, numerous spearheads and a colossal bronze head of the Roman Emperor Hadrian, which all now enhance London's museums. Enthusiasm for Thames-found artefacts was such that two illiterate rogues, Billy Smith and Charley Eaton, even began forging medieval trinkets and passing them off as the real thing, claiming they had found them during the digging of an East End dock. At the same time, impoverished children known as 'mudlarks' were also searching the Thames. Their haunt was the river's foreshore – the area of mud, sand, shingle and rocks exposed for a few hours twice per day when the river is at low tide. Their goal was to gather anything they could sell for a few pennies, including bits of rope, bones and copper nails, and, if they were lucky, a hammer accidentally dropped from a

*PREVIOUS PAGES.*
*Two views of the River Thames foreshore at Southwark, one including the author mudlarking among the rubble there.*

*OPPOSITE.*
*The author searching the River Thames foreshore at Tilbury, Essex, where London's rubbish was dumped at riverside landfill sites in the early twentieth century.*

*OVER.*
*Two boys mudlark on the Thames foreshore by the York Water Gate, a landing stage for London river traffic, in this painting by Henry Pether, c. 1850.*

*I.*
*A nineteenth-century shipbuilder's hammer, caulking irons and a barge lock, all discovered on the Thames foreshore by Jay Sisu.*

*II.*
*A mudlark wears a basket on his head to use later for his finds in this drawing by Beard taken from Mayhew's* London Labour and the London Poor, *1851.*

*III.*
*This 1805 engraving depicts mudlark Peggy Jones carrying her finds recovered on the foreshore near Blackfriars Bridge in her apron. She will be able to sell pieces of coal for eight pence a load.*

shipbuilder's hand. One such mudlark, aged fourteen, told journalist Henry Mayhew his father had died falling drunk between two river barges, and his mother was too weak to work. Searching the muddy foreshore at Wapping for many hours every day, his bare feet were often painfully pierced by shards of broken glass and rusty nails. However, he had no choice but to keep returning to the river in search of a few lumps of coal, as the family often had nothing to eat until he provided the cash from its sale.

In the twentieth century, destitute searchers vanished from the foreshore and the grand finds unearthed by the Victorian construction boom became rarer. But the practice of mudlarking continued, evolving into an offbeat leisure activity for the historically curious. Archaeologist Ivor Noël Hume

was one such enthusiast, observing in 1956 that 'many minor treasures [are found] not by builders, dredgermen or even skilled archaeologists but by enthusiastic antiquaries who have discovered the strange hobby of mudlarking.'[2] These hobbyists have since recovered many thousands of artefacts from the Thames foreshore, which have added greatly to our knowledge of London's past. Five years ago, I joined their number.

My first attempt to search the foreshore ended in failure. Not understanding it could only now be accessed at a few points, I ended up abandoning my quest while looking for riverside steps long since decayed. The next trip proved more successful, and I gradually learned how to scour the mud, rocks, bricks and shingle, without the aid of a metal detector, for bent pins, broken

*I.*

THE MUD-LARK.

[From a Daguerreotype by BEARD.]

II.

PEGGY JONES,
The well known Mud Lark.
at Black Friars.

Pub.d June 28 1805 by R.S. Kirby at London House Yard S.t Pauls

III.

buckles, arcane tokens, lost coins and fragments of discarded pottery. I also discovered the foreshore's miraculous preservative qualities – the mud's low oxygen conditions and soft cushioning safeguarding Roman leather boot soles, delicate glass medicine vials and even pages of century-old newspapers. At first my motivation was purely curiosity and the dopamine hit released by making a find, but it soon became clear that mudlarking provided a unique lens through which to examine the past. While studying for a history degree I never once handled an object from the past. Having grown up trawling a Victorian rubbish dump for bottles in the industrial Midlands, this always struck me as a missed opportunity. Objects from the foreshore, such as Georgian counterfeit coins (some perhaps with bite marks where their authenticity had been tested by a shopkeeper's teeth) or a Roman gaming counter with a wager crudely scratched into its underside, bring a degree of viscerality and emotional charge to the past that is missing when studying documents alone.

But mudlarking doesn't just provide the opportunity to find artefacts. It can also inspire the discovery of hidden histories – stories that disrupt what we typically know of the past. Like any histories, these start with raw materials drawn from an archive. But the foreshore is an archive like no other. The Thames' currents constantly erode the foreshore's surface, freeing objects and sorting them, not by period or purpose, but by weight and shape with no regard for rarity or value. Embracing this chaos as a starting point for investigating the past throws up unexpected connections, disrupting traditional hierarchies of information and overturning preconceptions. This is not least because the owners of many mudlarked objects were those marginalized or censured people who remain underrepresented in the history books. A Roman pin was perhaps last held by an enslaved hairdresser, a die last rolled by a Georgian gambler, a token last exchanged by an itinerant Victorian vegetable seller and a Jew's harp plucked by a forgotten street musician. Mudlarking can therefore become a redemptive act, aiding the creation of a people's history, the river's waters helping to fill the gaps in the stories we tell ourselves about the past.

# IN FOCUS—
# *Prehistoric Tools.*

Human activity in the Thames Valley began around 500,000 years before London's birth. Flint hand axes from the oldest phase of this occupation have been recovered from the river but mudlarks are more likely to encounter the area's prehistoric past as a tool lost or discarded by its Mesolithic ('Middle Stone Age') inhabitants.

Around ten thousand years ago, the ice sheets that had covered much of Britain retreated. With the new warmer, wetter climate, hunter-gatherers became a consistent presence along the Thames. Wild cattle, elk, deer and pigs were hunted, and fish were harpooned with spears incorporating tiny flint barbs, termed 'microliths' by archaeologists. These were designed to snag the flesh of an animal, making it harder for it to escape, and were produced from a piece of flint known as a blade. A second Mesolithic innovation was the tranchet adze (also known as a

'Thames Pick'). This cutting tool, similar to an axe but with the cutting edge perpendicular to the handle, was likely used in woodworking. The remains of a Mesolithic wooden structure (London's oldest known construction) has been discovered on the foreshore at Vauxhall: six enigmatic wooden piles preserved by the low oxygen conditions of the Thames mud, and visible only during especially low tides.

From the fourth millennium BC, forests were gradually cleared to provide land for growing cereals and herding animals. This more settled lifestyle saw the emergence of new rituals. Polished stone and flint axes – some of which had been traded from across Britain and beyond – have been found by a lucky few. Archaeologists believe these were probably placed into the Thames deliberately as offerings, perhaps the beginning of the river's longstanding spiritual significance to those living alongside it.

This Neolithic ('New Stone Age') culture would not endure, however. Ancient DNA analysis shows that around 4,500 years ago, Neolithic people were almost completely replaced in the course of just a few hundred years, following a wave of migration to Britain. The arrival of these newcomers was accompanied by a number of tools and cultural practices that had captured the imagination of peoples across Europe. One example was the exquisitely knapped 'barbed and tanged' arrowhead, which was used against both animals and humans, and placed in archers' graves. Another tool from this period was the mattock, used for digging, with a head fashioned from deer or elk antler attached to a wooden haft.

As the Bronze Age unfolded, metal tools gradually came to supplant those made of flint. Many bronze spearheads have been recovered from the Thames, some ritually damaged before being placed in the river.

I.

II.

Mesolithic microlith.

Mesolithic tranchet adze.

Early Bronze Age barbed and tanged arrowhead.

Middle Bronze Age spearhead.

*OPPOSITE.*
*I.*
*Mesolithic or Neolithic bone point; shaped by a flint tool and probably used for piercing animal hides.*

*II.*
*Bronze Age mattock fashioned from red deer antler; used for digging, butchery or carpentry.*

*ABOVE.*
*A selection of mudlarked prehistoric tools, spanning 9,000 years of human activity along the River Thames.*

*All finds made by Tony Thira with the exception of the spearhead, which was found by Łukasz Orliński.*

# Finds from the River Thames, revealing stories from around the world.

Below are shown the twenty-seven artefacts that the stories in this book take as their starting point, presented in the order in which the stories appear in the book. They have been photographed on the foreshore in the locations in which they were originally discovered. The other two hundred and ninety finds featured in *Mudlark'd*, and relating to the stories, have been shot on surfaces recovered from the river, including part of an eighteenth-century ship's rudder, a Tudor floor tile, a Roman roof tile and rubble generated by the aerial Blitz of the Second World War. While all were found in the River Thames, they reveal stories not only of London's inhabitants,

but also of forgotten people from across Britain and the world beyond. London was the busiest port in England for centuries, and the busiest in the world in the late eighteenth and nineteenth centuries. And so, mudlarking in London means discovering Britain's global connections forged through millennia of trade, warfare and colonialism.

Interspersed throughout the book are 'In Focus' pages, exploring the evolution of five different types of finds over time – prehistoric tools, buttons, clay pipes, pottery and ammunition. Concluding the book is a 'Mudlarking Primer', which provides practical advice and guidelines to mudlarking on the River Thames.

1. *Hairpin.*
150–400
(Ornatrices)

2. *Signet Ring.*
1450–1550
(Hanse)

3. *Lead Cloth Seals.*
1500–1700
(Strangers)

4. *Glass Bead Production Tube.*
c. 1635
(Black Georgians)

5. *East India Co. 1½ Paisa Coin.*
1791
(Lascars)

6. *Bartmann Jug Fragment.*
1550–1700
(Cunning-Folk)

7. *Counterfeit George III Shilling.*
1819
(Coiners)

8. *Candlestick.*
1550–1700
(Sex Workers)

9. *Cufflink.*
1662–1700
(Courting Couples)

10. *Pilgrim Ampulla.*
1220–1420
(Pilgrims)

11. *Doves Type.*
1899–1901
(Printers)

12. *British Fascists Badge.*
1924–c. 1933
(Fascists)

13. *Jew's Harp.*
1500–1800
(Street Musicians)

14. *Hudson's Bay Co. Trade Beads.*
c. 1680–1850
(Indigenous North Americans)

15. *Clay Tobacco Pipe Featuring Parachutist.*
c. 1890–1910
(Parachutists)

*BELOW.*
*Each of the twenty-seven finds shown here, which are key to the stories told in this book, is located on the map below in the London borough in which it was found.*

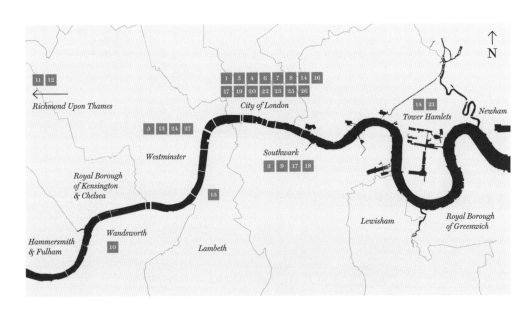

16 *Coin of Roman Emperor Caracalla.* 198–217 (Romans)

17 *Lead Tokens.* 1600–1800 (Mollies & Macaronis)

18 *Chauffeur's Uniform Button.* c. 1900–1920 (Cross-Dressing Women)

19 *Clay Tobacco Pipes.* 1610–1680 (Smokers)

20 *Bone Die.* 1600–1800 (Gamesters)

21 *Case Gin Bottleneck.* c. 1750–1850 (Gin Drinkers)

22 *Human Tooth.* date unknown (Montebanks & Dentists)

23 *Medicine Bottle.* 1700–1800 (Quacks)

24 *Spitalfields Market Token.* c. 1880–1900 (Costermongers)

25 *Turk's Head Clay Tobacco Pipe.* c. 1850 (Forgotten Heroes of the Crimea)

26 *Auxiliary Fire Service Uniform Button.* 1938–1941 (Auxiliary Firefighters)

27 *7.62×54mmR Rifle Cartridge Case.* 1944–1945 (The Red Army)

*OVER.*
*The Thames foreshore exposed at low tide. Top: Bankside, Southwark, once famed for its theatres, brothels and bear-baiting pit. Centre: Queenhithe Dock, City of London, a stretch of the river that has seen continuous activity for almost 2,000 years. Bottom: Wapping, Tower Hamlets, once inhabited by sailors, mast makers, shipbuilders and victuallers.*

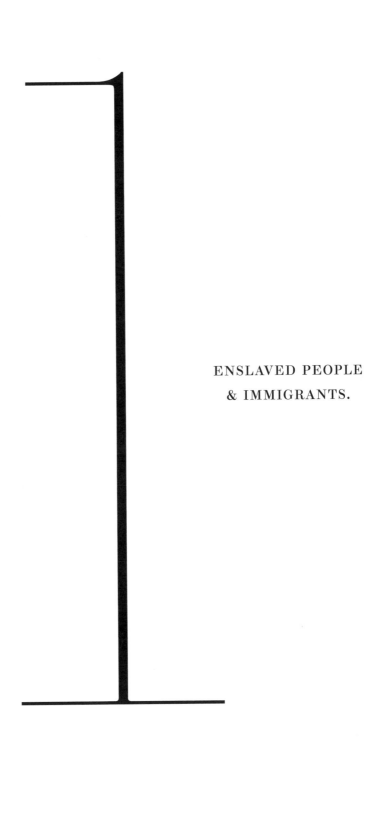

ENSLAVED PEOPLE
& IMMIGRANTS.

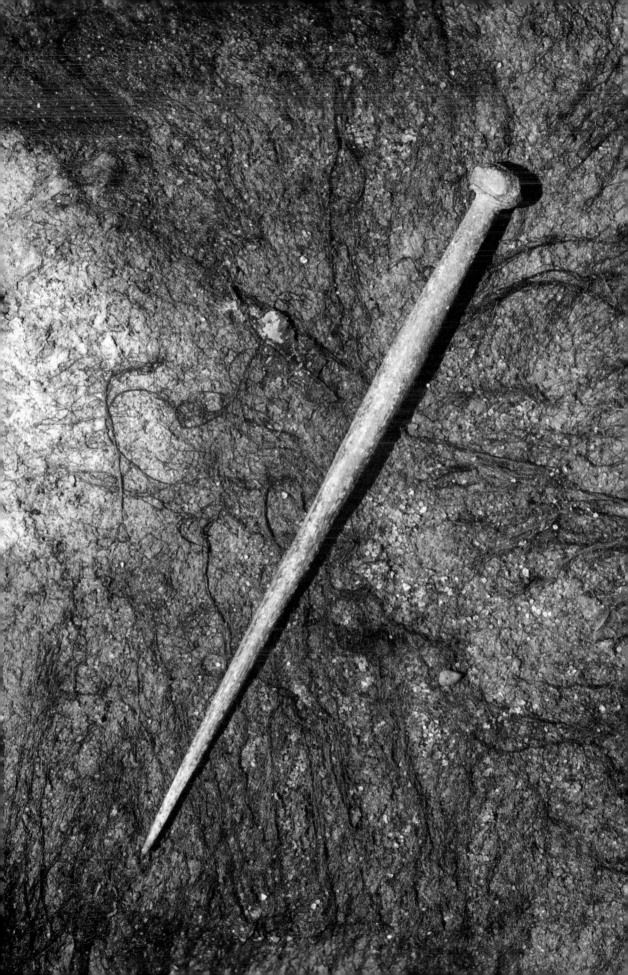

# *Ornatrices—*

The enslaved hairdressers of the Roman Empire, *revealed by a pin.*

**THERE IS A SMALL PATCH OF SHINGLE** on the Thames foreshore where bone pins wash up, sometimes hard to distinguish from the shredded plastic straws and decaying plant stems that litter the same area. They were last used nearly two millennia ago to help create the elaborate hairstyles worn by the female citizens of Londinium, the Roman precursor to today's London. Women could not create some of these styles themselves and so the last hands to touch these finds may have belonged to an *ornatrice*: a female hairdresser, who was often enslaved.

I.

Hair was central to Roman ideas of femininity, social status and even what it meant to be Roman itself. Much of the population of Londinium consisted of Britons who had become Romanized to varying degrees. For the socially ambitious, hairstyles, along with clothing, bathing and eating habits, could be used to signify their embrace of the Roman way of life.

When Britain was first colonized, the fashion was for especially tall and elaborate hair. Wearing one of these complex styles signified that a woman was wealthy enough to afford the time to style her hair. Natural hair was associated with barbarism – the uncivilized other of the Roman world. Hair was also directly intertwined with the exercise of power, through the fashion for hairpieces known as *crines empti*. Sometimes these were made from *captivos crimes* – 'captured hair' – obtained as a spoil of war. According to the poet Ovid, blonde hair from Germany was especially popular. In his book of poetry *Amores*, a male lover berates his mistress for ruining her hair through using curling irons, declaring: 'Now Germany will send you tresses from captured women; you will be saved by the bounty of the race we lead in triumph.'[3] The visit of Empress Julia Domna to Britain in AD 208–11, meanwhile, reportedly led many British women to adopt the Syrian style of hairdressing – crimped in waves on either side of the head with a large coil at the back.

Ornatrices, as hairdressers, were *familia urbana* – a type of enslaved person who worked inside the enslaver's home performing chores that freed their enslaver to live, in Roman eyes, nobly. Other roles for enslaved females of this type included cleaners, bedchamber servants, cooks, nannies, maids, wet nurses and laundresses, while males worked as attendants, gatekeepers, gardeners, animal keepers and in workshops. Regardless of the positions they ended up occupying, there were common routes leading to their enslavement.

After a successful battle, captives were considered part of the plunder and were rounded up and sold to slave dealers who followed the armies. Others were seized by pirates, born into slavery or sold into it as children. Once captured, an enslaved person was prepared for sale using various plant and animal products to 'improve' their body and command a higher price at market. Muscle was faked by fattening boys up, while wounds, scars and other defects were covered with clothing. The enslaved people were then presented to prospective buyers, some of whom were enslaved themselves. A wax and silver fir writing tablet found near the River Walbrook, a Thames tributary, records the sale of a Gaulish female named Fortunata (ironically, meaning 'Lucky') who was bought by an imperial enslaved person, Vegetus, who was himself owned by Montanus, who was in turn slave of the Emperor.

As the property of their enslaver, an ornatrice, or any other kind of enslaved person, could be sexually exploited, or receive harsh treatment for any perceived transgression. Clumsiness,

II.

muttering, noisiness, defiant looks, or simply their enslaver's bad mood, could result in punishment by whipping. Ovid warned any noble woman having a bad hair day against attacking her ornatrice with hairpins. He instead suggested she post a guard at her door to prevent anyone entering and seeing the sorry state of her hair:

And leave your maid alone!
To scratch her face or stick
Her arm with pins – that
makes me simply sick
She'll curse your head each time
you touch her; then she cries,
Bleeding on tresses you've
made her despise.
Bad hair? Well post a door guard;
that should work just fine.[4]

Notwithstanding such treatment, the enslaved person often played an active role in creating a life for themselves, albeit within a limited range of options. Some married, although this was not legally recognized, and any children were the property of their mother's enslaver. Acts of resistance included 'wandering' (taking longer than necessary to accomplish a task in order to visit friends), stealing food and money, and spreading malicious gossip about their enslaver with the goal of harming his reputation.

Some of the enslaved eventually succeeded in gaining their freedom, either by saving for a lengthy period to buy it, or as a reward for long service or for bearing children. Some who were freed rose high up in the Roman hierarchy. After Boudicca, queen of the Iceni tribe, led an uprising that devastated Londinium in AD 60, the Emperor Nero sent the formerly

III.

enslaved Polyclitus to Britain to head an inquiry. Polyclitus ordered the removal of the governor of Britannia, much to the amazement of the local tribespeople, who 'marveled that a general and an army who had completed such a mighty war should obey a slave'.[5]

Unlike the transatlantic slavery of the eighteenth century, there was no Roman literature of enslaved people and no abolition movement. The only written sources we have were created by Roman elites who wrote of enslaved people as possessions or vehicles for literary comedy. We can attempt to get closer to their day-to-day existence, however, through the objects they handled. Beakers and flagons were fetched and poured by enslaved waiters. Bowls, jars and pots were essential items in the kitchens of enslaved cooks. Oil lamps needed to be refilled regularly. Pins were used to create the hairstyles of the elites by ornatrices. Almost any visit to the Thames foreshore can turn up an object that is a testament to the pervasiveness of slavery in Roman society.

# *Finds Relating to Roman Women and Slavery.*

*I.*

*II.*

*III.*

*IV.*

*I.*
*Shale Bracelet.*
AD 43–410
*Found* at City of
London by Guy Phillips.

It is believed that
shale was used by
Roman jewelry makers
to imitate jet. This
was thought to hold
protective powers
for women, with the
philosopher Pliny
enthusing that 'the
kindling of jet drives
off snakes and relieves
suffocation of the
uterus.'⁶

*II.*
*Glass Beads.*
AD 43–410
*Found* at City of
London by Ed Bucknall.

Necklaces and
bracelets of glass beads
of mixed types, strung
on leather thongs,
copper alloy wire or
string, were a common
form of jewelry worn
by the women of
Roman Britain across
the social strata.

*III.*
*Roof Tile with*
*Dog Paw Print.*
AD 43–410
*Found* at City of
London by Ed Bucknall.

According to the
geographer Strabo,
Britain was most noted
for its exports of both
enslaved people and
dogs across the Roman
Empire. The most
renowned of the latter
was a squat animal
famed for its hunting
abilities, known as
an Agassian.

*IV.*
*Bowl Fragment*
*Featuring a Gladiator.*
AD 65–90
*Found* at City of
London by Ed Bucknall.

Most gladiators
were enslaved, with
hand-to-hand fighting
between them being
one entertainment
offered at Londinium's
amphitheatre,
alongside bear-baiting
and bullfighting.

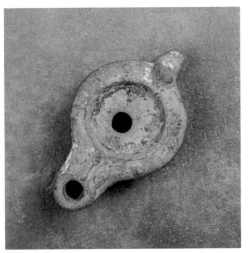

V.

VI.

VII.

VIII.

V.
*Oil Lamp.*
AD 70–140
*Found* at undisclosed
location by Monika
Buttling-Smith.

Enslaved people
could be assigned
responsibilities
for specific objects
including mirrors,
jewelry and oil lamps,
which required refilling
every couple of hours.

VI.
*Pipe Clay Figurine
of Venus.*
AD 100–250
*Found* at City of
London by Ed Bucknall.

As goddess of beauty,
sex, love and fertility,
Venus was of particular
significance to the
women of the Roman
Empire. Such pipe clay
figurines were part of
day-to-day religious
practices. They have
also been found in
women's graves, leading
some archaeologists
to suggest these are
burials of women who
died in childbirth.

VII.
*Flagon Neck.*
2nd–3rd century
*Found* at City of
London by
Ed Bucknall.

Flagons were used
for serving wine at the
table. Waiting on diners
was one duty fulfilled
by enslaved people
in wealthier Roman
households.

VIII.
*Pot with Original
Contents.*
AD 160–250
*Found* at City of
London by Ed Bucknall.

Enslaved people
sometimes toiled in
workshops belonging to
their enslavers. This pot
was found containing
eighteen scraps of
wood, leather and bone,
which may have been
waste materials from a
manufacturing process.

# *Hanse—*

The merchants who supplied Tudor England, *revealed by a ring.*

OPPOSITE.
*Signet Ring.*
*c.* 1450–1550
*Found* at Southwark
by the Author.

ABOVE.
*Detail from a portrait*
*of Georg Giese by Hans*
*Holbein the Younger, 1532.*
*The Hanseatic League*
*merchant is pictured*
*with a signet ring on*
*the table before him.*

TUDOR MERCHANTS USED SIGNET RINGS to personalize wax seals by imprinting their initials on to them. This example carries the initials R.D. under a crown. Who might this R.D. have been? A search of wills reveals at least six English merchants living in the immediate vicinity of the find spot with these initials. The ring's original owner may have been grocer Richard Druce, mariner Richard Dawton or, perhaps, one of the drapers Robert Drayton or the aptly named Robert Drape. Or maybe it belonged to Richard Dene or Race Delamare, both of unknown occupation.

I.

*Illustrated cover page of a
document published in 1497,
detailing the shipping laws of
the Hanseatic city of Hamburg.*

II.

*This 1538 portrait of a Hanseatic
merchant by Hans Holbein
the Younger was one of several
commissioned to display in the
League's London headquarters.*

III.

*Plan of the Hanseatic League's
London headquarters, the
Steelyard, situated on the Thames
near today's Cannon Street station,
showing the layout in 1667.*

I.

But another possibility is that its owner
may not have been English at all, and
was instead one of Tudor London's
foreign merchants.

In 1532, Georg Giese, a 34-year-old
German merchant living in London, sat
for Hans Holbein, considered to be one
of the greatest contemporary portraitists.
Giese had done well, rising to be the
highest-ranking representative for his
family's business interests in England.
The result was rich in symbolism. In a
vase on Giese's desk sits basil, believed
to offer protection from disease.
Rosemary sits alongside it, a symbol of
friendship. Giese's personal motto on his
office wall reads 'No joy without sorrow',
while correspondence from merchant
families shows his extensive trading
connections. The objects required to
help seal such correspondence are also
present – including Giese's signet ring.

The portrait was painted at the
Steelyard, the fortified London base of
the Hanseatic League on the north bank

of the Thames, near today's Cannon
Street station. This confederation of
Baltic city states, led by the cities of
Lübeck and Danzig, dominated trade
in northern Europe for three centuries –
by force when necessary. The Steelyard
saw squirrel pelts arrive from Russia,
garments from Bruges and herring from
Sweden, while English cloth was shipped
across the Continent. As much as 15 per
cent of the nation's imports and exports
was controlled by the Hanseatic League.
London was never officially a member,
but the organization was crucial to
meeting its demand for goods. This was
because England lacked the expertise
to make not only the luxuries demanded
by elites, such as wine, spices, velvets,
silks, satins, taffeta and tennis balls,
but also some of the most basic items,
such as needles, paper, soap and glass.
These items all had to be imported from
abroad, with foreign merchants, some
resident in London, ensuring demands
were met – and profiting handsomely
as a result.

Just as immigrant communities
often do today, these residents clustered
together for mutual support. Their
communities were focused in *liberties*:
areas where institutions, often
monasteries, ran their own affairs
with little interference from the city
authorities. Living in such areas allowed
immigrant merchants to avoid the
trade regulations normally imposed on
foreigners. To some of London's English
residents, this was perceived as giving
them an unfair advantage. Florentine
textile merchant Francesco de Bardi was
granted a licence to trade without paying
customs duties, much to the chagrin
of his English competitors. He also
attracted criticism through scandalously
persuading the wife of an Englishman

to move into his home, bringing along her husband's gold and silver plate as part of the arrangement. De Bardi then had the husband arrested for failing to pay the cost of his wife's lodging. Such actions were seized upon by those calling for anti-immigrant measures. In 1516, a notice was nailed to the door of St Paul's Cathedral complaining that immigrant merchants were monopolizing the wool trade. Early the following year, the Mercers' Company, a merchant's guild, asked for the Earl of Surrey's help in subduing foreign residents seen to be flaunting regulations. In mid-April, the broker John Lincoln convinced a firebrand preacher named Dr Bell to read a rabidly xenophobic speech from the cathedral pulpit on Easter Tuesday. In it, according to the Venetian ambassador, he 'abused the strangers in the town, and their manner and customs, alleging that they not only deprived the English of their industry, and of the profits arising therefrom, but dishonored their dwellings by taking their wives and daughters'.[7]

Bell's polemic accelerated ill feeling towards London's immigrant population, which exploded in the mob violence that came to be known as Evil May Day. A crowd of over a thousand people, consisting mainly of young apprentices, headed to Newgate Prison where they

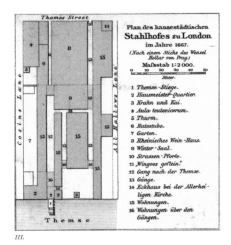

III.

freed several men who had been jailed for assaulting immigrants. The mob then went on to pillage the shops and homes of foreigners, both those of wealthy merchants and ordinary craftsmen. A house belonging to French merchant John Meautys, who had been accused of harbouring foreign pickpockets, was attacked and looted. Meautys reportedly only managed to escape with his life by hiding in his gutters. In St Martins, under sheriff of London, Sir Thomas More, attempted to persuade the rioters to cease. He had almost succeeded when his sergeant of arms was struck by bricks and hot water thrown by Dutch and French residents trying to defend themselves. His angry cry of 'Down with them!' in response was seized upon by the mob and the destruction intensified. By the time May Day morning dawned, the crowds had receded, but hundreds were arrested and many sentenced to death for attacking foreigners considered to be under the protection of the King. Most were subsequently pardoned, but fifteen, including the instigator, John Lincoln, were executed.

As the century progressed and England's industrial and commercial strength grew, the power of the Hanseatic merchants waned. The Steelyard was closed by order of the authorities in 1598 and the site rented to the Royal Navy for storage. Most of its buildings were destroyed in the Great Fire of 1666.

II.

# Finds Imported into Early Modern England.

I.

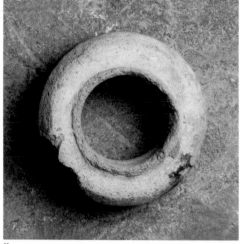

II.

III.

IV.

I.
*Venetian Soldino.*
15th century
*Found* at Southwark
by the Author.

Venetian merchants
sailed to England in
huge galleys crewed by
up to a thousand men.
There they would spend
their *soldini*, which the
English nicknamed
'galyhalpens' after
these 'Galley-men'.
The authorities tried
to outlaw their use,
sometimes raiding the
galleys to prevent their
distribution.

II.
*Spanish Olive Jar Rim.*
1500–1700
*Found* at City of
London by the Author.

As well as olives,
such jars were used
for importing capers,
chickpeas, wine, oil
and honey from Spain.
In the last decades of
the sixteenth century,
following the Anglo-
Spanish War, trade with
Spanish merchants was
outlawed. It continued
nonetheless, with rogue
English merchants
disguising their ships
as Irish or Scottish.

III.
*Martincamp Flask Neck.*
1500–1700
*Found* at City of
London by the Author.

Globular ceramic
flasks named after
the Normandy village
of Martincamp
were imported from
northern France.
Encased in wicker,
they were carried
by soldiers, travellers
and field workers.

IV.
*Thimble.*
16th century
*Found* at City of
London by the Author.

Tudor England
lacked the capacity
to produce brass at any
scale, so thimbles were
one of the everyday
items imported by
the Hanseatic League
from the metal-working
centre of Nuremburg.

*V.*

*VI.*

*VII.*

*VIII.*

*V.*
*Werra Ware Plate*
*Fragments.*
*c.* 1590–1625
*Found* at Westminster
by Seán O'Mara.

Given pride of place
on the wall when not
in use, high-quality
Werra ware plates were
made by potters in the
Werra valley (in today's
Germany) and exported
across northern
Europe. Their central
motifs, scratched using
a technique known
as '*sgraffito*', carried
Christian meanings,
such as hunting scenes
symbolizing the
chasing away of sin.

*VI.*
*Stoneware*
*Krug Fragment.*
Late 16th century
*Found* at City of
London by the Author.

Hanseatic merchants
imported huge
numbers of stoneware
vessels from the
Rhineland region of
today's Germany. This
example was probably
made in the Raeren
workshop of Jan
Baldems Mennicken,
whose work was
richly decorated with
Renaissance motifs
and religious mottoes.

*VII.*
*Jetton.*
Late 16th to
early 17th century
*Found* at Westminster
by Seán O'Mara.

Jettons were used
to perform numerical
calculations by traders
and officials. They were
moved around on a
chequered counting
board to perform
addition or subtraction.
This method of
calculation fell out
of use as the Hindu-
Arabic numeral system
replaced the use of
Roman numerals.

*VIII.*
*Montelupo Maiolica*
*Fragment.*
Early 17th century
*Found* at City of
London by the Author.

Until an outbreak of
plague killed off many
of its makers, this
luxury Tuscan tin-
glazed earthenware
was imported to
London via Antwerp,
the preeminent
commercial and
financial centre of
northern Europe in
the sixteenth century.
By 1540, more than a
hundred ships per year
were carrying goods
purchased there up
the Thames.

# *Strangers—*

The refugees who helped transform England's economy, *revealed by lead seals.*

*OPPOSITE.*
*Lead Cloth Seals.*
1500–1700
*Found* at City of London
by the Author.

*ABOVE.*
*In Isaac van Swanenburg's*
*painting* Washing the
Skins and Grading the
Wool, *1594–1596, Dutch*
*workers can be seen*
*preparing sheep skins*
*ready to be spun into yarn.*

*ON SOME PATCHES OF FORESHORE,* at especially low tides, the sand is scattered with small, twisted lead discs. Some carry a monarch's head, others feature harps, hearts, portcullises, initials and place names. These are the remnants of seals that were riveted to cloth at various stages of its manufacture. From weaving to dyeing – a malodorous process involving copious amounts of urine – seals were attached as guarantes of quality. A final lead seal was applied by an official known as an alnager, to indicate that taxes had been paid and the finished product was of the correct dimensions.

I.

*In this painting by Isaac von Swanenburg (1594–1596) Dutch women are shown spinning warp threads using spinning wheels, which they turn by hand.*

II.

*Portrait of Lord Thomas Howard of Walden, 1st Earl of Suffolk, 1598. His ruff was stiffened by the use of starch in laundering, introduced to England by Dutchwoman Mistress Dingham van der Plasse.*

Cloth was of crucial importance to the English economy, yet by the mid-sixteenth century, the country's weaving industry was falling behind that of its continental rivals. This was only reversed by an unprecedented influx of foreigners, often referred to as 'strangers': Dutch, Flemish and French religious refugees who helped transform England from an industrial backwater into a leading European economic power.

The spur for their seeking sanctuary was the Catholic Church's attempt to repel the advance of Protestantism. Amid a wave of iconoclastic fervour, in 1566 Dutch Protestants destroyed Catholic monasteries and images. In response, the ruler of the Netherlands, King Philip II of Spain, sought to aggressively reassert Catholic orthodoxy. In just four years, around eighteen thousand Dutch Protestants were

executed for their religious beliefs, driving many abroad. They were soon joined by co-religionists from France following anti-Protestant riots in which tens of thousands were murdered. By the end of the century an estimated thirty to fifty thousand continental Protestants had settled in England – a wave of immigration on a scale hitherto unknown.

One refugee was the Dutch weaver Clais van Wervekin. Writing from Norwich to his wife in Ypres, he enthused: 'the cost of living is very cheap so it's easy to earn a living and you'd never believe how friendly the people together are.'[8] Encouraging her to join him in England, he assured her that work was abundant and that he would be able to earn enough to support their three children. Like many immigrants, he was also missing the

I.

tastes of home and requested that she not forget to bring their bread-making equipment, since he found English bread 'disgusting'.[9]

The arrival of Van Wervekin and his fellow refugee weavers was transformative. Fifteen years before he arrived in Norwich, the city's weaving industry had collapsed, with one local official bemoaning that 'people had become poore, many lefte ther howses, and dwelte in the coutrye'.[10] One issue was that traditional English cloth was heavy, and ill-suited for export to the markets of warmer southern Europe, which were growing in importance. After thirty households of master weavers from the Low Countries moved in, bringing new skills and manufacturing innovations, the same official enthused that 'many ruinous houses are re-edified, the city profitted and the poor maintained by working from begging'.[11] In London, meanwhile, other strangers helped develop a lucrative new dyeing industry, dismissing claims that London water was not suitable for this purpose as a 'foul slander upon the famous river of Thames'.[12]

The beneficial impact of the refugees' presence extended beyond cloth-making. The Flemish woman Mistress Dingham van der Plasse was credited with introducing the English to starch, a new laundering technique that gave rise to the wearing of large ruffs we think of as quintessentially Elizabethan. New skills were also injected into occupations as diverse as goldsmithing, shoemaking, printing, papermaking, tapestry-weaving, bookselling, gardening, brewing and haberdashery.

Despite their role in this burgeoning industrial renaissance, London's strangers felt the antipathy of native artisans, who saw them as competitors. Refugees and other immigrants were accused of causing rising prices, higher rents and unemployment. Some were seen as leading insular lives, unwilling to divulge trade secrets or train English apprentices. There were also echoes of today's moral panic over economic

II.

migrants posing as asylum seekers, with claims that many strangers were 'not here for religion: but rather are here to take away the livings of our owne Citizens and countrimen, and to eat by trade the bread from their mouthes'.[13] Concerns were also voiced that the newcomers might include criminals and dangerous religious radicals among their ranks. The authorities responded to these concerns by carrying out regular surveys of the stranger population of London in order to ascertain its size and motivations. In the 1590s, hostility had increased further and attempts were made to expel all strangers from the country. A pamphlet ominously warned 'Flemings and Frenchmen' that it would be 'best for them to depart out of the realm of England between this and the 9th of July next. If not, then to take which follows.'[14] After several decades in London and the wider country, however, the economic benefits the strangers brought were clear to many in authority. This, aided by lobbying from the strangers' religious leaders and their supporters in Parliament, meant efforts to hound them out were quashed.

# Finds Relating to Early Modern England's Immigrants.

I.

II.

III.

IV.

**I.**
*'Cowmouth' Leather
Shoe Sole.*
1500–1550
*Found* at Royal Borough
of Greenwich by the
Author.

In the early sixteenth
century, the shoemaking
guild – the Company
of Cordwainers –
complained, whether
with justification or
not, that immigrant
leatherworkers
were undercutting
English craftsmen
by purchasing unfit
leather 'in Innes
Corners & other secrete
places' in order to
produce 'disceytfull
wares'.[15]

**II.**
*Copper Alloy Clothing
Hooks and Chatelaine
Hook.*
1500–1600
*Found* at City of London
and Westminster by
the Author and Seán
O'Mara.

To develop England's
resources more fully,
German mining expert
Daniel Höchstetter
was granted a patent
in 1565 to mine
copper in Cumbria.
The enterprise
proved problematic,
with Höchstetter
complaining about 'the
Laysie woorking of the
Englyshe' labourers
assigned to him.[16]

**III.**
*Book Clasp.*
1500–1700
*Found* at Tower
Hamlets by Mike
Walker.

Many of Tudor
London's leading
printers were
Protestant immigrants
who helped the new
religion prevail in
England through
their publications.
Stephen Mierdmaan,
for instance, moved
to Billingsgate from
Antwerp and turned
out fifty works,
including a blistering
attack on the papacy,
which he probably
penned himself.

**IV.**
*Venetian-Style Glass
Beaker Fragment.*
16th to 17th century
*Found* at City of
London by the Author.

In 1574, the Italian
glassmaker Jacob
Verzelini was granted
a monopoly to produce
Venetian-style glass in
London. This helped
to lower the price of
beakers and other
glass household wares,
making them available
to the middle classes
for the first time.

*V.*

*VI.*

*VII.*

*VIII.*

*V.*
*Bodkin.*
17th century
*Found* at undisclosed
location by Monika
Buttling-Smith.

Bodkins were used
for piercing cloth in
lacemaking, another
trade practised by
immigrant textile
workers in London.
This example features
an ear scoop at one end,
used to gather earwax
for use on thread to
keep the cut ends
from unravelling.

*VI.*
*Dutch Republic*
*One Duit Coin.*
1628–1632
*Found* at Southwark
by the Author.

Spanish rule in the
Netherlands, which
drove Protestant
refugees to England,
was eventually
overthrown in its
northern provinces
with the establishment
of the Dutch Republic.
In a reverse of the
previous flow of
migrants, English
Puritans now moved
to the Netherlands,
seeking greater
religious freedom.

*VII.*
*French Double*
*Tournois Coin.*
1610–1643
*Found* at Southwark
by the Author.

In the 1620s, rebellions
by French Protestants,
known as Huguenots,
resulted in an erosion
of their religious
freedoms. Ongoing
persecution culminated
in Protestantism being
declared illegal in
France sixty years
later, prompting forty
to fifty thousand to
flee to England.

*VIII.*
*Tin-Glazed Tile*
*Fragment.*
Late 17th to 18th century
*Found* at City of
London by the Author.

Imported Dutch-
made, tin-glazed wall
tiles were immensely
popular in London, yet
the city's tile makers
struggled to replicate
them. This changed
when the Dutch potter
Jan Ariens van Hamme
moved to England and
established a pothouse
for the manufacture
of tiles on the Thames
at Lambeth.

# *Black Georgians—*

London's eighteenth-century Black residents, *revealed by a glass tube.*

OPPOSITE.
*Glass Bead Production Tube.*
*c.* 1635
*Found* at City of London
by the Author.

ABOVE.
*British sailors shipwrecked*
*in Africa are shown repaying*
*their rescuers by enslaving*
*them in this print based on*
*a painting by George Morland,*
*first exhibited in 1788 and*
*probably used in support*
*of the abolitionist cause.*

*IN 1635, LONDON MERCHANT* Sir Nicholas Crispe began manufacturing glass beads at his estate on the bank of the Thames at Hammersmith. The process involved creating tubes of glass which were then cut into shorter lengths to make individual beads. Two years later, Crispe had a ship fitted out 'to take nigers and to carry them to foreign parts'.[17] The two events were intimately connected: Crispe held a controlling interest in the Guinea Company, an organization with exclusive control over English trade with the coast of West Africa.

I.
Sample card, c. 1900, illustrating
the extensive catalogue of designs
developed by European bead
manufacturers for trade in
Africa between the seventeenth
and early twentieth centuries.

II.
Portrait of abolitionist, writer,
composer, London shopkeeper
and former slave, Ignatius Sancho,
by Thomas Gainsborough, c. 1768.

Beads were one commodity the Guinea Company and its successors exchanged for a wealth of African goods, including redwood, hides, wax, gum, pepper, sugar and enslaved people.

Most enslaved Africans were not captured directly by Europeans, but by local participants in the trade. This drew on practices that predated European contact, such as debt slavery and the enslavement of war captives and criminals. Traditional African forms of slavery gave certain rights to those captured, but Europeans regarded the enslaved as commodities, simply to be bought and sold. Europeans expanded, brutalized and incentivized local practices by offering trade goods, including firearms, to deliberately exacerbate regional conflicts and hence increase the supply of captives.

A plethora of different products were exchanged for people and other commodities under this system. In 1687,

a male was bought on the Gold Coast for twenty-six bed sheets, while the price of enslaved people at New Calabar in today's Nigeria was thirty-six copper rods for a man and thirty for a woman. In 1704, an individual was purchased for two trumpets and a piece of blue cotton cloth. More beads were shipped to Africa than any other commodity, typically traded on strings or in bundles. Their colours and shapes were designed to cater to local preferences, beads having been used long before European imports for adornment, to signify social rank and in religious rituals.

Once forced on to British vessels, the enslaved people were transported across the Atlantic to work on the sugar and tobacco plantations of the West Indies and the American colonies. The vast majority toiled and died in brutal conditions there, but by the late eighteenth century, around ten to fifteen thousand people of African descent were living in London. Some were brought to Britain as the servants of administrators, planters and soldiers; others were transported to be offered for sale; while some were freemen who made their own way as sailors.

As slavery on British soil was technically illegal, these Black residents of Georgian London enjoyed an unclear status. Some lived in *de facto* servitude, while others forged their lives relatively independently, if often in poverty. They worked as coachmen, bargemen, sex workers, dock hands, sailors, cooks and performers at fairs, while the liveried Black servant became fashionable among the wealthy.

The most famous Black residents of Georgian London were those who found literary success through their own accounts of their experiences. From the

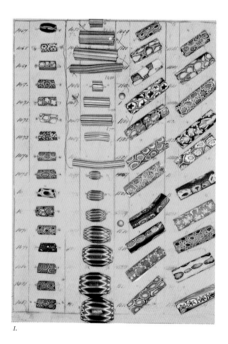

I.

mid-eighteenth century, some Africans and people of African descent began to write accounts of their lives in poems, pamphlets and longer publications that found a wide audience among the reading public. These were important voices in the movement that sought the abolition of slavery.

II.

One such figure was Ignatius Sancho. Sancho gained fame as 'the extraordinary Negro', becoming a symbol of the humanity of Africans and the immorality of the slave trade. According to the biography that prefaced his collected letters, Sancho was born into slavery aboard a ship sailing along the same Guinea coast where Sir Nicholas Crispe had traded a century earlier. At the age of two, he was brought to London and given to three sisters in Greenwich who maltreated him, but he found a patron in the Duke of Montagu, who encouraged him to read. In 1766, he entered into correspondence with the celebrated writer Laurence Sterne, encouraging him to advocate for the ending of the trade. As country-wide debate over slavery gathered steam, their correspondence became a potent weapon for the abolitionist cause. Some of these letters reveal Sancho's feelings of isolation. Despite being the first African to have a British newspaper obituary that celebrated his life and the first to vote in a General Election, and despite having lived in Britain since the age of two, Sancho noted that he still felt 'only a lodger, and hardly that'.[18]

Sancho's *Letters of the Late Ignatius Sancho, an African*, published posthumously in 1782, was followed five years later by Ottobah Cugoano's scything *Thoughts and Sentiments on the Evil and Wicked Traffic of the Slavery and Commerce of the Human Species*. Cugoano had been sold into slavery at the age of thirteen and forced to toil on a Caribbean plantation. Purchased by a British merchant, he was taken to England, given his freedom and joined the anti-slavery group comprising Africans living in Britain: Sons of Africa. Another member of the group was the former sailor Olaudah Equiano – known as Gustavus Vasso for most of his life. In the 1780s, Equiano was appointed to the highest-ranking position to which a Black Briton had ever been assigned by the British state, when he was appointed commissary for a scheme to transport London's 'Black Poor' to the new colony of Sierra Leone. Conceived by the adventurer and botanist Henry Smeathman, to 'remove the burthen of the Blacks from the public for ever', the plan nevertheless found favour among some of London's Black residents.[19] Equiano's enthusiasm waned, however, as he became suspicious that money intended for the care of those who signed up was being siphoned off. After writing a letter to the press voicing his concerns, which attracted the ire of Smeathman's successor, Equiano was dismissed.

These writings of Sancho, Cugoano and Equiano helped ease the passage of the Slave Trade Act of 1807, which made the buying and selling of enslaved people illegal across the British Empire. The ownership of enslaved individuals was eventually outlawed in 1833. This was accompanied by £20 million being paid in compensation to enslavers for the loss of enslaved people as business assets. The number of Black people in London declined with the ending of the trade, and would not reach a similar level again until more than a century later.

# Finds Relating to the Transatlantic Slave Trade.

*I.*

*II.*

*III.*

*IV.*

*I.*
*Lead Shot.*
17th to mid-19th century
*Found* at undisclosed
location by Monika
Buttling-Smith.

Firearms were traded
extensively for enslaved
people in Africa, with
Europeans bringing
several hundred
thousand guns and
millions of pieces of
shot a year to West
Africa by the second
half of the eighteenth
century. The African
states of Asante
and Dahomey built
formidable armies
around these weapons,
using them in warfare
and in raids for captives.

*II.*
*Token.*
1648–1672
*Found* at City of
London by Ed Bucknall.

This token – issued to
compensate for a lack
of small denomination
coins – features a
figure holding an ale
mug and a clay pipe,
with the text 'At the
Black Boy'. This was
a common sign used by
coffee-houses, taverns
and tobacconists. It
probably originated in
the nickname given to
the swarthy Charles II
by his mother, but
subsequently took
on associations with
enslaved Africans.

*III.*
*Token Issued by T. Dry*
*at the Three Sugar*
*Loaves in Wapping.*
1650
*Found* at Tower Hamlets
by Ed Bucknall.

This token features
the shop sign consisting
of three loaves of sugar,
suggesting that Mr Dry
was a grocer. At the
time he issued this
token, most of London's
sugar was produced
using slave labour on
Portuguese-owned
plantations in Brazil.

*IV.*
*Sugar Mould Fragment.*
Late 17th to 19th
century
*Found* at Southwark
by the Author.

Ninety per cent of the
sugar shipped from
England's Caribbean
colonies was semi-
processed muscavado
and required refining
in London. After being
boiled, sugar was
poured into ceramic
moulds and left to
mature for several
months. When ready,
the mould was turned
upside down and the
sugar, in a conical form
known as a sugarloaf,
was removed.

V.

VI.

VII.

VIII.

V.
*Button.*
18th century
*Found* at City of
London by the Author.

Buttons featuring
a Tudor rose were
associated with the
Royal Navy. In the
eighteenth century,
Britain's naval force
was firmly enmeshed
in the slave trade: using
enslaved Africans in its
dockyards in Jamaica
and Antigua, escorting
slave ships down the
African coast and
fighting battles for
control of the sugar-
producing islands
of the Caribbean.

VI.
*Sugar Crusher.*
19th century
*Found* at undisclosed
location by
Florence Evans.

Households would use
metal pincers to remove
a 'nip' of sugar from a
sugar loaf for use. Once
added to a drink of tea,
coffee or hot chocolate,
a glass crusher was
used to break it up.

VII.
*Hawkes & Co. Button.*
*c.* late 19th century
*Found* at Westminster
by the Author.

The tailors Hawkes
& Co. were renowned
for dressing explorers,
including Welsh-
American journalist
Henry Morton Stanley
who, in 1871, travelled
to Africa in search
of David Livingstone.
Livingstone believed
that Christianity and
commerce would help
end Arab-directed
slave trading on the
continent. His efforts
were used to justify the
expansion of European
control of Africa.

VIII.
*Clay Tobacco Pipe.*
*c.* late 19th century
*Found* at Tower Hamlets
by Claire Everitt.

Black and other 'exotic'
people from across the
British Empire were
featured on Victorian
clay tobacco pipes,
reflecting notions
of racial and cultural
superiority that
lingered long after
the abolition of the
slave trade.

# *Lascars—*

The Indian seamen who manned British ships, *revealed by a coin.*

*OPPOSITE.*
*East India Company*
*1½ Paisa Coin*
1791
*Found* at Westminster
by the Author.

*ABOVE.*
*In* Train Up a Child in
the Way He Should Go
*by William Mulready,*
*1841, a child is shown being*
*taught the importance of*
*charity by aiding three*
*destitute Indian seamen*
*stranded in England.*

*THIS COPPER COIN WAS MINTED IN 1791*
for the East India Company, the private
corporation which functioned as the
*de facto* government of much of the
Indian subcontinent for a century.
The East India Company issued its own
currency, raised a private army larger
in size than the British Army, and had
a transformative impact on British social
habits: changing the food people ate and
the fabrics they wore, turning tea into
the national drink, and – almost by
accident – creating the British Empire.
None of this would have been possible
without the labour of Indian seamen
known as 'lascars'.

I.
An official of the East India
Company is depicted smoking
a water pipe, attended by
his Indian servants, c. 1760.

II.
Three lascar crew members of the
RMS Viceroy of India, a mail ship
on the Tilbury-Bombay route, stand
behind the wheel of one of the ship's
tenders in this 1930s photograph.

Their presence in London would come to constitute one of the largest migrant communities in the city in the eighteenth and nineteenth centuries.

From the early seventeenth century, East India Company ships set sail for India crewed by British sailors. By the time they reached their destination a mix of disease, accidents and brawls had often depleted their number. To make up the shortfall, lascars were recruited as pre-assembled crews for the return journey. The pay was attractive for men who were otherwise poor rural farmers, but brutal treatment at the hands of British captains was not uncommon. Some voyages proved fatal. When Company vessel the *Elizabeth* sank in 1810, its captain, Robert Eastwick, turned it into a lifeboat and proceeded to beat off with an oar any lascars attempting to join him in it, contributing to the deaths of 310 Indians.

The lascars who landed in London were supposed to be sheltered and fed during their time in the city by the owners of the ships that had brought

them to England. These owners were also required to promptly provide them with a passage back to India. Nonetheless, some unprincipled operators simply dismissed the lascars who had served on their vessels on to the cold and unfamiliar streets of London. Some froze to death without clothing suitable for the British winter, while others fought to be properly provided for in the British courts – and won. A few married and found employment, but many more quickly spent their pay on alcohol, sex and gambling, or were robbed of their earnings, making destitute Indian sailors a visible feature of London street life.

In the eighteenth century, their presence increased as the East India Company's influence in India grew. For the first one hundred and fifty years of its existence, the Company operated from the fringes of India, confined to small coastal trading posts. With the rapid decline of India's Mughal rulers, in what historian William Dalrymple aptly termed 'the supreme act of corporate violence in world history',[15] it subdued and seized the entire Indian subcontinent in less than half a century, assuming the functions of a ruling power while draining India of its resources. This greater control led to an aggressive expansion of trade on the Company's terms.

More trade meant more lascars making the voyage to London, and growing attacks on their presence. Complaints centred on accusations that lascars sold or pawned charitable donations of clothing to raise cash for drinking or for buying sex. Violence also attracted the attention of the press. In 1806, one hundred and fifty Indian sailors fought three hundred Chinese, while a few years later Irish dock workers

I.

known as 'lumpers' fought lascars whom they accused of taking work from them. Other disputes in which lascars fell foul of the authorities were more personal. One lascar, whose name was recorded at the Old Bailey only as 'Abdulah', was accused of murdering another lascar during a fight over a cooked potato. Found guilty of manslaughter, he was fined one shilling and sentenced to three months' imprisonment.

In 1802, the East India Company finally decided to make proper provision for lascars awaiting a return passage to India. Accommodation was opened in the Thames-side neighbourhood of Shadwell, but the loss of the Company's trade monopoly would lead to its closure. At the same time, more lascars were arriving in the city as more merchants began trading with India. The result was the emergence of the Oriental Quarter, an area of London's East End populated by a largely working-class Asian community. While for many Indians the area provided shelter, food and companionship in an unfamiliar city, the Oriental Quarter came to hold dangerous connotations for many Londoners, fuelled by exaggerated press reports. Christian missionaries such as Joseph Salter, who focused his efforts on London's 'Asiatics', added to the clamour, railing against the Oriental Quarter as 'Satan's stronghold'.[20] For Salter, the area's depravity was epitomized by the sight of two lascars lost in an opium daze, while another lay dead on the floor beside them covered by an old rug.

Despite the challenges of life in London, some lascars managed to establish sustainable, if precarious, existences in the city. Some worked as artists' models when an 'exotic' person was required, while others toiled alongside destitute veterans of the Napoleonic wars, sweeping London's street crossings clear of horse dung for the feet of the rich. Selling Christian tracts or matches on the street were also means by which lascars generated an income.

II.

Long-standing antipathy towards the presence of lascars increased following the Indian Rebellion of 1857. The mutiny of the East India Company's Bengal Army evolved into a wide-scale rebellion against its rule. Reports of the violence transformed the way India was perceived in Britain. In many British minds, the subcontinent went from seeming to be a land of fabled wealth and wisdom to an impoverished colony, exporting cheap labour and raw materials. Lascars were now sailing back to India on ships carrying cheap cotton made in Lancashire mills, to be sold in a country that had previously led the world in its production. Technological change also altered the status of the lascars on board ships. Where once a lascar could rise to work as a petty officer, the advent of steam-powered vessels often reduced them to the more lowly job of shovelling coal into the steamships' furnaces.

The lascars' contribution to Britain's trade was sometimes publicly acknowledged in their time, but the indispensable role they played in building Britain's maritime wealth, the agency they exercised fighting for their rights in an unfamiliar land and the community they created in London are all still only slowly being recognized.

# Finds Relating to Seafaring and the East India Company.

I.

II.

III.

IV.

**I.**
*Porcelain Tea Bowl Fragment.*
1662–1722
*Found* at Westminster by the Author.

The East India Company shipped huge quantities of porcelain from China, which was much admired in Europe for its durability and delicacy. It was packed into crates padded with rice straw and placed around the sides of the ship's hold to provide stability and help protect the inner core of the cargo: tea.

**II.**
*Fid.*
17th to 18th century
*Found* at City of London by the Author.

A fid, hewn from sheep bone, was a tool used to help splice together two pieces of rope. With as much as forty miles (sixty-four kilometres) of rope aboard a sailing vessel, this was an essential skill for sailors to master. Alternative uses for such tools may have included coring apples and taking samples from cheeses to test their ripeness.

**III.**
*Chinese Coin.*
18th century
*Found* at Royal Borough of Kensington and Chelsea by Seán O'Mara.

As well as sailors from India, the East India Company also recruited Chinese seamen. Officially, it was forbidden for Chinese to serve on foreign vessels, but many made their way to the East India Company's base in Canton where they were smuggled aboard its ships.

**IV.**
*Sail Needle.*
18th to 19th century
*Found* at Southwark by the Author.

Needles were used in the making and mending of ships' sails. Sail menders were known as 'idlers' aboard ship because, along with carpenters and cooks, they were exempt from watch duty at night. In London, sailmakers supplying ocean-going vessels could be found in the Thames-side lofts of Limehouse Hole.

V.

VI.

VII.

VIII.

V.
*Knives.*
18th to 19th century
*Found* at undisclosed location by Monika Buttling-Smith.

Sailors used their personal knives for slicing salted meat, crafting trinkets, trimming rope and sometimes interpersonal violence. In the eighteenth century, British naval courts tried scores of men for murders committed aboard ship using their own knives.

VI.
*Shipwrecked Mariners' Society Membership Token.*
1858
*Found* at Royal Borough of Greenwich by Nicola White.

The Shipwrecked Mariners' Society was a charity established after the tragic loss of a fleet of fishing vessels off the north Devon coast in 1838. Its aim was to help seafarers and their dependants who were suffering hardship as a result of accidents, illness, death or retirement. The Victorian era saw an expansion of such maritime philanthropy.

VII.
*Button, Ranken & Co, Calcutta.*
19th century
*Found* at Southwark by the Author.

The tailors Ranken & Co. was established in Calcutta in 1770, making uniforms for East India Company officials and officers in its private army. During the era of the British Raj, it also maintained outlets in the imperial summer capital of Shimla, Lahore, and on Delhi's Connaught Place, where it dressed higher ranking colonial administrators in the latest London fashions.

VIII.
*Oriental Club Plate Fragment.*
*c.* late 19th century
*Found* at Westminster by Seán O'Mara.

The Oriental Club was founded in 1824 to provide high-ranking members of the East India Company with a place to relax or meet while in London. Club chef Richard Terry published anglicized recipes for Indian food. London's first Indian restaurant, the Hindoostane Coffee House, had been opened by Company surgeon, Sake Dean Mahomed, over a decade earlier.

CRIMINALS.

PREVIOUS.
*Detail from* The Mock
Trial, 1812, *by Francis
Greenway, who painted
the scene inside Newgate
Prison, Bristol, while
awaiting transportation
to Australia for forgery.*

# *Cunning-Folk—*

The fight against witchcraft,
*revealed by a pottery fragment.*

*OPPOSITE.
Bartmann Jug Fragment.
1550–1700
Found at City of London
by the Author.*

*ABOVE.
A Bartmann jug with its
bearded man motif features
in* Still life with Herring,
*c. 1635, by Georg Flegal.*

*THE TOUGHEST CERAMIC MATERIAL*
available in the sixteenth and
seventeenth centuries was German
salt-glazed stoneware. Its most common
form was that of a bulbous jug with a
neck featuring a bearded face. These
bore a range of expressions from smiling
amusement to open-mouthed rage.
Primarily used for storing liquids in
kitchens, taverns and on board ships,
these Bartmann jugs, as archaeologists
describe them, were also used in the
creation of 'witch bottles'. These objects
were used to counter acts of witchcraft,
often on the advice of local healers
known as 'cunning-folk'.

I.

was to engage the services of a cunning man or woman. These folk magicians specialized in countering *maleficium* (malevolent sorcery), but also used magic to help recover stolen property, find buried treasure, tell fortunes and rekindle the love of husbands and wives. London had many such practitioners, including, in 1620, 'the cunning man on the Bank side, Mother Broughton in Chicke-Lane, young Master Olive in Turnebole-street, the shag-hair'd wizard in Pepper-Alley, the churgion with the bag pipe cheeke' and 'Doctor Fore-man at Lambeth'.[22] Their magical abilities were variously said to have been learned, acquired or to have been present from birth. Joan Wilmott claimed she obtained her powers after William Berry 'willed her to open her mouth, and hee would blow into her a Fairy which should doe her good'.[23] The seventh sons of seventh sons were said to be born with magical powers. Richard Gilbert, the seventh son of a Somerset husbandman, began his healing career at only one day old, and by the age of five was curing the sick at his weekly Monday sessions.

A first visit to a cunning person might involve diagnosing whether an affliction had indeed been caused by witchcraft. One divination technique was to examine the patient's urine or wash the patient using a preparation containing the herb vervain. If this ran off the body containing many hairs, witchcraft was detected. Another method was to burn a piece of thatch from the roof of the suspect's house to see if they immediately came running. Once bewitchment had been diagnosed a remedy could be created to undo its power. One solution was to prepare a witch bottle. The clergyman Joseph Glanvill wrote of a cunning man who was asked to treat a woman who had 'been a long time in a languishing condition, and that she was haunted with a thing in the shape of a Bird that would flurr near to her face'.[24] The cunning man advised her husband to 'take a Bottle, and put his Wife's Urine into it, together with Pins and Needles and Nails, and Cork

In early 1646, Norfolk butcher's wife Katherine Parsons stopped her husband from selling Ellen Garrison a pig. Garrison vowed vengeance, and shortly afterwards Parsons felt 'extremely tormented all over as if someone were pulling her into pieces'.[21] Next, her two young children died. This tragedy, Parsons believed, was the result of Garrison bewitching them. Similarly, in 1621, Agnes Ratcleife of Edmonton found one of Elizabeth Sawyer's sows eating her soap. Shortly after striking the animal to retrieve it, Ratcleife died unexpectedly. Sawyer was accused of causing Ratcleife's death, a suspicion confirmed when local women found a witch's mark – a permanent marking of the Devil – near her anus. At her trial it was revealed that a demon, in the form of a dog named Tom, had appeared before her and seduced her into serving Satan. Aside from such instances of illness and death, witchcraft was also blamed for an array of everyday misfortunes, from houses burning down, milk not turning into butter, bread not rising, cows unable to give milk and livestock dying.

One response when it was feared someone had been afflicted by witchcraft

them up, and set the Bottle to the Fire.'[25]
The husband followed these instructions
and felt something moving inside the
bottle as he held it fast in the fire with
a shovel. Unfortunately, the cork popped
out, along with the bottle's contents, and
his wife's ailment continued unabated.
On hearing this, the cunning man
advised preparing another bottle, but
this time instructed that it should be
buried in the ground. The husband did
this and his wife began to feel better.
Shortly afterwards, a woman came to
the house crying that they had killed
her husband, who was a wizard and
who had bewitched the afflicted woman.

Another report of the successful use
of a witch bottle recommended placing
nails, salt and urine in a bottle under
certain astrological conditions. The
bottle was said to represent the witch's
bladder, and by inserting pins and the
victim's urine into it she was caused
intense pain, forcing her to remove the
spell from her victim. In some cases,
a more aggressive attack on the witch

was made by including a piece of felt
pierced with pins, which represented
the perpetrator's heart.

In northern Europe and the American
colonies during the period 1560 to 1680,
almost one hundred thousand witch trials
took place amid heightened concerns
over *maleficium*. Alongside economic
pressures enhancing interpersonal
tensions, this wave of witch persecution
was exacerbated by religious upheaval.
Medieval Catholicism had offered
an array of protections against the
supernatural, such as guardian angels,
consecrated herbs, holy water and
the sign of the cross. The arrival of
Protestantism swept these protections
away, leaving the believer to surrender
to the unpredictable mercies of God.
This left little recourse to the afflicted
other than to pursue a suspected
witch in the courts, in the belief that
a successful prosecution would undo
any malevolent spell, or, alternatively,
to enlist the services of a cunning
person to fight magic with magic.

*II.*

# Finds Relating to Witchcraft.

*I.*

*II.*

*III.*

*IV.*

*I.*
*Pins.*
15th to 18th century
*Found* at City of
London by the Author.

Many witch bottles
have been found to
contain pins, included
with the intent of
causing the witch
pain or death.

*II.*
*Pipkin Handles.*
1500–1700
*Found* at City of
London by the Author.

A pipkin was a
globular cooking pot.
It was also the vessel
recommended by one
cunning woman for
preparing a concoction
to establish whether
two children had been
bewitched. She advised
their mother to 'take
the two children's first
water in the morning,
and put it in a pipkin
on the fire; and if, when
it is boiled, all colours
of the rainbow came
out of it visibly, she
could cure it.'[26]

*III.*
*Charles I Rose Farthings.*
1636–1644
*Found* at City of
London by the Author.

One eighteenth-century
cunning man's cure
for scrofula was a
glass of water in which
thirteen Charles I
farthings had been
boiled. This was almost
certainly influenced
by the tradition of
the monarch touching
sufferers of the disease
– also known as the
King's Evil – in the
belief this would
cure them.

*IV.*
*Knife.*
17th century
*Found* at City of
London by the Author.

Objects were concealed
beneath hearths, in
rafters and in front
of doors as a form
of counter-magic
to protect against a
witch entering a home.
Knives were considered
ideal for this purpose,
as drawing blood from
a witch was believed
to be a highly effective
way of neutralizing
a spell, and iron was
said to repel them.

V.

VI.

VII.

VIII.

V.
*Keys.*
17th to 18th century.
*Found* at Southwark
and Tower Hamlets
by the Author and
Ed Bucknall.

A key and a Bible were
used to identify a witch
from a list of suspects.
The key was tucked
inside the Bible and the
names of the suspects,
written on separate
pieces of paper, were
placed at the end of the
key. When the piece of
paper bearing the name
of the guilty party was
inserted, the book was
said to 'wag' and fall
out of the hand of the
person holding it.

VI.
*Holy Water Stoup
Backplate.*
18th century
*Found* at Westminster
by Seán O'Mara.

Holy water stoups
were common objects
in Catholic households.
They contained
consecrated water into
which family members
would dip their fingers
to trace the sign of
the cross as a blessing
or to ward off evil.
Protestantism's removal
of such traditional
supernatural assistance
contributed to a
heightened sense
of vulnerability to
bewitchment.

VII.
*Horseshoe.*
19th century
*Found* at Lambeth
by the Author.

Horseshoes have long
been considered to
provide protection
against bad luck
and evil spirits. One
possible origin of this
belief was the future
St Dunstan, who, in
the tenth century, was
said to have nailed a
horseshoe to the Devil's
foot. He supposedly
removed it only after
extracting a promise
that the Devil would
never enter a household
that had a horseshoe
nailed to the door.

VIII.
*Spell.*
21st century
*Found* at Southwark
by the Author.

Witchcraft continues
to be practised in
London today. This
spell consists of a
plastic dinosaur toy
pierced by a knitting
needle and wrapped,
together with several
wooden blocks, in
snakeskin and linen.
One interpretation is
that it was created to
encourage a child to
take on some of the
misfortune of another
and thereby to develop
greater empathy.

# IN FOCUS—
## *Pottery.*

Following the invasion of AD 43, Roman incomers revolutionized pottery production in Britain. Most vessels were now produced using a potter's wheel, often on an industrial scale and utilizing a multitude of new forms and decorative techniques. Black burnished ware, so named by archaeologists because its surface was finished by polishing it with a pebble, was used in kitchens for preparing and storing food. Samian ware, imported from Gaul, was the Roman's 'best china', its distinctive glossy red making it easy to spot on the foreshore. Following its demise, local potters filled the gap by producing drinking beakers decorated using barbotine – a mixture of clay and water – and often featuring dogs, hares or stags chasing each other around the outside of the vessel.

Medieval pottery can appear crude by comparison. Some includes pieces of shell, known as temper, which was added to the clay to prevent shrinking and cracking during firing. Coarse Borderware, made from the mid-fourteenth century along the Surrey–Hampshire border in England, carries splashes of green glaze and sometimes stab marks, made to prevent vessels exploding during firing.

During the sixteenth and seventeenth centuries England's pottery industries and imports were transformed. Borderware, identified by its off-white clay with a yellow,

green, olive or brown glaze, took the form of early modern essentials, such as porringers, pipkins, fuming pots and costrels, with output evolving swiftly to reflect the fashions of the day. Salt-glazed stoneware was imported in huge quantities from today's Germany, in particular brown jugs from Frechen and grey vessels decorated with cobalt blue from Westerwaldkreis. Its imperviousness made it ideal for liquids, while its decoration brought Renaissance-style motifs – coats of arms, royal portraits and even anti-papal propaganda – into English homes. Tin-glazed earthenware, its white enamel glaze allowing brightly coloured painted decoration for the first time, was imported from the Netherlands – until two Antwerp potters settled in London. Several Thames-side potteries emerged in their wake, producing chargers, ointment pots, bleeding bowls, candlesticks and salt pots.

At the same time, large amounts of Chinese porcelain began to be shipped into the city and auctioned off to dealers known as chinamen. The prestige and popularity of this highly coveted 'white gold' paralleled that of the new intoxicants that went in it: tea, coffee, sugar and cocoa. Efforts to replicate porcelain in Europe led to the emergence of 'refined earthenware', which would replace tin-glazed pottery. One easily spotted type of refined earthenware is Mochaware, its seaweed-like decoration created by dripping a solution of ingredients including urine, tobacco juice, ground iron scale and hops on to the surface of a vessel covered in liquid clay. This was said to resemble moss agate imported from Mukha in Yemen, giving rise to its name.

In the same period, the development of transfer printing replaced the hand painting of pottery. This enabled complex decoration to be applied to relatively cheap pottery, and placed the matching dinner service set within reach of the middle classes.

*Roman.*
1st to 5th century.

*Medieval.*
11th to 15th century.

*Tudor
and Stuart.*
16–17th century.

*Georgian.*
18th century.

*Victorian to
Edwardian.*
19th–early
20th century.

*OPPOSITE.*
*Print of 1808 depicting
flower pots being made
on a potter's wheel, which
is being turned by an
assistant using a crank.*

*ABOVE.*
*Fragments of pottery types
commonly found on the
Thames foreshore, from
the Roman era to the
early twentieth century.*

1. *Jar fragment.*
   Black burnished ware.
2. *Bowl fragment.*
   Samian ware.
3. *Drinking beaker
   fragment.*
   Colour-coated ware.
4. *Vessel fragment.*
   Shell-tempered ware.
5. *Jug fragment.*
   Coarse Borderware.
6. *Jug fragment.*
   Kingston-type ware.

7. *Jug fragment.*
   German stoneware.
8. *Vessel fragment.*
   Borderware.
9. *Charger fragment.*
   Tin-glazed
   earthenware.
10. *Jug fragment.*
    Westerwald stoneware.
11. *Vessel fragment.*
    Staffordshire slipware.
12. *Bowl fragment.*
    Porcelain.

13. *Jug fragment.*
    Mochaware.
14. *Jug fragment.*
    London salt-glazed
    stoneware.
15. *Plate fragment.*
    Transferware.

*All finds made by the
Author with the exception
of Samian ware and colour-
coated ware fragments,
both found by Ed Bucknall.*

# *Coiners—*

The forgers transported to Australia,
*revealed by counterfeit coins.*

**SOME COINS FOUND ON THE FORESHORE**
are not what they first seem. When you
wrap what appears to be a George III
shilling in tinfoil with a little spit and
gently rub the package between your
thumb and forefinger, it might fail to
omit the sulphurous smell that indicates
the presence of silver. You may find a
seventeenth-century guinea with a dull
grey colour, rather than the gleaming
lustre that gold retains in the Thames
mud. You might come across a 1935
George V half-crown with a chunk wrested
out of it, whilst a 1911 florin, supposedly
made of silver, may show signs of 'tin pest'
– a deterioration of the less desirable
metal that occurs at low temperatures.

*OPPOSITE.*
*Counterfeit George III*
*Shilling.*
1819
*Found* at City of London
by the Author.

*ABOVE.*
*Convicts stand outside*
*Sydney's Hyde Park Barracks,*
*in which transportees from*
*Britain were accommodated*
*upon arrival in Australia.*
*Illustration by Augustus*
*Earle, 1826.*

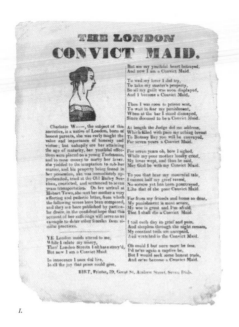

### THE LONDON
## CONVICT MAID.

Charlotte W——, the subject of this narrative, is a native of London, born of honest parents, she was early taught the value and importance of honesty and virtue; but unhappily ere her attaining the age of maturity, her youthful affections were placed on a young Tradesman, and to raise money to marry her lover, she yielded to the temptation to rob her master, and his property being fixed in her possession, she was immediately apprehended, tried at the Old Bailey Sessions, convicted, and sentenced to seven years transportation. On her arrival at Hobart Town, she met her mother a very affecting and pathetic letter, from which the following verses have been composed, and they are here published by particular desire, in the confident hope that this account of her sufferings will serve as an example to deter other females from similar practices.

YE London maids attend to me,
While I relate my misery,
Thro' London Streets I oft have stray'd,
But now I am a Convict Maid.

In innocence I once did live,
In all the joy that peace could give,

But on my youthful heart betrayed,
And now I am a Convict Maid.

To wed my lover I did try,
To take my master's property,
So all my guilt was soon displayed,
And I became a Convict Maid.

Then I was soon to prison sent,
To wait in fear my punishment,
When at the bar I stood dismayed,
Since doomed to be a Convict Maid.

At length the Judge did me address,
Which filled with pain my aching breast,
To Botany Bay you will be conveyed,
For seven years a Convict Maid.

For seven years oh, how I sighed,
While my poor mother loudly cried,
My lover wept, and thus he said,
May God be with my Convict Maid.

To you that hear my mournful tale,
I cannot half my grief reveal,
No sorrow yet has been portrayed,
Like that of the poor Convict Maid.

Far from my friends and home so dear,
My punishment is most severe,
My woe is great and I'm afraid,
That I shall die a Convict Maid.

I toil each day in grief and pain,
And sleepless through the night remain,
My constant toils are unrepaid,
And wretched is the Convict Maid.

Oh could I but once more be free,
I'd ne'er again a captive be,
But I would seek some honest trade,
And ne'er become a Convict Maid.

BIRT, Printer, 39, Great St, Andrew Street, Seven Dials.

*I.*

The trial of James Coleman, age thirty-three, at London's Old Bailey on 4 December 1828, helps shed some light on these peculiarities. The policeman John Vann testified that on 14 November he visited Coleman's house in Bethnal Green to carry out a search. In the yard he discovered a shed containing a donkey, some chickens and a tub filled with straw. Under the straw he found two plaster of Paris moulds which contained the impression of a shilling coin, some spoons, rags and sandpaper. Vann promptly arrested Coleman for the offence of 'coining' – manufacturing counterfeit coins. At the trial Coleman protested his innocence, but was found guilty and executed the following January.

The role of these objects in counterfeiting was later explained by the journalist John Binny in his lurid account of the Victorian coiners' craft. First, a mould was created by pressing a legitimate coin into plaster of Paris; utensils such as spoons were then melted, and the molten metal poured into the mould. Next, the coin had its edges trimmed with scissors and was sanded before being electroplated using a battery, sulphuric acid and cyanide of silver (before the availability of batteries in the 1840s, a wash of nitric acid was used to provide a silver appearance).

Finally, it was 'slummed' – made to look used through rubbing with a mix of lamp blacking and oil.

Once counterfeit coins had been made, they were sold on to agents such as John Abrahams. In May 1828, Abrahams was found guilty of supplying counterfeit shillings following a police sting operation. It was discovered he kept his stash of forgeries in his privy after an officer climbed down into the toilet pit on a rope. Abrahams's customers were *utterers* – the name for those who attempted to pass off counterfeit coins as the real thing in shops, public houses and other businesses. Amid widespread fears that London was suffering under a growing 'criminal class', uttering was often punished just as severely as the practice of manufacturing counterfeit coins itself. John Hall was tried in 1838 for attempting to spend a counterfeit sixpence on a glass of gin at an inn in St Luke's. In his defence, Hall pleaded poverty:

> My mother died in child-bed, and my father died when I was nine years old – I was left to my grandfather – my grandmother died when I was about twelve years old, and my grandfather turned me out of doors... I lost my money by misfortune, and came to poverty, and had nothing to do but to utter base coin – I hope you will have mercy on me.

*II.*

I.

II.

III.

*Lyric sheet of the nineteenth-
century ballad, 'The London
Convict Maid'. This version tells
the story of Charlotte W., a servant
transported to Australia for seven
years for robbing her master.*

*A 1828 etching by Edward William
Cooke of HMS* Discovery, *former
ship of explorer James Cook,
after conversion into a prison
hulk on the Thames at Deptford.*

*In this satirical print of 1792 two
prostitutes sit weeping on the dock
at Plymouth while two shackled
convicts about to be transported
to Australia stand beside them.*

Mercy was not forthcoming, however, and he was sentenced to transportation to Australia for ten years.[27]

Transportation emerged from the quest to find a punishment for serious crimes that were not seen to merit the death penalty. From the mid-sixteenth century, coining was judged to be an act of treason, forcing judges to sentence those found guilty to the most severe punishment the state could inflict: death by hanging for men and burning at the stake for women. As with others ordered to the gallows for a multitude of offences, however, there was often no intention of carrying out all sentences; those able to demonstrate basic literacy were often pardoned. This discrepancy left the legal system open to criticism and prompted a search for a secondary punishment.

The answer was found in transportation: the forced migration of felons, first to America, and to Australia from 1787. Of 160,000 convicts shipped to the territory, around 3,000 were coiners, the slang term for whom was 'bit-faker'. Before being transported, prisoners were kept on disused ships moored on the Thames, known as hulks. From 1816, they were interred in Millbank Prison, which occupied a site next to the river in Pimlico. The largest penitentiary in Europe, Millbank's layout was so confusing even the prison warders got lost, and it closed before the century was out.

On arrival in Australia, after a voyage lasting up to six months, life was especially harsh for female convicts. Ann Barrett, age fifty-three, was sentenced to be transported for seven years in 1839 for attempting to spend a counterfeit shilling on rhubarb at Covent Garden market. Women like Ann were sometimes sold off as domestic servants, known locally as 'London Maids', and

BLACK-EYED SUE and SWEET POLL of PLYMOUTH.

III.

preyed upon by male members of the household in which they served. Others worked in one of the 'Factories' established to provide them with work and shelter. In reality, however, these functioned as brothels and marriage outlets for male settlers and convicts. Many women had to resort to prostitution in order to survive and save enough to pay for their passage back to England at the end of their sentence. Men, in contrast, could pay for this by acting as a crew member on board ship.

Colonizing Australia with forced convict labour brought economic success. In 1824 a visitor remarked 'that colony is certainly the fruit of the convict's labour'.[28] Nevertheless, with convicts overwhelmingly represented as indolent, disobedient and unswervingly committed to vice, by the mid-nineteenth century, the Australian colonies were beginning to resent being a dumping ground for British criminals. Humanitarian reformers, inspired by the ideas of the Enlightenment, mounted pressure on the British government to replace transportation with imprisonment in Britain. As a result, coiners were instead sentenced to penal servitude, with the Penal Servitude Act of 1864 stipulating a minimum sentence of five years.

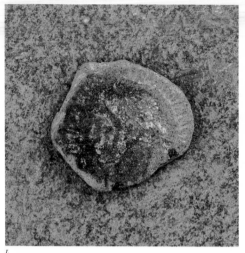

I.

II.

III.

IV.

CRIMINALS.

2. CRIMINALS.

I.
*Ceramic Coin Mould.*
AD 222–235
*Found* at City of
London by Jason Sandy.

The methods used by
Roman counterfeiters
were similar to those
of the Victorian era.
A mould was made by
pressing a legitimate
coin into clay. After
firing, the mould was
filled with molten
metal, which contained
less silver than official
coins.

II.
*Elizabeth I Silver
Threepence.*
1565
*Found* at City of
London by the Author.

Silver and gold coins
were susceptible to
the treasonous crime
of clipping: shaving
metal from the coin's
circumference. Another
method of debasement
was sweating: shaking
coins in a bag and
collecting the dust left
behind. Bounty hunters
were sometimes deployed
to find perpetrators,
and were rewarded
with a share of their
property – including
any clippings recovered.

III.
*Coin Weights.*
1550–1658
*Found* at City of
London by the Author
and Ed Bucknall.

Coin weights allowed
tradespeople to guard
against clipped, worn or
counterfeit coins. They
corresponded to the
lowest weights at which
specific high-value
gold coins remained
legal tender, with the
denomination indicated
in their design.

IV.
*Stoneware Jug Fragment.*
1580–1620
*Found* at City of
London by the Author.

The unicorn figure on
this pottery fragment
was the mark of
stoneware shipper,
Jan Allers. An Allers
jug was found on the
wreck of the *Batavia*,
a seventeenth-century
Dutch ship that was
run aground off
Western Australia by
mutineers. Rescuers
punished two of them
by leaving them there –
the first Europeans to
live on the Australian
continent.

*V.*

*VI.*

*VII.*

*VIII.*

*V.*
*Charles I Rose Farthing.*
1636–1644
*Found* at Southwark
by Nina Russell.

We might think of coins
consisting of two metals
as a modern innovation,
but copper farthings
issued during the reign
of Charles I had a small
plug of brass inserted
into them to make
them harder to forge.

*VI.*
*William III Silver
Sixpence.*
1696–1697
*Found* at Southwark
by the Author.

In 1696 all existing
silver coins were
withdrawn and new
machine-made coins
issued. This ensured a
uniform diameter and
allowed the application
of graining to their
edges, both acting as
a deterrent to clippers.

*VII.*
*Convict Department
Prison Warder's Button.*
19th century
*Found* at Westminster
by the Author.

In the nineteenth
century, 'convict'
referred to those
prisoners who had been
tried, convicted and
imprisoned for serious
crimes such as murder,
burglary, robbery and
coining. London's
convict prisons included
the notorious Millbank,
situated on the bank
of the Thames, where
convicts were held
before being transported
to Australia.

*VIII.*
*Metropolitan Police
Plate Fragments.*
19th to early 20th
century
*Found* at Westminster
by Seán O'Mara.

The formation of
London's Metropolitan
Police in 1829 gave
fresh impetus to the
pursuit of coiners.
Sergeant James
Brannan arrested
many, including Henry
Brown in 1844, who,
when surprised by
the sergeant, put two
shillings in his mouth,
prompting Brannan to
seize him by the throat.

INTIMATES.

# *Sex Workers—*

Prostitution in early modern London,
*revealed by a candlestick.*

*IN THE SEVENTEENTH CENTURY*,
candlelight was used by painters and
writers as a device to illuminate the
sexually deviant behaviour that took
place under the cover of darkness. Light
thrown from a candle was often used to
create an erotic and illicit atmosphere
in an intimate scene. It was deployed by
the well-known London dramatist and
pamphleteer Thomas Dekker in *Lantern
and Candlelight* in which a candle carrying
night-watchmen visits London's notorious
suburbs: those areas of London that were
part of the urban area but beyond the
official limits of the city, and thus
outside the control of its officials.

I.

Etchings by Wenceslaus Hollar (1607–1677) depicting four sex workers. Their names and charges are written beside their portraits.

II.

Thomas Rowlandson's 1808 hand-coloured etching of female prisoners at Bridewell waiting to be 'passed' into the care of their parishes. Sex workers were commonly committed to Bridewell.

It was in these districts that prostitution flourished, especially on the south bank of the Thames, directly opposite the City of London. This had been the location of a cluster of brothels known as the 'stews', which in 1161 had been placed under the control of the Bishop of Winchester. That a leading cleric should profit from prostitution was in keeping with the Catholic Church's belief that it provided a sexual safety valve for unmarried apprentices and journeymen, who might otherwise engage in rape or sodomy. The greater moral scrutiny ushered in by the Reformation, along with concerns over disease, led to periodic attempts to close or regulate the stews, but the trade simply spread into an array of alehouses, taverns, lodging houses, former mansions and back alleys across the city.

What is known of the women who worked in these establishments during the seventeenth century suggests that most were compelled to do so by economic necessity. Some poor relief was available, but if a woman was unmarried, without children and capable of work she was ineligible for help, and even if she was, it was often too little too late. This led some women to use prostitution as a temporary means of earning money in between more desirable jobs, while for others it became a longer-term occupation. The fish seller Mary Knight, for instance, married a seaman whose profligate spending impoverished her. In court on trial for being 'a common nightwalker', she claimed she had only turned to prostitution to 'keep herself from starving'.[29]

Some women toiling as sex workers experienced greater degrees of coercion. In the late sixteenth century, the age of consent was lowered from twelve to ten. Children were sold into prostitution by destitute parents, or if orphaned might be left with little alternative. There was no shortage of willing customers, as it was believed that intercourse with virgins could cure venereal disease. This meant large profits could be made by offering men virgins – or at least claiming to. One pamphlet of 1635 alleged 'a bawd sold one maidenhead three or four hundred times', while other accounts mentioned the use of herbs to tighten the vaginal wall, or the use of a small bladder of animal blood to mimic the result of a broken hymen.[30]

Some sex workers were managed by bawds or pimps who brought them clients, offered the sex worker some protection, bribed the authorities and sourced medical help if venereal infection occurred. They also taught new girls how to deliver maximum sexual pleasure for their client in the minimum time, while

I.

*II.*

extracting as much money as possible from the customer.

Bawds were often former sex workers themselves. According to the pamphlet *The Devil and the Strumpet: Or, the Old Bawd Tormented*, former 'Hackney Jilt' Jane Freeman could no longer offer her own body for sale because potential clients thought her 'not worth throwing their legs o'er'.[31] Instead, she became a bawd, making money deluding 'poor Innocent Creatures, to satisfie the Lust of ungrateful Sinners, almost as bad as herself'.[32] Other sex workers-turned-bawds amassed fortunes. Damaris Page became known as 'the great bawd of the seamen', running two premises near the docks in Ratcliffe, one for ordinary sailors and another for officers.[33] She also specialized in importing costly and supposedly highly skilled Venetian sex workers to London, and died a wealthy woman. Priscilla Fotheringham, meanwhile, built her fame and fortune by offering a novelty sex act. Proprietress of the Six Windmills on the corner of Whitecross Street and Old Street, she was renowned for standing on her head naked with her legs apart and having customers throw coins into her vagina – an activity described as 'chucking'.

What rewards prostitution brought for some were not gained without great risks. Many women succumbed to disease, and if arrested and found guilty they might be sent to the pillory or 'carted': carried through the streets sitting in a cart or backwards on a horse. Such punishments were often accompanied by a spell in a house of correction, known as a 'Bridewell'. Here, women toiled beating hemp with wooden mallets or were sent to work on the treadmill, a large human-powered system for grinding corn. Around the same time as the Bridewells were established, women apprehended for prostitution also began to be transported to the English colonies of the Caribbean and America – often expected to service crew members during the lengthy voyage across the Atlantic.

The threat of such punishments, however, was inadequate in stemming the growth of London's sex trade. With poor relief remaining inadequate, thousands of impoverished migrants arriving each year and the spirit of libertinism growing with every decade, the sex trade would become an even greater force shaping lives in London in the following century.

# *Finds Relating to Prostitution.*

I.

II.

III.

IV.

I.
*Chafing Dish Handle.*
1450–1550
*Found* at Southwark
by the Author.

Tudor brothels were
known for selling
food to clients at
highly inflated prices.
Woodcuts show vessels
known as chafing dishes
being used to keep
food warm at the table.
A pamphlet of 1592
described this sharp
practice, claiming that
customers 'shall pay
for a pippin-pie that
cost in the market
fourpence, at one
of the trugging
houses [brothels]
eighteenpence'.[34]

II.
*Money Box Fragments.*
1550–1650
*Found* at Southwark
by the Author.

Money boxes were
used in London's
early modern theatres
to collect takings.
Among those paying
the entrance fee
were numerous sex
workers for whom the
theatre was a venue
for picking up clients.
A disapproving poem
of 1691 made the
connection explicit
in its opening lines:
'The Play-house is their
Place of Traffick, where
/ Nightly they sit, to sell
their Rotten Ware.'[35]

III.
*Chamber Pot Fragment.*
17th century
*Found* at Southwark
by the Author.

It was believed that
urinating as much
as possible after
intercourse helped
prevent disease.
Seventeenth-century
brothels kept chamber
pots for this purpose.
One customer
described himself as
'pissing...till I made it
whurra and roar like
the tide at London
Bridge...for I know
no better remedy
more safe than pissing
presently to prevent
the French pox.'[36]

IV.
*Clothing Stud Featuring
Copulating Couple.*
18th century
*Found* at undisclosed
location by Anna
Borzello.

By the late eighteenth
century, the turnover
of London's sex industry
was on a par with the
value of goods handled
by the city's docks.
Sexual themes even
made their way into
fashion, being sported
on buttons, cufflinks
and clothing studs.

DISPATCH OR JACK PREPARING FOR SEA

*ABOVE.*
*A sailor, with glass of wine*
*in hand, sits astride a woman*
*while fondling another's breast*
*in Thomas Rowlandson's*
*etching entitled* Dispatch or
Jack preparing for sea, *1815.*

# *Courting Couples—*

The early modern journey to marriage, *revealed by a cufflink.*

*ON 23 AUGUST 1662, A RIVER PROCESSION* took place that the diarist Samuel Pepys described as 'the most magnificent Triumph that certainly ever floted on the Thames'.[37] The pageant, which saw ten thousand barges on the river, celebrated the arrival of Charles II's new queen, Catherine of Braganza, at Whitehall Palace, following their marriage in Portsmouth a few months earlier. The occasion spurred the sale of commemorative cufflinks featuring two hearts underneath a crown, a motif that continued to represent romantic affection or marriage for the next few decades.

I.

*This beadwork basket, used to hold a child's clothes during a christening ceremony, features a design celebrating the marriage of Charles II and Catherine of Braganza; after 1662.*

II.

*Frontispiece of* The Academy of Complements, *1684, by John Gough, containing 'elegant expressions of love and courtship... for the use of ladies and gentlewomen by the most refined wits of this age'.*

III.

*A couple hold a glowing heart aloft between them in this popular woodcut, entitled* The Happy Marriage, *c. 1700. Such woodcuts were pasted on to the walls of cottages and taverns.*

Romance had nothing to do with what brought the couple together in marriage, however. Charles had never met Catherine, daughter of King John IV of Portugal, prior to their union, but her dowry included the territories of Bombay and Tangier, full trading privileges for England in the Indies and a large sum of money for the cash-strapped King.

Such wholly mercenary motives for marriage were not reflective of most unions at the time. Couples generally passed through recognizable phases of courtship in which their feelings towards each other ultimately dictated the outcome, but were influenced by the interests and actions of parents, family and friends along the way.

Once a person had reached marriageable age – typically in their mid-twenties – the first step in finding a spouse was to identify suitable candidates. According to a proverb of the day, these should be of 'like blood, like good and like age'.[38] Servants and apprentices met prospective partners at work, fairs and dances, where games such as 'cod-piece kissing' provided physical intimacy. Among the middling sort, parents might initially

vet candidates, while friends across all classes could act as matchmakers. Typical was yeoman Leonard Wheatcroft, who met Elizabeth Hawley on the suggestion of a mutual friend. 'I had some intelligence of a young maid... by one of her relations, who told me she was very fortunate, besides beautiful [and] lovely,'[39] he wrote in his detailed narrative of the courtship.

Once a prospect had been identified, they had to be courted and won, with the man typically playing the role of pursuer, and women either granting or holding off affection in response. The aim was to develop 'mutual liking' through visiting, letter-writing (for the literate), conversation and a range of gifts. These were sometimes collectively referred to as 'tokens'. Merchant John Hayne wooed Susan Henley in 1634, giving her a Puritan tract, four pence of ribbon, bracelets, stockings, 'two yards of scarlet kersey', 'a cabinet made in Rouen', green silk garters and six pairs of ash-coloured gloves.[40] Deliberately bent coins figured prominently as tokens of affection, and could be given at various stages of the relationship. Hayne gave Henley half a twenty-shilling piece which, he wrote, 'we brake together' as part of the ritual of their engagement.[41] In 1598, Thomas Kennet gave Bennet Dunnye a sixpence, 'bending yt once, as a tooken and pledge of the bargen and promis passed betwene them'.[42] When William Singer felt his relationship with Margaret Smith was advancing nicely he sent her some ginger and a nutmeg, while Margaret, feeling the same, sent him a bent groat in return. If the courtship fizzled out, however, such tokens could be returned. This was unfortunately experienced by musician Thomas Whythorne. As the affections of an unnamed widow he was

I.

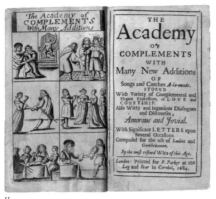

II.

attempting to woo cooled, he bemoaned that she had the token he had given her delivered back to him, although he refused to accept it. Perhaps the multitude of bent coins found in the Thames attest to it being a convenient place to dispose of unwelcome reminders of spurned advances.

Once the couple had decided to marry, some entered into a binding contract referred to as 'spousals' or 'handfasting'. This consisted of a promise to marry and could be regarded as legally binding, as long as any conditions stipulated were met, such as the provision of property. Nonetheless, by no means all couples were contracted, and the practice declined in the later seventeenth century with the actual wedding ceremony being regarded as the pivotal moment of commitment.

All sexual activity outside of marriage was officially forbidden, but once a couple was contracted, or had simply decided to wed, it was widely thought acceptable for it to progress from kissing and fondling to full sexual intercourse. Analysis of parish registers shows around a fifth of women were pregnant by the time they got married in church. This premarital intercourse could spell disaster if a contract was not followed through, as a multitude of court cases attests. In 1590, John Baker testified how George Thompson, who had promised to marry his daughter, had died before the ceremony leaving her with an illegitimate child. Such a situation attracted not only moral but also financial concern – with the cost of raising the child having to be borne by the ratepayers of the parish. Religious reformers such as Richard Greenham lamented that 'many marriages have been punished of the Lord for the uncleanness that hath been committed betwixt the contract and the marriage', and by the early seventeenth century the courts were paying greater attention to punishing bridal pregnancy.[43]

Next, a date was set for the wedding ceremony and banns were read three times in the couple's parish church. For those desiring greater privacy, a licence could be acquired allowing marriage in a parish away from home. Such 'clandestine marriages' allowed a couple to marry in haste, avoid public scrutiny or simply mitigate the expense of having a multitude of hungry and thirsty neighbours as guests. Two popular venues for such unions were the Tower of London and the less than romantic Fleet Prison. For poorer folk, the alehouse often sufficed as a wedding venue, with rooms on hand for consummation.

During the wedding ceremony itself, the placement of a ring on the woman's finger provided the crowning token of commitment and indicated her married state thereafter. It might be the same ring given earlier in courtship, perhaps inscribed on the inside with a short saying or 'posey'. The use of rings was not without controversy. For some hardened Puritans it was a superstitious popish hangover to be purged from the ceremony. Their use managed to survive such concerns, however.

III.

# *Finds Relating to Early Modern Courtship and Marriage.*

I.

II.

III.

IV.

I.

*Spindle Whorls.*
1300–1500
*Found* at City of
London by Ed Bucknall.

Spindle whorls
helped give a spindle
momentum while
spinning fibres into
yarn, an activity
undertaken in medieval
times by women known
as spinsters. Later,
'spinster' came to refer
to an unmarried woman.
This was perhaps
because married women
took on higher-status
economic activities,
leaving the unwedded
with more lowly
occupations, such
as spinning.

II.

*Bent Elizabeth I
Sixpence.*
1580
*Found* at City of
London by Jason Sandy.

Bent coins were given
as tokens of affection.
Joseph Addison's
'The Adventures of
a Shilling', mentions
this practice, with
the shilling recalling:
'This wench bent me,
and gave me to her
sweetheart...This
ungenerous gallant...
pawned me for a dram
of brandy, and drinking
me out next day, I
was beaten flat with
a hammer, and again
set a running.'[44]

III.

*Gold Finger Ring
with 'Posey' Inscription.*
Mid-17th century
*Found* at Wandsworth
by Blain French.

'Posey' rings – given as
gifts during courtship
or used as betrothal or
wedding rings – derived
their name from the
French word 'poésie',
or poem, referring to
the inscriptions they
carried inside. This
example reads: 'The
love is true that I O U.'

IV.

*'Merryman' Plate
Fragment.*
Late 17th century
*Found* at Lambeth
by the Author.

Often given as a gift to
newly married couples,
Merryman plates were
made in sets of six.
Each carried one line
of verse and, when
the plates were put
together, the whole
rhyme, commenting
on married life, could be
read: 'What is a merry
man / Let him do what
he can / To entertain
his guests / With wine
and merry jests / But if
his wife do frown / All
merriment goes down.'

*ABOVE.*
*The marriage of a London lawyer*
*and his bride is depicted in this*
*conversation piece by William*
*Hogarth, entitled* The Wedding
of Stephen Beckingham and
Mary Cox, *1729.*

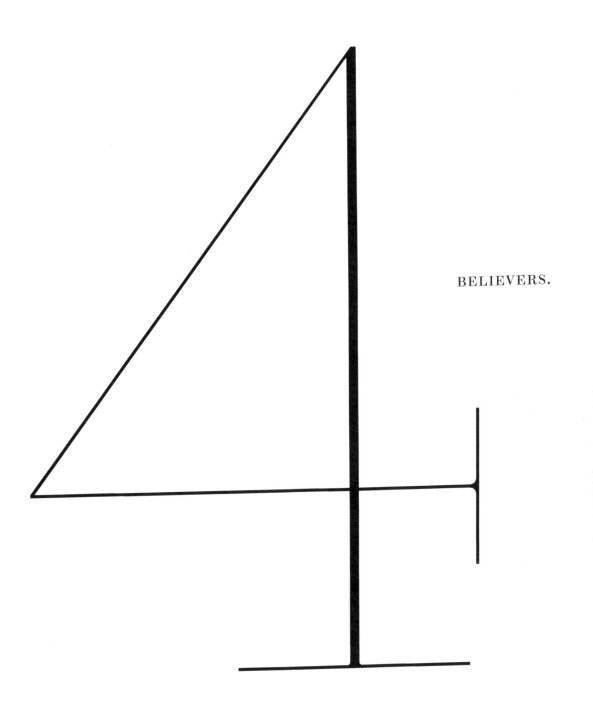

BELIEVERS.

# *Pilgrims—*

Medieval religious travellers,
*revealed by an ampulla.*

OPPOSITE.
*Pilgrim Ampulla from the
Shrine of St Thomas Becket.*
1220–1420
*Found* at Wandsworth
by Łukasz Orliński.

ABOVE.
*In this oil panel detail,
c. 1520–1530, two pilgrims
observe a miracle performed
by St James the Elder. Pinned
to their hats are scallop shells
associated with the shrine of
St James at Santiago de
Compostela, Spain.*

*FROM AROUND THE SIXTH CENTURY,*
'ampulla' came to refer to miniature
containers produced to hold relics such
as holy water from the River Jordan.
Such receptacles were brought back
to England by travellers who had made
the lengthy and arduous pilgrimage
to the Holy Land. With the murder of
the Archbishop of Canterbury, Thomas
Becket, in 1170, England was to get a
Jordan of its own. Across a series of
positions of state, Becket had proved
himself a highly capable official and
had won the trust and friendship of
King Henry II.

Soon after his appointment as Archbishop of Canterbury, however, the relationship began to sour over a series of disputes about the respective rights and privileges of the Church and Crown. After a period of exile in France, Becket returned to England as Henry decided to have his eldest son crowned successor. Rather than follow custom and have the Archbishop of Canterbury perform this act, he chose three alternative clerics. Incensed, Becket promptly excommunicated the trio, prompting Henry to exclaim in exasperation: 'Who will rid me of this turbulent priest?' Taking his words literally, four enterprising knights set off for Canterbury, and with a fifth accomplice, brutally assaulted Becket in a side chapel of his own cathedral. This culminated with one of the five, a subdeacon who subsequently became known as 'Hugh the evil clerk', slicing the top off the dead Archbishop's head, scattering his brains and blood across the chapel floor.

Recognizing the significance of what had occurred, some monks anointed their eyes with the spilled blood, while others brought vessels in which to capture it or else dipped their clothes

II.

I.

in it. Very soon, the blood was believed to have miracle-making qualities. A monk from Reading had his leprosy cured after drinking the blood mixed with water and washing his face with a piece of cloth tinged with it, while a woman with an abdominal growth was said to have been cured immediately and was able to wear her closest-fitting dress again. Becket was canonized in 1173, and miracles involving him occurred 'throughout the whole church of Christ throughout the world', spurring a religious cult that made Canterbury the most important centre of pilgrimage in England and one of the most visited across Europe.[45]

Pilgrims who visited the shrine were able to take away a small quantity of the 'Canterbury water', as the diluted blood became known, in ampullae made from lead alloy. Large enough to hold a ladleful, these were suspended on a cord or chain around the neck, some inscribed in Latin with the words: 'Thomas is the best doctor of the worthy sick'. They were not merely souvenirs, but wonder-working objects in their own right. The water might be rubbed on to a body part that needed healing, or else taken home for sick family members, unable to make the journey themselves. The ampulla might be kept as a talisman – attached to a rosary, given to a local church or handed down as a family heirloom. Some found their way into the Thames, perhaps as offerings made as an expression of gratitude for a safe return home.

*I.*

*This illuminated manuscript leaf by an anonymous illuminator active in France and England, known as The Master of Sir John Fastolf, depicts the martyrdom of Thomas Becket, c. 1430–1440.*

*II.*

*One of Canterbury cathedral's medieval stained-glass windows depicts pilgrims at St Thomas' tomb. The holes carved in the side of the tomb enabled pilgrims to get closer to the remains of the saint.*

*III.*

*This portrait of Geoffrey Chaucer decorates the Ellesmere Manuscript of* The Canterbury Tales *in which pilgrims travelling to St Thomas' shrine pass the time by regaling one another with stories.*

Not all pilgrims were expecting to encounter miracles or seeking cures. Many travelled to the shrine in fulfilment of a vow to undertake a pilgrimage, often made in a moment of personal danger or sickness. In 1336, a Yorkshireman made the journey to Canterbury because he had vowed to do so should he recover from sickness. A group of pilgrims from Lincolnshire, fearful they would perish in a thunderstorm, had vowed to visit Becket's shrine. After surviving, they fulfilled their promise. John de Holderness of Danbury in Essex, while in peril at sea, vowed to visit 'all the shrines of the saints in the king's realm'.[46]

The opportunity to gain indulgences motivated others to take to the road. Late medieval Christians overwhelmingly believed in heaven, hell and purgatory – a place where the souls of moderate sinners would go for purification before being allowed into heaven. The time a soul would spend suffering the pains of purgatory could be reduced by people acquiring indulgences – the absolution of past sins. More worldly benefits played a role too; a visit to a shrine might coincide with a nearby fair, or satisfy a feeling of wanderlust, with the returning pilgrim becoming something of a local celebrity in an age where most people lived their entire lives within a short distance of home.

Some pilgrimages were meted out as punishments by the ecclesiastical courts. Adulterer William Covel was ordered to go on pilgrimage to Canterbury naked except for his breeches; while John Mayde was sent all the way to St James's shrine in Spain for fornicating with his godmother. Journeys could also be initiated by a bequest in a deceased's will. In 1361, Hugh Peyntour requested in his will that a pilgrimage to Canterbury be undertaken barefoot. If the deceased's children or wife did not wish to travel, such requests might be undertaken by a 'palmer' – a professional pilgrim who could be paid to travel on behalf of another. It was said that palmers were in the habit of selling pilgrim ampullae and badges to one another to appear more experienced in the role. Pilgrimage was also a way of life for Norfolk mother-of-fourteen, Margery Kempe. Clad all in white, often to be found weeping incessantly with religious fervour and gaining audiences with some of the leading religious figures of the day, Kempe was a well known figure on Europe's pilgrimage routes, travelling to Jerusalem, Rome, Santiago de Compostela and a host of English shines.

Attracting pilgrims for a multitude of reasons, the cult of Becket's blood lasted for two hundred years. Thereafter thousands continued to visit, with badges replacing ampullae as the most popular pilgrim 'sign'. The Protestantism of the English Reformation had little time for pilgrimage, however. In 1538, St Thomas's shrine was destroyed, along with most of England's other pilgrimage destinations.

*III.*

I.

II.

I.
*Pilgrim ampulla from the shrine of St Thomas Becket, c. 1170–1220. Found at Hammersmith and Fulham by Łukasz Orliński.*

II.
*Pilgrim badge from the shrine of St Thomas Becket, c. 1300–1500. Found at Wandsworth by Łukasz Orliński.*

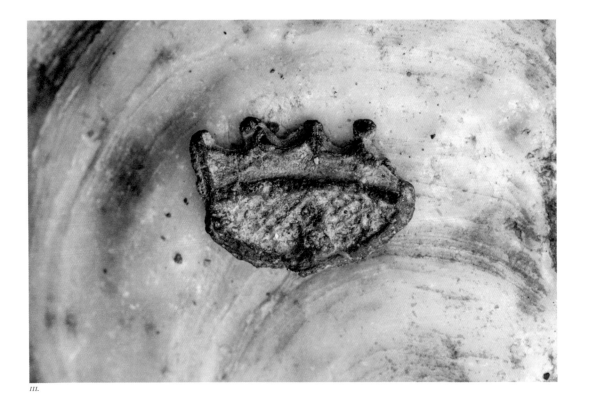

*III.*

*IV.*

*III.*
*Pilgrim badge from the shrine*
*of St Edward the Confessor at*
*Westminster Abbey, c. 1350–1420.*
*Found at an undisclosed location*
*by Monika Buttling-Smith.*

*IV.*
*The side of a pilgrim ampulla,*
*showing the face of St Thomas*
*Becket, c. 1220–1420. Found*
*at Wandsworth by Łukasz*
*Orliński.*

# Finds Relating to Pilgrimage and Religion.

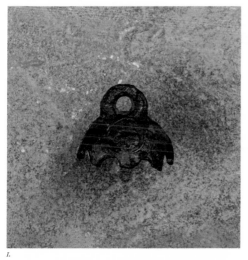

*I.*

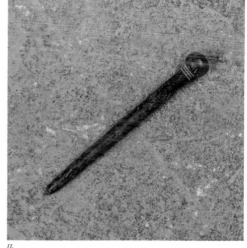

*II.*

*III.*

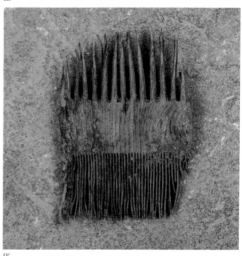

*IV.*

I.
*Crotal Bell.*
Late 13th century
*Found* at Wandsworth
by Mark Iglesias.

Crotal bells were
attached to a horse's
harness to warn other
road users of its
approach. This example
features the arms of
Edmund, 2nd Earl of
Cornwall, who joined
the Ninth Crusade in
1271. The Crusades were
initiated when Pope
Urban II raised the
plight of pilgrims to
the Holy Land being
forced to pay high fees
to enter Christian sites.

II.
*Parchment Pricker.*
13th to 16th century
*Found* at Westminster
by Seán O'Mara.

Biblical manuscripts
written on parchment
were essential to all
aspects of medieval
religious life. This
object, known as a
parchment pricker,
and originally equipped
with a small metal
point, is believed to
have been used to
prick multiple small
holes on each side of
a manuscript page to
mark evenly spaced
horizontal lines for
writing on.

III.
*Henry VI Groat.*
1422–1427
*Found* at City of London
by the Author.

A religious cult
developed around
King Henry VI
following his death
in 1471. Posthumous
miracles attributed to
him include preventing
the death of Thomas
Fuller, who was wrongly
accused of stealing
sheep and had been
sentenced to be hung.
The long-dead Henry
was said to have placed
his hand between the
man's neck and the
rope to prevent his
death.

IV.
*Comb.*
c. 1500–1550
*Found* at City of
London by Ed Bucknall.

The closely spaced
teeth on this comb were
for the removal of lice.
Suffering from lice
was sometimes said to
be an aid to religious
contemplation or a
form of penance. As
the murdered Thomas
Becket's body cooled,
it was observed that the
lice in his shirt 'boiled
over like water in a
simmering cauldron',
and the irritation they
must have caused him
was taken as a sign
of his piety.[47]

*V.*

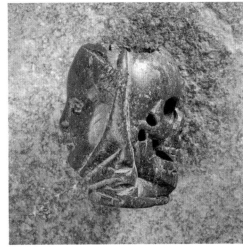

*VI.*

*VII.*

*VIII.*

V.
*Touchpiece.*
15th to 16th century
*Found* at Southwark
by the Author.

This copper disc
features the letters
'IhS', an abbreviation
for Jesus Christ derived
from the first three
letters of the Greek for
Jesus: iota-eta-sigma.
It may have functioned
as a touchpiece: a
personal protective
charm that had to be
touched for its power
to be obtained. It was
found folded in half,
recalling the practice
of folding a coin at the
moment of making
a vow of pilgrimage.

VI.
*Rosary Bead.*
Early 16th century
*Found* at City of
London by Caroline
Nunneley.

Rosaries were used as a
means of keeping count
of recitations during
the saying of prayers.
They sometimes
incorporated beads
juxtaposing depictions
of the living with
representations of
death – most often in
the form of the skull.
Known as *memento mori*
(Latin for 'remember
you must die'), these
reminded their owner
of their inevitable
mortality.

VII.
*Henry VIII Half Groat.*
1526–1532
*Found* at City of
London by Ed Bucknall.

Early in his reign,
King Henry VIII was
a model of Catholic
devotion, visiting
Canterbury on the
350th anniversary
of St Thomas's
martyrdom, and
making an offering
at the saint's shrine.
However, his split with
the Roman Catholic
Church in order to
divorce Catherine
of Aragon, led to the
destruction of such
sites and the end of
pilgrimage in England.

VIII.
*Statuettes of Hindu
Goddess Saraswati and
Spiritual Master Sai Baba.*
21st century
*Found* at Lambeth by
the Author.

For some Hindu
festivals, a new idol
is sanctified for its
duration. Once the
festival is over the
idol can no longer be
worshipped. To cleanse
it of its holiness and
return it to its material
form, it is submerged
in running water. In 1970
the Thames was blessed
to become a sacred
river in the Hindu faith,
allowing it to be used
for this purpose.

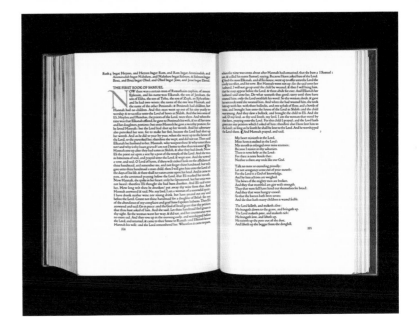

# *Printers—*

The Arts and Crafts Movement,
*revealed by pieces of type.*

*OPPOSITE.*
*Doves Type.*
1899–1901
*Found* at Richmond
upon Thames
by Robert Green.

*ABOVE.*
*Pages from Volume 1*
*of the Doves Press's*
*masterpiece, the English*
*Bible, published in 1903.*

**THE GREAT EXHIBITION OF 1851**
attracted six million visitors, displaying
the gamut of British manufacturing to
the world. But not everyone was impressed.
Seventeen-year-old William Morris, taken
by his parents, found the exhibition's
contents deeply and viscerally deplorable.
Over the next few years, Morris's critical
view of Victorian industrial society
hardened further. He became convinced
that mass-production had resulted in
a grotesque glut of ostentatious and
poorly made goods, accompanied by
a transformation of the workplace into
one of grinding misery.

The lot of the factory worker was in stark contrast to that of the medieval craftsman who, in Morris's view, had found joy in his work and seamlessly fused utility and ornament in the goods he produced.

Guided by this reformist zeal, Morris set about applying his prodigious creative urges to textile design, fantasy fiction, conservation and socialist campaigning. He eventually turned his hand to printing books, drawing on the expertise of engraver and printer Emery Walker. In 1900, four years after Morris's death, Walker was asked by bookbinder Thomas James Cobden-Sanderson to become his partner in establishing a new press for printing fine books by hand. They named it the Doves Press after 'The Dove', a Thames-side pub in Hammersmith, their centre of operations. As became customary for such a press, Doves had its own typeface devised, a process overseen by Walker. It was described as 'the most beautiful that had ever been made'.[48]

While Cobden-Sanderson and Walker had both been in Morris's circle, they were rather different men. Walker, reticent and of humble background, had attracted the attention of the burgeoning Arts and Crafts movement after giving an inspirational but stumbling lecture on typography, attended by Morris. Cobden-Sanderson was a former lawyer, who had left the profession after suffering a breakdown caused by toiling over a tedious legal tract, eventually finding renown as a bookbinder. He saw his move into printing as a spiritual quest for 'The Ideal Book'.

A printing of *Agricola* by the Roman historian Tacitus – the Doves Press's first book – was deemed a great success, and subsequent publications sold out in advance. Relations between Cobden-Sanderson and Walker were amicable, although such was the former's perfectionism that he remarked bitterly in his diary about mistakes Walker had failed to spot in one edition. The pair then embarked on their magnum opus: an edition of the Bible printed in five calfskin-bound volumes, which took four years to complete. For Cobden-Sanderson, this was his life's highest purpose and he worked tirelessly on it, personally checking every proof to eliminate even the tiniest flaws. That Walker, who was not a hands-on printer, did not share in this task was resented by Cobden-Sanderson. The Doves Press Bible was nevertheless a resounding success and hailed as 'a masterpiece of workmanship'.[49] Such adoration notwithstanding, Cobden-Sanderson wrote to Walker in 1906 requesting that they dissolve their partnership.

The next decade saw a series of bitter negotiations between the two, mediated by their long-suffering friends. Walker and Cobden-Sanderson had made an agreement whereby Walker could have a set of the Doves type for his own personal use. But Cobden-Sanderson feared this would be used for commercial purposes and offered to pay Walker off. Walker declined, and a new agreement was proposed that would allow Cobden-Sanderson to dissolve the partnership

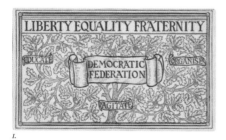

*I.*

_II._

_III._

five years later. However, when the day eventually came to give notice, Walker claimed he had never made such an agreement. Instead, he instructed his solicitors to claim his right to half of everything connected with the Doves Press. Incensed, Cobden-Sanderson refused, and barred Walker from the Press's premises. Eventually, they agreed that Cobden-Sanderson would enjoy exclusive use of the type as long as he lived, but on his death this would revert to Walker, if he was still living. With Cobden-Sanderson a decade older, it seemed likely the type would eventually end up in Walker's hands.

Still fearful that Walker would use the type for less exalted purposes and angered at his demand for half ownership, Cobden-Sanderson developed a plan to ensure it would never fall into his partner's possession. He decided he would cast his beloved type into the River Thames. After a period of procrastination, on 31 August 1916, with his quest for the ideal book achieved and his health declining, the time finally came for the destruction of the type. That night in his journal he recorded: 'I had gone for a stroll...when it occurred to me that it was a suitable night and time; so I went indoors, and taking first one page and then two, succeeded in destroying three. I will now go on till I have destroyed the whole of it.'[50] And he did. Over the next five months, the frail septuagenarian made perhaps one hundred and seventy trips to Hammersmith Bridge under the cover of darkness, casting more than a tonne of type from the bridge. The disposal was eventually completed on 24 November, with Cobden-Sanderson wishing: 'May the river in its tides and flow pass over them to and from the great sea forever...untouched by other use.'[51]

Walker learned of this illegal act of destruction in a review of a Doves Press publication that Cobden-Sanderson had mailed to the _Times Literary Supplement_. On Cobden-Sanderson's death in 1922, his widow finally settled with Walker for financial compensation, twenty years after tensions had first emerged.

For the next century it was believed that only one block of type remained in existence, but in 2014, designer Robert Green found three pieces on the foreshore after painstakingly retracing Cobden-Sanderson's steps. Determined to recover more, he hired divers to scour the riverbed for two days, and one hundred and fifty more pieces were recovered. These were enough to help Green refine his digital revival of the type, finally rescuing it from the river.

4. PRINTERS.

99

a a a a a a a a a a a

a a a a a a a a a a a

a B B c d d d e e f f

F G G G G h h h h h h

h h h h h h h h h h i

i i i L L L L o o o o

o o o o o o o o o o o

o o o o o o o o o o o

o o o o o o o o o o R

u v x x x x x x x x X

X X X y y Y Y z ! ~ ~

# IN THE BEGINNING

GOD CREATED THE HEAVEN AND THE EARTH. ⟨AND THE EARTH WAS WITHOUT FORM, AND VOID; AND DARKNESS WAS UPON THE FACE OF THE DEEP, & THE SPIRIT OF GOD MOVED UPON THE FACE OF THE WATERS. ⟨And God said, Let there be light: & there was light. And God saw the light, that it was good: & God divided the light from the darkness. And God called the light Day, and the darkness he called Night. And the evening and the morning were the first day. ⟨And God said, Let there be a firmament in the midst of the waters, & let it divide the waters from the waters. And God made the firmament, and divided the waters which were under the firmament from the waters which were above the firmament: & it was so. And God called the firmament Heaven. And the evening & the morning were the second day. ⟨And God said, Let the waters under the heaven be gathered together unto one place, and let the dry land appear: and it was so. And God called the dry land Earth; and the gathering together of the waters called he Seas: and God saw that it was good. And God said, Let the earth bring forth grass, the herb yielding seed, and the fruit tree yielding fruit after his kind, whose seed is in itself, upon the earth: & it was so. And the earth brought forth grass, & herb yielding seed after his kind, & the tree yielding fruit, whose seed was in itself, after his kind: and God saw that it was good. And the evening & the morning were the third day. ⟨And God said, Let there be lights in the firmament of the heaven to divide the day from the night; and let them be for signs, and for seasons, and for days, & years: and let them be for lights in the firmament of the heaven to give light upon the earth: & it was so. And God made two great lights; the greater light to rule the day, and the lesser light to rule the night: he made the stars also. And God set them in the firmament of the heaven to give light upon the earth, and to rule over the day and over the night, & to divide the light from the darkness: and God saw that it was good. And the evening and the morning were the fourth day. ⟨And God said, Let the waters bring forth abundantly the moving creature that hath life, and fowl that may fly above the earth in the open firmament of heaven. And God created great whales, & every living creature that moveth, which the waters brought forth abundantly, after their kind, & every winged fowl after his kind: & God saw that it was good. And God blessed them, saying, Be fruitful, & multiply, and fill the waters in the seas, and let fowl multiply in the earth. And the evening & the morning were the fifth day. ⟨And God said, Let the earth bring forth the living creature after his kind, cattle, and creeping thing, and beast of the earth after his kind: and it was so. And God made the beast of the earth after his kind, and cattle after their kind, and every thing that creepeth upon the

27

*II.*

I.
*Pieces of Doves type recovered from the Thames by type designer Robert Green, together with the corresponding digital letters and punctuation recreated by him.*

II.
*The opening page of Genesis from Volume 1 of the English Bible, set in the Doves type and published by the Doves Press in 1903.*

# *Fascists—*

Britain's first fascist organization,
*revealed by a badge.*

*FASCISM IN BRITAIN IS SEEN BY MANY* as the sole preserve of Sir Oswald Mosley's British Union of Fascists and the thuggish activities of its Blackshirts in the 1930s. But a badge mudlarked from the Thames reveals a movement with deeper and sometimes perplexing roots. Featuring a letter 'F' surrounded by the inscription 'For King and Country', it would have been worn by a member of the British Fascists. This organization, the first avowedly fascist group in Britain, was founded in 1923, a decade earlier than Mosley's. Its founder was not the male archetype associated with fascist leaders but a woman: Rotha Lintorn-Orman.

I.
*Two new male recruits to the
British Fascists learn the fascist
salute, standing beside a banner
bearing the organization's
insignia; 1924–1933.*

II.
*Photograph of Colonel Victor
Barker, born Lillias Irma Valerie
Barker, leading member of the
National Fascisti. Barker's gender
assignment at birth was seemingly
unknown to other members.*

Lintorn-Orman had demonstrated a liking for authority from an early age. Born into a middle-class family in Bournemouth, by the age of fourteen she was proudly leading her own Girl Scout troop. During the First World War, like many adventurous young women of her day, she sought service overseas, driving ambulances in Serbia before contracting malaria, returning to Britain and working for the Red Cross. Six months after Mussolini's rise to power, Lintorn-Orman decided to form her own fascist organization. Bankrolled by her mother, she launched the British Fascisti (renamed British Fascists a year later to avoid accusations of foreign influence).

Like other fascists of the 1920s, Lintorn-Orman saw society as being on the cusp of a crisis that would only be averted by facing down the 'Red Menace', ridding the country of foreigners, defending the monarchy, protecting children from subversive influences and preventing strikes. In her eyes

Britain was being debased, and taking a stand through fascism was the answer. The British Fascists soon attracted sympathizers from the right wing of the Conservative party, with which it would maintain close ties. Other members included minor aristocrats, former military figures and 'toughs' drawn from the working classes, who relished engaging in direct street confrontations with communists.

Like its founder, a significant proportion of the British Fascists' members were women. Some were former suffragettes who had become disenchanted with the feminist movement, but liked its action-oriented methods and the paramilitary-style structure of the Women's Social and Political Union. Many had served in the women's auxiliary services in the First World War and were seeking a similar sense of status, purpose and adventure. They were welcomed into the British Fascists' Women's Units and tasked

I.

with organizing an array of fundraising activities: dinners, carol singing, dances, garden parties and even a Fascist Dogs' Club. First-aid training was provided in preparation for the predicted crisis, while instruction in ju-jitsu was offered to those who might be required to eject protesters from meetings and participate in fascist street patrols.

*II.*

Another important duty fulfilled by women members was organizing Fascist Children's Clubs, with the movement's official newspaper declaring: 'women especially should make it their task and duty to prevent the spirit of the Red Menace to influence the future citizens of the Empire.'[52] Club activities included singing patriotic songs, playing games and distributing books such as the vehemently anti-Semitic *The Alien Menace* (1932), by former soldier Arthur Lane. Such initiatives were sometimes met with violence by opponents. In 1927, Lintorn-Orman explained to a sympathetic journalist how she and fourteen other fascist women had organized a meeting to promote Fascist Children's Clubs in east London. At the encouragement of communist infiltrators, the two hundred children present surged towards the fascists, hurling missiles at them and striking Lintorn-Orman in the face in the process.

The General Strike of 1926 saw the British Fascists at the peak of their popularity. Rallies were organized in London's Hyde Park which attracted crowds of several thousands, anti-strike divisions were formed and members joined government-sponsored initiatives to keep essential services running. But the collapse of the strike and the dissolution of the crisis through which the fascists had hoped to gain influence, led to disillusionment within the organization. Lintorn-Orman took on the day-to-day leadership of the British Fascists around this time (despite being its founder, she had previously left this to others). Her leadership drew criticisms of divisiveness and indecisiveness, while some members thought the British Fascists were not fascist enough – merely 'conservatism with knobs on' – and desired an approach more directly aligned to that of Mussolini.[53]

The first split in the organization had come in 1924, when sixty members left to form the more militant National Fascisti. That group floundered, however, when its brawling leader in London, Colonel Victor Barker, was, on his imprisonment for contempt of court, revealed as a woman, born Lillias Irma Valerie Barker. Barker was subsequently convicted of having made a false statement to a marriage registrar in order to marry one Elfreda Haward.

A more serious rival arose with the founding of Oswald Mosley's British Union of Fascists in 1932. Lintorn-Orman regarded the charismatic former Labour MP as a near communist, and the two organizations soon ran into conflict. This saw some of Mosley's Blackshirts raid the British Fascists' headquarters, smashing property and assaulting members. Despite defections, Linton-Orman refused calls to merge the two groups. At the same time her health began to fail, and it was reported she was recovering from a heart attack. The following year a friend complained to police that some of the British Fascists were constantly plying Lintorn-Orman with drink and drugs, 'with a view of extracting money from her'.[54] By 1934, she was being treated for an alcohol-related illness which would eventually lead to her death aged forty. The British Fascists were dissolved shortly afterwards.

ENTERTAINERS.

# Street Musicians—

London's sonic culture wars,
*revealed by a Jew's harp.*

OPPOSITE.
*Jew's Harp.*
1500–1800
*Found* at Westminster
by Seán O'Mara.

ABOVE.
Boy with a Jew's Harp,
*1621, by Dirck van Baburen. Asian in origin, the Jew's harp had become a popular musical instrument in Britain by the fourteenth century. Its name may have originated as an anti-Semitic slur or as a reference to Jewish sellers.*

**GIVEN THE QUANTITY OF JEW'S HARPS** found on the Thames foreshore, its distinctive twang may once have been one of London's most ubiquitous sounds. The owner of this example might have been among the city's legion of street musicians, with whom the Jew's harp was perennially popular, along with fiddles, pipes, drums known as tabors, and stringed instruments of many kinds. One such player was Peter Kelly, renowned for playing two Jew's harps at the same time in return for small change, around his local alehouses and taverns.

At his trial for murder in 1726, Kelly was condemned for 'Whoring, Drinking, and idling away his Time', yet the ingenuity with which he played on his two Jew's harps was complimented.[55] This condemnation of Kelly's character mixed with admiration for his skill highlights the simultaneous high and low status enjoyed by musicians – bringers of pleasure who have struggled throughout history to establish their respectability.

The century and a half following the Reformation was a particularly precarious time to be a musician. Those travelling between towns in search of temporary employment were caught up in a crackdown on 'pardoners, fortune tellers, fencers, minstrels and players' who, if unlicensed, faced being whipped on two consecutive days.[56] Other attacks were religiously motivated, with Puritans fearing that music would divert people away from organized worship and encourage debauchery. In 1583, pamphleteer Philip Stubbes ranted that learning to play music would make a man's son 'softe, wommannish, uncleane, smoth mouthed, affected to bawdrie, scurrilitie, filthie rimes and unsemely talking...transnatured into a woman'.[57] By 1656, the new Cromwellian regime had prohibited all fiddlers and minstrels from playing in taverns or offering their services in public. This left unemployed musicians with no alternative but to riskily 'wander with their instruments under their cloaks'.[58]

With the restoration of the monarchy in 1660, the ban was repealed and singers, fiddlers, pipers and Jew's harp players

II.

returned to the streets of London. Nevertheless, concern about street music did not abate in the eighteenth and nineteenth centuries, but instead shifted to focus on another issue: noise. As London's population rose, street music proliferated. By the mid-nineteenth century it provided a much needed income for many working-class players. Some were former mudlarks, turf-cutters and errand boys, who blackened their faces to become minstrels known as 'negro serenaders', performing on the ferries plying the Thames. Others were Italian organ grinders fleeing poverty at home or German brass bands equipped with cheap instruments. A member of one singing troupe admitted that most of its performers had little or no previous musical experience and rehearsed on the job, but such musicians also provided cheap and accessible entertainment.

Some members of the Victorian middle classes took exception to this musical entrepreneurship, dismissing it simply as a sonic nuisance to be silenced. The charge was led by brewery magnate and parliamentarian Michael Bass, who pressed for the regulation of street music, receiving thousands of letters of support. One, signing himself 'Paterfamilias', contacted *The Times*, complaining that his daughter's

I.

*I.*

*In* The Enraged Musician, *1741,*
*William Hogarth depicts a violinist*
*unable to rehearse as the noisiest*
*inhabitants of London pass by his*
*window, including street musicians*
*playing a hautboy and a drum.*

*II.*

*A man plays a Jew's harp, also*
*known as a jaw harp or mouth*
*harp, at home before his children*
*and dog in this painting by*
*John Burnet, c. 1809.*

*III.*

*An Italian street musician plays*
*a harp on the pavement in this*
*photograph taken from* Street
Life in London, *1877, by John*
*Thomson and Adolphe Smith.*

piano lessons were being deliberately
interrupted. He claimed that her tutor's
arrival was immediately followed by
a band of two blind clarinettists and
three blind cellists known as the 'Scotch
Crawlers'. After paying them to go away,
a series of other acts appealed for the
same treatment, including the 'notorious
widow, whose infant phenomena
perform irritating sonatas on a jangling
pianoforte placed on a…vegetable truck,
drawn by a small donkey'.[59] Charles
Dickens also joined the fray, writing that
'professors and practitioners of one or
other of the arts and sciences…are daily
interrupted, harassed, worried, wearied,
driven nearly mad, by street musicians.'[60]

Bass's most vociferous supporter,
however, was the mathematician Charles
Babbage, who advocated banning street
music completely. Babbage railed that
street musicians disturbed the sick and
destroyed the time of the intellectual

classes, costing him a (carefully
calculated) full quarter of his working
potential. His attempts to bring steet
musicians before the courts made him
a hate figure among them and their
supporters, who decided to fight back
against this assault on players' livelihoods.
According to Babbage, several neighbours
purchased, and regularly blew, worn-out
wind instruments they were incapable
of playing simply to annoy him, while
another tormented him nightly with
a penny whistle from his attic, which
overlooked Babbage's garden. Others
penned humorous verses of criticism,
which appeared on placards placed in
shop windows across the West End.

Bass succeeded in giving the police the
power to arrest any street musician who
refused to move on. This concession to
bourgeois concerns, however, was not
enough to prevent street musicians from
continuing to enliven the streets of London.

*III.*

# Finds Relating to Street Music.

I.

II.

III.

IV.

**I.**
*Bone Tuning Pin.*
1200–1500
*Found* at City of
London by the Author.

This find held a string
in place on a medieval
stringed instrument
such as a harp, enabling
it to be tuned. Small,
portable and capable
of brilliant monophonic
compositions, the harp
was a mainstay of the
era's minstrels.

**II.**
*Tin-Glazed Tile
Fragment.*
Late 17th to early 18th
century
*Found* at City of London
by the Author.

The musician featured
on this fragment of tile
is probably playing a
hautboy, precursor to
the oboe and popular
with street troupes.
It was also the main
melody instrument in
military bands, until
being succeeded by
the clarinet.

**III.**
*Whistle.*
*c.* 18th century
*Found* at Southwark
by the Author.

Whistles were played
in military bands,
taverns, on the street
and aboard ships.
They helped transport
the ballads, jigs and
marches of the British
Isles to the American
colonies. There they
would blend with other
European and African
musical influences
to create what would
later become known
as country music.

**IV.**
*Ice Skate.*
850–1800
*Found* at undisclosed
location by Tony Thira.

Between 1400 and 1835,
there were twenty-four
recorded winters when
the Thames froze over,
allowing skating. Ice
skates were fashioned
from the shin bone of
cattle or horses. Frost
fairs, featuring musical
performances, were
held on the frozen
water. In the words of
a 1684 ballad, 'a famous
river now become a
stage' for 'cheating,
drunken, leud, and
debauch'd crew'.[61]

FROST FAIR ON THE RIVER THAMES

THE FAIR ON THE THAMES, FEB.Y 4. 1814.    LA FOIRE SUR LA TAMISE, FEVRIER 4. 1814.

ABOVE.
Music and dancing features
in both these prints depicting
the frost fair held on the frozen
River Thames in February
1814. Towards the centre of

the top view people dance as
a fiddler plays in front of a
tent offering 'Good Ale Porter
& Gin', while ballad singers
are featured at right. In the

second image, at left, sailors
and a girl dance to a band
of musicians playing a hurdy-
gurdy, drum, panpipes and
a tambourine.

# Indigenous North Americans—

Native travellers and performance, *revealed by beads.*

Hudson's Bay Company
Trade Beads.
*c.* 1680–1850
*Found* at City of London
and Tower Hamlets
by the Author.

*ABOVE.*
*Print depicting a war dance*
*being performed by members*
*of an Ojibwe troupe who visited*
*London in 1844. J. Harris's*
*lithograph is based on a*
*painting by George Catlin,*
*who travelled to England in*
*the mid-nineteenth century,*
*giving lectures on Indigenous*
*North Americans.*

IN 1843, A GROUP OF NINE OJIBWE
'Indians', led by their 75-year-old chief,
Ah-quee-we-zaints ('The Boy Chief'),
visited the newly opened Thames Tunnel
running beneath the river between
Wapping and Rotherhithe. As the
first tunnel successfully constructed
underneath a navigable river, it had
instantly become a tourist attraction.
Around two million visitors a year paid
a penny to pass through and some
hailed it as the eighth wonder of the
world. The Ojibwe's reaction was
recorded at the time as follows:

When they entered the tunnel,
and were told that they were under
the middle of the Thames, and
that the great ships were riding
over their heads, they stood in utter
astonishment, with their hands over
their mouths (denoting silence), and
said nothing until they came out.
They called it the 'Great Medicine
Cave' and gave the medicine dance
at the entrance of it.[62]

*II.*

How did 'The Boy' and his fellow Ojibwe
come to be in London? Small, red glass
beads with green centres, found on the
foreshore twenty-five yards (twenty-
three metres) above the tunnel, help
illuminate the chain of events. Many
such beads have been excavated over
five thousand miles (eight thousand
kilometres) away in the Canadian
province of Manitoba, on the site of the
York Factory trading post. Built in 1684,
for most of its three hundred years of
operation York Factory was controlled by
the Hudson's Bay Company. Functioning
as the *de facto* government in parts of
North America for nearly two centuries,
the Hudson's Bay Company traded in
beaver pelts with Indigenous North
Americans. To tie the Indigenous
barter economy to the market-oriented
enterprise of the company, the currency
of the 'Made Beaver' was created. This

was defined as one prime quality skin
from an adult beaver. In 1776, Indigenous
traders could exchange four Made
Beaver for a pound of beads, a trunk,
or a gallon of brandy, along with a
host of other European commodities.

As Indigenous North American and
British interests became more entwined,
in addition to beaver pelts crossing the
Atlantic to London, so did an increasing
number of Indigenous people. Some
of these came as captives, others as
emissaries eager to discuss land claims
and alliances with the ultimate source of
power in America before the Revolution:
the British Crown. All aroused intense
curiosity. In 1603, two 'Virginians'
demonstrated their canoe-handling skills
on the Thames, for which they were
paid sixpence each. Three Cherokee
warriors who arrived in London in
1762 were followed across the city by
gawping crowds, and wax figures of them
were put on display at Mrs Salmon's
Waxworks in Fleet Street. This curiosity,
coupled with the ubiquity of Indigenous
imagery around the selling of tobacco,
made the Indigenous North American –
not the colonist – the predominant icon
of America in London before the War
of Independence.

Amid this intense interest, some
Indigenous North Americans began to
be brought to London specifically for the
purpose of display. One such spectacle
was curated by the American artist
George Catlin, who incorporated 'The
Boy' and his troupe into an exhibition
of his paintings of Indigenous North
Americans, held in London from 1843.
Their addition had an immediate impact

*I.*

I.

Officers of the Hudson's Bay
Company photographed by
H. N. Robinson at the company's
trading post in Rigolet, Labrador,
Canada, 1880s.

II.

Painting of Ojibwe performing the
Snow Shoe dance by George Catlin,
1860s. According to Catlin, it was a
dance of thanks to the Great Spirit
after the first winter snowfall, to
improve success in hunting.

III.

Poster commemorating the
performance of Buffalo Bill's Wild
West show in London for Queen
Victoria in 1887 as part of the
Golden Jubilee celebrations.

as previously Catlin had been dressing
up white Englishmen in Indigenous
clothing. After performing dances in
between Catlin's lectures on Indigenous
culture, 'The Boy' and his fellow Ojibwe
were met with 'a roar of applause' and
women 'screamed quite as loud as the
Indians as they were making a rush for
the door'.[63] In a show of appreciation,
audience members pressed money, trinkets
and jewelry into the troupe's hands. At
the end of each performance Catlin was
barraged with questions demonstrating
the spectators' ignorance. These
included 'in what way the Indians were
taken – whether with a lasso or in a sort
of pit', 'whether they eat the scalps' and
whether they were capable of reason.[64]

During their time in London, the
Ojibwe were struck by the poverty,
hunger, inequality and rampant
drunkenness they saw on its streets.
Factory smoke they described as 'the
prairies on fire', while they supposed
that men wearing sandwich boards were
doing so as a form of punishment. Queen
Victoria was also a topic of discussion,
with the troupe surprised at 'the
government of the greatest and richest
country in the world being in the hands
of a woman, and she no larger than many
of the Indian girls at the age of twelve
or thirteen years'.[65] Their partnership

with Catlin eventually fell apart after the
group's interpreter, 'Strong Wind', fell in
love with and married an English woman.

Later in the nineteenth century,
Indigenous people from across North
America visited London in a variety of
roles as entertainers. The runner named
Deerfoot drew huge crowds to the east
London suburb of Hackney Wick, to
witness his feats of athleticism. A total
of 2.5 million Londoners, meanwhile,
experienced Buffalo Bill's Wild West
Show. This sensationalized representation
of frontier life featured over 800
performers, 180 horses, 18 buffalo, 10 elk,
2 deer and 5 Texas longhorns. The climax
of an early tour came when Albert,
Prince of Wales, boarded a stagecoach
along with the kings of Belgium,
Denmark, Greece and Saxony, plus the
future Kaiser Wilhelm II. Buffalo Bill
then personally raced the stagecoach
around the arena, while a Lakota
mounted a mock attack, reinforcing
the prevailing perceptions of Indigenous
North Americans as dangerous savages.

Much about this entertainment
was exploitative: for example, female
performers were given immodest
costumes and male headdresses. Such
motifs carried over into Western movies,
the first of which was filmed in 1899, not
in America but in Blackburn, Lancashire.

III.

# *Parachutists—*

The aerial entertainers of the Edwardian age, *revealed by a clay pipe.*

OPPOSITE.
*Clay Tobacco Pipe
Featuring a Descending
Parachutist.*
*c.* 1890–1910
*Found* at Lambeth
by the Author.

ABOVE.
*Detail from poster
advertising Thomas
Baldwin's parachute
descent over Alexandra
Palace on 28 July 1888.
Baldwin was the first
American to descend
from a balloon by
parachute in 1887.*

IN 1861, SELINA YOUNG (billed as 'Madame Genevieve' to add some continental exoticism) crossed the Thames on a high wire from Battersea to Cremorne Gardens on the opposite bank. It was considered an act so outrageous to public decency that on her first attempt the guy lines that stabilized her wire were slashed by angry male onlookers. Eleven years later, the aptly named Leona Dare hung by her teeth from the basket of an airborne balloon. This prompted one MP to propose legislation regulating such outlandish performances.

*I.*

*Selina Young is shown crossing the Thames from Battersea Bridge to Cremorne Gardens on a tight rope on 12 August 1861 in this engraving from the* Illustrated London News.

*II.*

*Parachutist Dolly Shepherd ascending with her parachute under a hot air balloon from Alexandra Palace, 1903. She is holding on to a trapeze bar with one hand and waving to the crowd with the other.*

But aerial entertainment continued, with parachutists becoming its most popular figures by the turn of the century. Drawing huge crowds at fetes, fairs and galas across the country, the appeal of these performers inspired the creation of memorabilia for purchase by fans. Such items included clay tobacco pipes featuring a descending parachutist on each side of the bowl.

Making a parachute jump before the invention of the aeroplane involved ascending by balloon. At around 2,000 feet (500 metres), the parachutist launched themselves over the side of the balloon's basket or was released from beneath it. Unlike today, the parachute was not attached to their body. Instead, they descended to the ground sitting on a trapeze bar suspended below the parachute. The most popular parachutists were young women, some of whom met tragic ends. Fourteen-year-old Louisa Evans ('Mademoiselle Albertina') claimed to be age twenty in order to be taken on by parachute team leader Auguste Gaudron. On her maiden

jump in Cardiff, the wind unexpectedly carried her out above the Bristol Channel, where she drowned upon landing. Another tragic case was that of Edith Maud Cook, who landed safely on a factory roof only to have the wind drag her parachute on to the street below, causing her to fall to her death. When such incidents happened, Gaudron would simply report that the parachutist in question had 'left the team'.[66]

Another member of Gaudron's team, Dolly Shepherd, had better luck. Shepherd entered the world of parachuting as a result of her determination to see a concert by American musician John Philip Sousa at north London's Alexandra Palace. Tickets had sold out, so she sought work as a waitress in the venue's cafe. During one performance, her customers included the Wild West showman Samuel Cody. The previous night, during his stage show *The Klondike Nugget*, Cody had shot an egg balanced on his wife's head and the bullet had grazed her skull, leaving her unable to perform. Shepherd offered to take her

5. ENTERTAINERS.

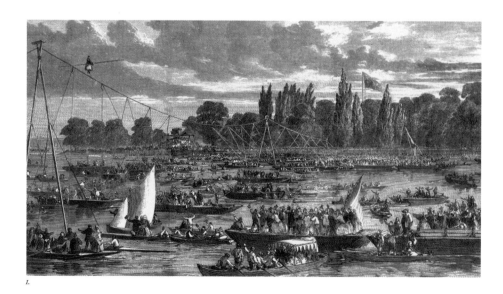

*I.*

place, and as a reward for her successful performance, Cody took her on a tour of the workshops at Alexandra Palace used by a small group of aeronauts. It was here that she encountered Gaudron, who had been making balloon ascents and parachute jumps at the site since 1898. As one of Gaudron's performers had recently 'left the team', he asked Shepherd if she would like to make a jump. After a mere thirty minutes of basic training she did so, earning £2/10 for her efforts.

Shepherd went on to make over one hundred jumps between 1903 and 1912. These were not without incident. At the top of her ascent above one Leicestershire showground, when she attempted to release the hot air balloon pulling her up, the mechanism jammed. This left her with only one option: to hang on to her parachute's trapeze bar until enough gas had escaped from the balloon to allow it to descend. In the meantime, she continued rising, higher into the air than she had ever been before. At 12,000 feet (3.7 kilometres) the air became cold, numbing her hands. When she was 2 miles (3 kilometres) above the showground, darkness fell. After three hours clinging on, having drifted for 35 miles (56 kilometres), she eventually descended, exhausted and dehydrated.

Her most notorious near miss, however, was during a planned dual descent with maiden jumper Louie May. The two ascended over Longton, Staffordshire, with both their parachutes suspended beneath a single balloon – but May's parachute suffered the same mechanism jam that Shepherd had experienced in Leicestershire. The pair continued upwards, with Shepherd recalling in her memoir that at 11,000 feet (3.4 kilometres) May was 'a limp figure hanging grimly on to life, but her lips were blue with cold, her eyes wide open and staring with suppressed fear'.[67] Figuring May was not strong enough to hold on to the trapeze bar until the balloon descended, Shepherd improvised the first ever mid-air rescue.

II.

Pulling May's parachute towards hers, she ordered May to cling on to her body and let go of the faulty parachute. Shepherd then pulled her own release cord and they both descended on a single parachute. May was unhurt, but Shepherd endured spinal injuries and it was feared she would never walk again. However, after a course of experimental electric shock treatment she eventually recovered, returning to parachuting for the next four years.

Shepherd's last jump took place during the spring of 1912 at Alexandra Palace, where she had begun her parachuting career nine years earlier. As the balloon carrying her into the air rose, she claimed she heard a voice telling her 'Don't come up again, or you'll be killed.'[68] Consequently, upon landing, she gave away her jumping accessories to members of the assembled crowd and settled into full-time work at her aunt's feather emporium. Soon after, her surviving fellow jumpers followed suit, as the aeroplane came to dominate the skies and parachuting became a more serious business.

# Finds Relating to the Life of Dolly Shepherd.

I.

II.

III.

IV.

*I.*
*Brick Commemorating*
*the Coronation of*
*Edward VII.*
1902
*Found* at Newham
by the Author.

Dolly Shepherd
saw herself as very
much a product of
the Edwardian age.
This brick, made to
commemorate Edward
VII's coronation,
features the original
planned month for
the event – June 1902.
Due to developing
appendicitis, however,
Edward was not
crowned until August
that year.

*II.*
*Women's Volunteer*
*Reserve Shoulder Badge.*
*c.* 1916–1918
*Found* at Westminster
by the Author.

A few days after the
outbreak of the First
World War, Shepherd
volunteered for the
Women's Emergency
Corps, which would
become the Women's
Volunteer Reserve.
Her duties included
driving ambulances
to ferry wounded
soldiers to hospitals
around London.

*III.*
*Cartridge Case Used in*
*a Martini-Henry Rifle.*
1871–1918
*Found* at Westminster
by the Author.

Shepherd wrote of her
fear when experiencing
a bombing raid on
London by a German
airship during the First
World War. Obsolete
Martini-Henry rifles
were used to fire
incendiary bullets at
airships. However, the
ships failed to explode
because of the lack
of oxygen in their
hydrogen bags.

*IV.*
*Royal Air Force Club*
*Teacup Fragment.*
*c.* 1922–1930
*Found* at Westminster
by the Author.

In her autobiography,
Shepherd mourned
the demise of the
aerial stage as a place
of pure entertainment.
The First World War
made the skies a more
serious and deadly
place: by the end of
the conflict, nearly
ten thousand British
airmen had been killed
and the Royal Air Force
emerged as the largest
in the world.

*ABOVE.*
*Portrait of Dolly Shepherd*
*wearing a late version of her*
*parachuting outfit and holding*
*the silk Union Jack that she*
*would wave at crowds as she*
*ascended; 11 September 1911.*

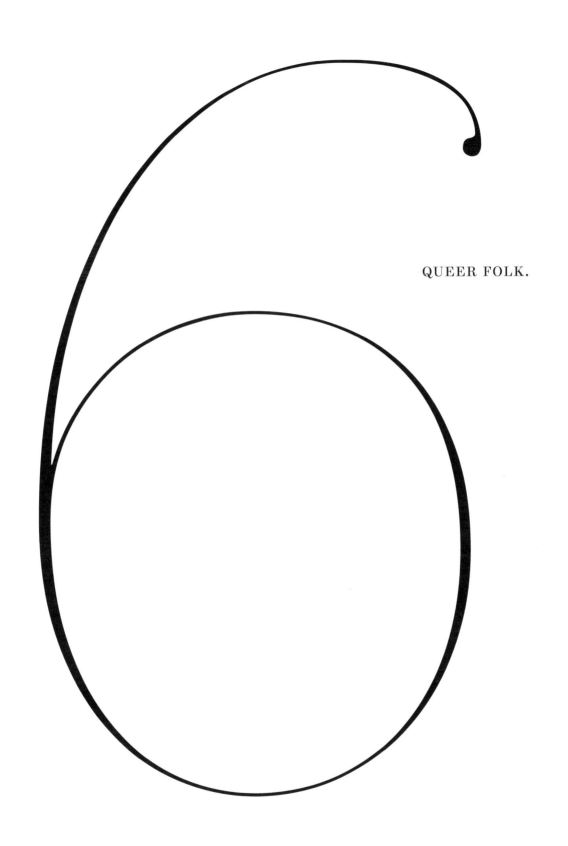

QUEER FOLK.

# Romans—

The men of antiquity who had sex
with men, *revealed by a coin.*

*THIS ROMAN COIN, FOUND LANGUISHING*
on the foreshore near to the site of an
ancient bathhouse, features the bust of
the notorious second-century Emperor
Caracalla. Frequently portrayed as
a tyrant, the young ruler remained
childless throughout his reign and
was subject to gossip about his sexual
activities. He was variously said to have
married his stepmother and debauched
a Vestal Virgin, before becoming impotent
and spending his time in the company
of male courtiers, by whom he enjoyed
being penetrated.

Whether this was politically motivated rumourmongering or true, what was seen as problematic was not that Caracalla was said to be having sex with men, but that the proper protocols were not being followed. In ancient Roman culture the sexual identities of today associated with heterosexuality, homosexuality and bisexuality did not exist. Instead, the dominant sexual delineation was between the penetrative partner, who was deemed to be 'masculine', and the receptive partner, who was deemed to be 'feminine', regardless of their gender. What this meant on a day-to-day level is bluntly brought to life by the poet Horace, who advocated sex with both enslaved males and females when a man's sexual appetite was high:

Now really, when your throat is parched with thirst, you don't ask for golden goblets, do you? When you're hungry, you don't turn your nose up at everything but peacock and turbot, do you? When your crotch is throbbing and there is a slave-girl or home-grown slave-boy ready at hand, whom you could jump right away, you don't prefer to burst with your hard-on, do you? I certainly don't. I like sex that is easy and obtainable.[69]

The fact that Horace specifically advocated sex with enslaved people reveals another tenet of Roman sexuality. Convention dictated that a Roman man

II.

should not only play the penetrative role in sex, but also avoid coupling with any citizen apart from his wife. This left enslaved people, sex workers (who were mostly enslaved) and other non-citizens of either gender as acceptable partners. Enslaved people were deemed to be the enslaver's property, and how this property was used was for him to decide. This permissibility of sex with enslaved people helps explain why – in a story told by writer Valerius Maximus – one Calidius of Bononia, who having been caught in a married lady's bed chamber, sought to extricate himself from trouble by claiming he was only there to for sex with one of her slave boys. It also accounts for why Emperor Hadrian, of wall-building fame, who visited London in AD 122, escaped censure for his relationship with Antinous – a handsome Greek, around thirty-five years the emperor's junior. While it is not completely clear whether Antinous was an enslaved person or not, he did not live as a freeborn Roman, which made their relationship acceptable.

Not all enslaved males were equally desirable in the eyes of Roman men. There was a clear preference for adolescents who were between the onset of puberty and the arrival of a full beard. Such an enslaved boy was known as a *pullus*, Latin for 'chick', which also functioned as an insult. Consul Fabius Maximus was given the nickname 'Jupiter's Chick' after being struck by lightning on his buttocks.

I.

*I.*

*This first century silver drinking cup depicts an older bearded man engaging in anal sex with a beardless youth who is lowering himself into position to be penetrated, using a strap.*

*II.*

*Roman mosaic depicting Zeus in the form of an eagle abducting Ganymede, the handsome young Trojan. Ganymede functioned as a symbol for young males who attracted desire from older men.*

*III.*

*Coin depicting the Greek youth Antinous (left), lover of Roman Emperor Hadrian, and another depicting Emperor Hadrian (right), who celebrated his affection for Antinous in erotic verse.*

It was thought the resulting injury gave him the appearance of having been raped by the king of the gods. The preference for beardless and smooth-bodied youths also gave rise to a plethora of treatments to mask the bodily advance of puberty. The philosopher Pliny the Elder recommended using ants' eggs as a depilatory for armpit hair along with bats' brains, fried viper, gall from a hedgehog and the milk of a bitch who had given birth to her first litter.

While it was seen as acceptable for Roman men to have sex with enslaved boys, some wives voiced concerns about their husbands' activities if they were seen to indulge excessively. In response, the poet Martial rebuffs a fictional wife who finds him penetrating an enslaved boy. She mentions that she too can offer him anal intercourse, but he replies that while he is perfectly happy to take up the offer, her anus is not as pleasurable as a boy's, akin only to a second vagina.[70] More troubling for a man's reputation, however, was being regarded as effeminate, which would lead to him being labelled a *cinaedus*, or 'slut'. According to the historian Suetonius,

even Julius Caesar was accused of being 'every woman's man and every man's woman'.[71] Such was the taboo surrounding being the receptive partner that making this accusation against enemies and rivals could be a potent weapon. Martial humorously suggests that some men thus accused should take remedial action to redress the balance: 'With doors wide open you screw big boys, Amillus, and you want to be caught when you do it – in order to prevent your freedmen and your father's slaves from gossiping.'[72]

Playing the receptive role was not the only way to get a reputation for effeminacy. The wearing of excessive perfume, being a womanizer, aiming to please a woman in a sexual encounter through performing cunnilingus and curling one's hair – could all fuel the gossip mill.

Roman sexuality defined what we might call homosexuality today as an act, rather than an identity – a reminder that while desire might be grounded in biology, how it manifests itself is constantly evolving under the influence of human culture.

*III.*

I.

II.

III.

IV.

I.
*Bronze Finger Ring
Intaglio.*
AD 43–410
*Found* at City of
London by Ed Bucknall.

This find features
three symbols related
to the god Apollo:
a raven, a serpent and
a laurel wreath. Apollo
had many male lovers,
including the Spartan
prince, Hyacinthus.
A discus thrown by
Apollo was blown off
course by the jealous
Zephyrus, killing
Hyacinthus instantly.
Apollo, filled with grief,
created a flower out
of Hyacinthus's blood
and named it after him.

II.
*Box Flue Tile Fragment.*
AD 43–410
*Found* at City of
London by the Author.

In Roman bathhouses,
box flue tiles carried
hot air through walls
from underfloor
heating. Numerous
contemporary sources
attest to bathhouses
as spaces where some
men admired other
men or had sex with
them. The Emperor
Elagabalus (officially
Antoninus) is said
to have constructed
a public bath so he
could fill it with well-
endowed young men
of his choosing.

III.
*Fragment of Samian
Ware.*
AD 150–185
*Found* at Westminster
by Seán O'Mara.

The maker of this
high-end tableware
chose to mark his work
not only with his name,
'MACRINI', but also
with the image of a
phallus. In contrast to
ancient Greece, where
a small penis signified
rational self-control,
for the Romans phallic
endowment was admired
as an embodiment of
masculine potency.
Phallic charms were
thought to ward off evil
and were ubiquitous.

IV.
*Emperor Constantine
One Follis Coin.*
AD 309–337
*Found* at Westminster
by the Author.

Constantine was the
first Roman emperor to
convert to Christianity.
The writings of the
early Christian Church
contained strong
condemnations of
same-sex acts which
came to underpin the
cultural and legal
prohibitions that would
govern such behaviour
after Britain had fully
adopted the religion.

ABOVE.
*First century erotic fresco
from the House of the Vettii,
Pompeii, showing the god
Priapus weighing his penis.*

# Mollies & Macaronis—

Queerness in Georgian London,
*revealed by lead tokens.*

*Lead Tokens.*
1600–1800
*Found* at Southwark and
City of London by the Author.

*ABOVE.*
The Macaroni. A real
Character at the late
Masquerade, *mezzotint
by Philip Dawe, 1773. The
extravagant and effeminate
dress of the 'macaroni', was
often satirized in the press.
The name was given to
fashionable young men
following the high fashion
of the Continent during
the second half of the
eighteenth century.*

BY THE 1730S, LONDON HAD AT LEAST
six thousand alehouses. Remnants of
this vivacious drinking culture abound
on the foreshore, including crude lead
tokens, some of which were used
as chits for service in such drinking
establishments. These often bear designs
evoking the names of the premises they
were used in: anchors, feathers, rising
suns and crossed keys; while others
feature drinking paraphernalia such
as bottles or glasses. The alehouse
provided a space for male socializing
and an escape from domestic drudgery.

For some men who were patrons of alehouses known as 'molly houses', they also offered a place to meet and have sex with other men. The molly house took its name from the pejorative term for men perceived as effeminate who engaged in such relations. Satirist and publican Ned Ward sought to lift the lid on the phenomenon for the reading public in his *The History of the London Clubs*. The molly house, according to Ward, was a place where a 'curious band of fellows' met and held parties. Mollies, he claimed, 'rather fancy themselves women, imitated all the little vanities that custom has reconcil'd to the female sex, affecting to speak, walk, tattle, curtsy, cry, scold, and mimick all manner of effeminacy'.[73] Whether molly house patrons thought of themselves in these terms remains unknown.

Most of what we can discover of these men and the spaces in which they fraternized comes from the records of trials initiated by the prudish vigilante organization, the Society for the Reformation of Manners. After targeting the city's brothels, in the last months of 1725 this self-appointed suppressor of lewdness turned its attention towards molly houses. Four of its agents were sent to make clandestine visits and gather evidence, guided by a young 'molly' named Mark Partridge. Partridge had quarrelled with another 'molly' named William Harrington, and seeking revenge had turned informant. By February 1726, enough evidence had been amassed to bring to trial eleven men and one woman for running molly houses, and against sixteen other men for visiting these premises and 'acting sodomitical practices'.[74] Other arrests soon followed, with an unprecedented total of fifty-six men charged with sodomy and seventeen molly houses revealed, mostly alehouses with back rooms reserved for 'mollies'. Several were situated around Charing Cross, while others were in Moorfields, an area notorious for prostitution. A third cluster lay near the latrines, known as bog houses, at Lincoln's Inn, which were also used for making pick-ups.

The most popular house seems to have been that run by Margaret Clap, whose patrons called her 'Mother'. Ostensibly a coffee-house and private residence, Mother Clap's molly house ran as an alehouse with alcohol sourced from the tavern next door. The court heard that Clap had beds in every room for 'the more convenient entertainment of her customers'.[75] Samuel Stevens, a member of the Society for the Reformation of Manners, who had posed as a 'molly' to visit Mother Clap's, testified that he saw a large group of men hugging and kissing, sitting in each other's laps and 'making love...in a very

I.

indecent manner'.[76] Men who paired off retired to another room, and when they re-emerged 'would tell what they had been doing, which in their dialect they called *marrying*'.[77] To his horror, Stevens also recounted how one William Griffin had tried to grope his breeches while other men danced and made curtsies.

Another molly house was infiltrated by Society member Joseph Sellers while pretending to be the 'husband' of the informant Partridge. This ruse, designed to shield Sellers from the unwanted advances experienced by Stevens, failed to prevent one Martin Mackintosh, who went by the name of Orange Deb, from thrusting his hand into Sellers's breeches and his tongue into his mouth. After attempting to persuade Sellers to let him sodomize him, Mackintosh offered to be the receptive partner himself and sat down naked on his lap. In response, and having now gathered all the evidence he needed, Sellers repelled Mackintosh with a hot poker from the fire, threatening to 'run it into his arse'.[78] Similar scenes were observed at a third molly house near Moorfields, which also featured the singing of obscene songs such as 'Come let us fuck finely'.[79]

In his defence, George Whitle, who ran the Royal Oak on St James's Square, claimed the men seen exposing themselves in his tavern were venereal disease patients being examined by surgeons. He was acquitted, but

Margaret Clap was not so lucky. Found guilty as charged of running a molly house, she was pilloried and sentenced to two years' imprisonment. Her fate thereafter is unknown.

In the second half of the eighteenth century, another figure that became associated with the 'sodomite' in the public mind was the 'macaroni'. The term originated as a reference to wealthy young men who had travelled extensively in Europe and supposedly picked up a taste for Italian pasta and all things foreign and exotic. Known for the habit of wearing outlandishly tall and elaborate wigs, face powder, rouge, flashy accessories and tight clothing, the macaroni was sometimes described as connoting a deviant third gender. The molly and the macaroni should not be seen as interchangeable. Most macaronis were not accused of being mollies and not all mollies were macaronis. Nevertheless, numerous commentators viewed the fashion as either a symptom or a cause of homosexuality, and a series of scandals in the 1770s reinforced the connection. In 1772 'military macaroni' Captain Robert Jones was tried for sodomizing a thirteen-year-old boy. One of Jones' defenders was macaroni, bookseller and luxury trinket retailer, Samuel Drybutter. Having been arrested for sodomy on several occasions, Drybutter, like Jones, was forced into Parisian exile after a mob of several hundred besieged his home.

# Finds Relating to Macaroni Fashion.

I.

II.

III.

IV.

V.

VI.

A MACARONI DRESSING ROOM.

*Pub according to Act June 26, 1772 by M. Darly (39) Strand.*

I.
*Wig Curlers.*
1650–1800
*Found* at City of London
by the Author.

Curlers made of
pipe clay were used
to keep wigs in
shape. In the 1770s,
macaronis replaced
the smaller wigs of
the older generation
with elaborate
hairstyles matching
the extravagance of
female coiffure. These
combined a very tall
toupee at the front of
the head, which might
be topped by a tiny hat,
with thick club of
natural hair behind.

II.
*Pocket Watch Winder.*
18th century
*Found* at Tower Hamlets
by Ed Bucknall.

The wearing of
pocket watches grew

in popularity during
the eighteenth century.
In keeping with their
taste for extravagance,
many macaronis took
to wearing two watches
– one functional, and
the other a much more
decorative dummy
watch, or *fausse-montre*,
as it was known by
the fashion conscious.

III.
*Fob Seal.*
18th century
*Found* at City of London
by Sarah Weston.

Carrying family crests,
initials or classical
motifs, seals were
supposed to be used for
making a personalized
impression in sealing
wax on documents
or correspondence.
Attached to fobs at the
waist, they were often
worn as part of the
macaroni style simply
as ornamentation.

IV.
*Buckle.*
18th century
*Found* at Tower Hamlets
by Mike Walker.

Elaborate and often
oversized buckles were
another indispensable
macaroni accessory.

V.
*Ivory Pot Lid.*
18th century
*Found* at undisclosed
location by Florence
Evans.

This lid may have
belonged to a small
pot for holding beauty
spots known as
'patches'. Often made
from black felt, these
were used for covering
spots or pockmarks,
turning a flaw into
a feature. *Bon Ton
Magazine* lamented in
1791 that the macaroni
needed no such excuse
to don a beauty patch.

VI.
*Silver and Bristol
Stone Cufflink.*
Late 18th century
*Found* at Southwark
by the Author.

Cufflinks and buckles
set with chips of quartz
(known as 'Bristol
stones'), paste (lead
glass), or diamonds
for the wealthiest,
were staple macaroni
accessories.

*ABOVE.*
A Macaroni Dressing
Room, 1772. *In this
satirical etching,
published by M. Darly,
several macaroni are
depicted dressing with
the help of servants.
A seated man has his wig
powdered, while another
plays with a parrot.
Behind them a macaroni
lunges towards the open
door with his sword,
causing a servant
behind it to drop a tray.*

# Cross-Dressing Women—

The emergence of a lesbian identity, *revealed by a button.*

OPPOSITE.
*Button Featuring the Name and Address of Chauffeur's Uniform Supplier, Alfred Webb Miles & Co.*
c. 1990–1920
*Found* at Southwark
by the Author.

ABOVE.
*Britain's first female chauffeur, Vera 'Jack' Holme, dressed in her chauffeur's uniform at the wheel of the Pankhursts' car, photographed with fellow members of the Women's Social and Political Union, c. 1911.*

*IN THE YEARS BEFORE* the First World War, business was booming for Alfred Webb Miles & Co., the gentleman's outfitters and supplier of chauffeurs' livery. The motor car was rapidly replacing the horse-drawn carriage for the wealthy, and the new profession that emerged to facilitate the use of these vehicles even had its own magazine, *The Chauffeur.* In 1911, its pages announced the appointment of Britain's first female chauffeur: Vera 'Jack' Holme.

*I.*

*Cover of the sheet music for
'The Latest Chap On Earth' as
performed by the most successful
male impersonator of the music
hall era, Vesta Tilley; 1899.*

*II.*

*Vera 'Jack' Holme at the age
of twenty-two, photographed
performing one of her cross-
dressing music hall acts for a
theatrical publicity picture, 1903.*

*III.*

*Radclyffe Hall (right), whose
novel* The Well of Loneliness
*was banned in Britain for its pro-
lesbian stance, photographed with
her lover, Una Troubridge, 1927.*

Wearing a uniform of the kind made by Alfred Webb Miles, Holme was one of a growing number of women in the early twentieth century who adopted clothing conventionally associated with men. The reasons for this were diverse and were not necessarily expressions of lesbian or transgender identities. But by the late 1920s, these choices contributed to the emergence of a distinct lesbian identity.

Prior to becoming a chauffeur, Holme had worked as a touring music-hall actress. Often performing in a suit and tie, she was one of the many cross-dressing music-hall acts popular at the time. She also used her performance skills to campaign for women's suffrage. *A Pageant of Great Women*, a theatrical production celebrating the achievements of women throughout history, saw her play the role of Hannah Snell, an eighteenth-century woman who disguised herself as a man and became a soldier. The same year she also hid

inside the organ at Bristol's Colston Hall during a meeting of the ruling Liberal Party, hijacking the proceedings by calling out 'Votes for Women!' through one of the organ pipes, and garnering much publicity for the suffragette cause.

These actions brought her to the attention of Women's Social and Political Union co-founder, Emmeline Pankhurst. After successfully driving Pankhurst from London to Scotland, using motoring skills she probably picked up on theatre tours, Holme was appointed her personal chauffeur. For Pankhurst and her activist daughters, Christabel and Sylvia, the motor car was an important enabler of their cause. It let them campaign freely around the country, as well as providing a fast getaway vehicle when the movement's tactics became more violent, including bombings and arson. The employment of a woman as a chauffeur also acted as a clear political statement.

With the outbreak of war in 1914, most suffrage societies suspended militant campaigning, but opportunities for women to step outside gender norms abounded. Holme and her partner Evelina Haverfield joined the transport wing of the Scottish Women's Hospitals for Foreign Service, an organization that provided women nurses and medical support overseas. Stationed in Serbia, Holme became an ambulance driver.

In their uniforms, Holme and Haverfield were two of the thousands of wartime women, who, in the words of the *Daily Express*, could be found 'in offices, shops, railway companies, banks, acting, writing, driving taxis, ploughing the land, taming vicious horses, felling trees in all kinds of uniforms…khaki, blue, brown, or grey, with slouch hat, round hat, or no hat at all, in skirts as short as ballet girls

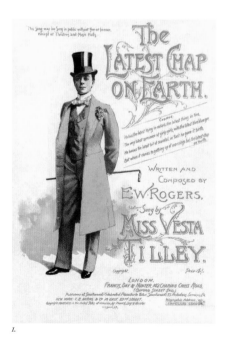

*I.*

*II.*

of Loneliness in 1928. The isolation felt by the gay female character, Stephen Gordon, acted as a plea for toleration. The book's lesbian author Radclyffe Hall was an established writer known for her fashionable masculine clothing. Following a campaign by the *Sunday Express* for the book's suppression, its publisher was tried on obscenity charges. During the trial, the newspaper published numerous photographs of Hall dressed in masculine clothing to emphasize her gender nonconformity. But by 1928, the boyette look was on the way out, with women's magazine *Eve* declaring: 'it looks as if everyone will dress...with just an added touch of femininity. The masculine woman is as dead as the dodo in the streets of fashion.'[82] It was also the year that women finally gained the same voting rights as men, eliciting alarm in the conservative press about potential gender role reversals.

From this point on, women adopting a masculine look became more overtly connected with lesbianism in the public consciousness. Pioneering war correspondent and lesbian, Evelyn Irons, recalled how 'the minute [*The Well of Loneliness*] came out if you wore a collar and tie, "Oh you're Miss Radclyffe Hall, Miss", the truck drivers used to call on the street.'[83] Despite such stereotyping, women who wanted to clearly signal their same-sex desires now had a visual identity they could assume to claim their place in the 'newly emerging lesbian subculture'[84] of the interwar years.

or in masculine breeches. Everywhere but in the Home, which they have deserted *en masse*.'[80] After the war ended, most women did not keep their wartime jobs, but these masculine military styles influenced the women's fashion of the 1920s. A look emerged incorporating severely tailored suits, short cropped hair, ties and monocles, which was variously described as boy-girl, boyette, hard-boiled flapper or boyish female. It has been suggested that for certain cliques of upper-class lesbians adopting this look, the style cues may well have been deliberate signals of same-sex desire, but for most women it was simply mainstream fashion.[81] Working-class women who passed as men to work as labourers, waiters or truck drivers, meanwhile, were treated by the press as amusing tricksters seeking to get ahead.

As historian Laura Doan has demonstrated, this was to change with the publication of the novel *The Well*

*III.*

# Finds Relating to the Women's Movement, Fashion and Identity.

I.

II.

III.

IV.

V.

VI.

I.
*Skirt Lifter.*
Late 19th century
*Found* at Westminster
by Seán O'Mara.

Late Victorian skirts
were long, heavy and
layered, requiring
a device known as
skirt lifter to keep
them off dirty ground
and help facilitate
movement. The
emergence of the 'New
Woman' – independent
and career-minded –
alongside the boom in
bicycle riding, helped
usher in less restrictive
dress, such as bloomers,
shorter dresses and
looser or no corsets.

II.
*Halfpenny Stamped
'Votes for Women'.*
1899; stamped 1910s
*Found* at undisclosed
location by Florence
Evans.

Perhaps influenced
by the actions of
anarchists, the
defacement of coins
was seen as an effective
way to raise awareness
of the suffragette
cause, with each coin
hand stamped by an
unknown individual.

III.
*Elizabeth Arden,
'Chariot' Lipstick.*
Early 20th century
*Found* at Westminster
by the Author.

In the Victorian era,
lipstick was seen to
signify promiscuity.
Some suffragettes
sought to reclaim it
as a sign of women's
freedom. British beauty
entrepreneur Elizabeth
Arden participated
in the movement by
supplying a red shade
to campaigners marching
in New York City.

IV.
*'Boyette' Pendant.*
1920s
*Found* at Westminster
by Seán O'Mara.

The masculine styles
donned by women
who served during
the First World War
carried over into the
fashions of the 1920s.
The woman depicted
on this pendant sports
the main components
of the 'boyette' look:
short cropped hair
and a tailored suit.

V.
*Dubarry Powder
Compact.*
*c.* 1930
*Found* at Westminster
by the Author.

This powder compact
was launched, by
Brighton cosmetics
maker Dubarry, to
help create the more

conventionally feminine
look that became
fashionable from the
late 1920s, replacing
the boyish style popular
earlier in the decade.

VI.
*Plate Fragment
from Dolphin Square.*
Mid-20th century
*Found* at Westminster
by Seán O'Mara.

Radclyffe Hall, author
of *The Well of Loneliness*,
lived in the Thames-
side Dolphin Square
apartment complex
– the largest in Europe
when it was built –
shortly before her
death in 1943.

*ABOVE.*
*Leading suffragette
Christabel Pankhurst
addresses a
predominantly male
crowd from a car in
central London, c. 1910.*

# *Buttons.*

Widespread use of buttons only began from the later medieval period onwards. Before then, the predominance of open-weave fabrics made pins, hooks or brooches more effective methods of fastening clothes. While a seemingly mundane find – the button – provides a wealth of opportunities for exploring the fashions of London's past.

Some of the earliest buttons commonly found on the foreshore date to the late fifteenth and sixteenth centuries. Made in one piece from copper alloy, these often feature a long shank, perhaps designed to allow them to pass through the padding of a doublet: a snug-fitting jacket, buttoned at the front, which remained a staple of the male wardrobe for three centuries. In the later phase of its use it might feature pewter 'nipple' buttons – easily identified by the raised point at their centre – which were also used to fasten jerkins and buff coats.

In the eighteenth century, buttons could be found on the front, cuffs and pocket flaps of the justacorps, a knee-length coat worn by wealthier men, which replaced the doublet. It was at this time that the button reached its zenith as a fashion accessory. Buttons could be made of cloth, cut steel, porcelain, gold or silver, but it is those made of tombac – a brass alloy featuring zinc to give it a silvery appearance – that predominate on the foreshore. The geometric and floral designs often featured on these buttons were either made using a lathe or carefully engraved by hand. The amount of daily buttoning and unbuttoning this preponderance of buttons required was rumoured to have driven a disgruntled colonel to take his own life.[85] This was not an issue for the macaronis (see p.135) of the period, who adopted the high fashion of France and Italy: narrow-cut, luxurious clothing with lavish use of lace and ornate cut-steel buttons. Remnants of another type of eighteenth-century button – the Death's Head – can be found on the foreshore in the form of bone discs with a single hole in the middle. This button's ominous name arose from the 'X' pattern created by the colourful silk thread wrapped around it, said to resemble a skull and crossbones.

In the years following the French Revolution, the more understated look of the dandy emerged, featuring simple yet elegant gilt buttons. These were manufactured by adding at least five grains of gold per gross to mercury, which was brushed on to brass buttons that were then heated. Unscrupulous manufacturers were accused of gilding their buttons with too little gold, prompting the use of marks such as 'Treble Gilt' (indicating three times the legally required amount) to provide an assurance of quality. Later in the nineteenth century, the mass-produced four-hole button became ubiquitous. Some feature the specific name and address of the tailor to whose wares they were once sewn. Researching these often reveals long gone premises that fell victim to the Blitz or were swept away in London's post-war redevelopment.

Tudor.
15th–16th century.

Jacobean.
17th century.

Georgian.
18th century.

Georgian.
18th century.

Georgian.
18th century.

Regency.
Early 19th century.

Victorian.
19th century.

Victorian to
Edwardian.
Late 19th–early
20th century.

Edwardian to
First World War.
Early 20th century.

*LEFT.*
*The evolution of button design from the fifteenth to twentieth century. All finds made by the Author.*

1. *Pyramidal button with elongated shank.*
2. *Pewter 'nipple' button.*
3. *Tombac button with geometric pattern.*
4. *Pewter button with floral decoration.*
5. *Bone disc from a Death's Head button.*
6. *Maker's mark on the back of a gilt button.*
7. *Servant's uniform button.*
8. *Four-hole button with tailor's name and address.*
9. *Metropolitan Police uniform button.*

*OPPOSITE.*
*Portrait of Don Miguel de Castro, Emissary of Congo, sporting a doublet with 'nipple' buttons, by Jaspar Beckx, 1643.*

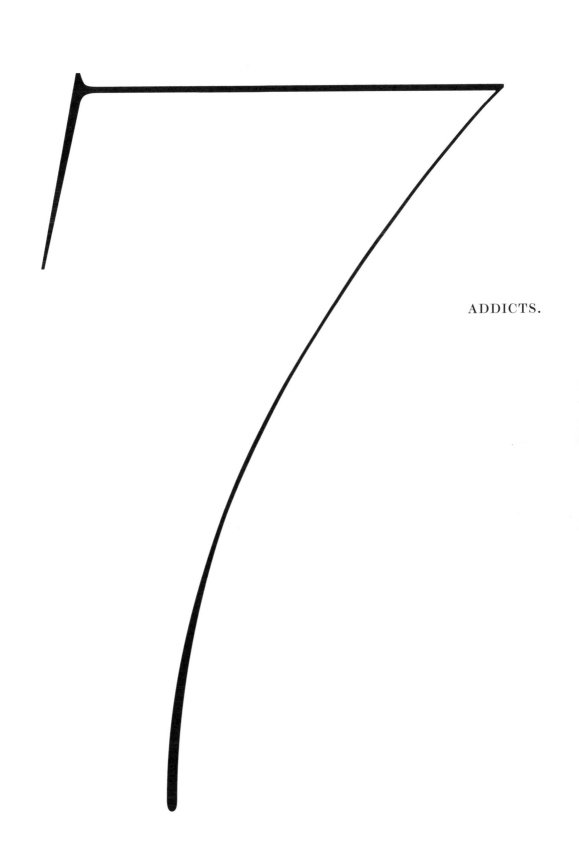

ADDICTS.

# *Smokers—*

Consumers of a new intoxicant,
*revealed by clay tobacco pipes.*

IN OCTOBER 1492, ITALIAN NAVIGATOR Christopher Columbus was offered a bunch of dried leaves by the Indigenous people of the Bahamian island he called San Salvador. Not knowing their use, his crew reportedly threw them overboard. When he reached Cuba a couple of weeks later, two of his sailors observed men and women holding a 'firebrand of weeds to take in the fragrant smoke'.[86] They tried this for themselves and went on to smoke habitually during the three months they spent in the region.

*I.*
*Frontispiece of* Panacea; or
The universal medicine, being
a discovery of the wonderfull
vertues of tobacco taken in a pipe,
with its operation and use both
in physick and chyrurgery, *1659.*

*II.*
*Trade card for eighteenth-century*
*London tobacco and snuff seller,*
*James Norris. Depictions of*
*Indigenous North Americans*
*on such cards implied direct*
*access to the source of the tobacco.*

*III.*
*Trade card for the tobacconist*
*Lacroix, c. 1790s, after Hogarth.*
*It depicts a typical tavern scene*
*with four gentlemen sitting round*
*a table, smoking and drinking,*
*three others standing behind them.*

These were the first known European encounters with tobacco, a substance Indigenous people applied to wounds for its analgesic and antiseptic qualities, ingested in high doses to commune with the gods, smoked to seal oaths and declare war, and also for pleasure.

During the following decades, descriptions of tobacco and smoking featured in many accounts of the 'New World'. Seeds were brought back across the Atlantic and tobacco was cultivated in Europe, fuelled by an interest in the plant's medicinal potential. In one influential pamphlet of 1571, Spanish doctor Nicolás Monardes enthused that tobacco was an effective treatment for a wide range of maladies, including kidney stones, tapeworms, illnesses of the internal organs, toothache, bad breath – especially, he claimed, in children who had eaten too much meat – and could be applied to any type of wound. The smoking of tobacco meanwhile, found favour among Spanish seamen, for

whom it helped alleviate hunger and thirst during long months at sea. But in Spain this new habit was to remain confined within the maritime fringe. In the country of the Inquisition, smoke was seen as the stuff of the Devil and smoking the habit of the ungodly Aztecs.

It was in England that smoking for pleasure first developed into a mainstream habit. Its sailors probably first encountered the practice among their Spanish counterparts, and the earliest recorded instance of an Englishman smoking was when, in 1556, a Bristol sailor created a spectacle by blowing smoke from his nostrils in the street. It was not until three decades later, however, that smoking reached polite society, popularized by an association with England's colonial ambitions. Between 1585 and 1587, statesman and explorer Sir Walter Raleigh made two attempts to establish the first permanent English colony in North America. When the first attempt was abandoned due to lack of supplies and conflict with the local Indigenous people, many of the returning colonists brought home a smoking habit. With further colonial plans in the works, tobacco smoking became an expression of this expansionist ambition – a fashionable badge of adventure that retained its medicinal associations.

Raleigh and his returning colonists also helped popularize what would become England's preferred means of inhaling tobacco smoke – the pipe. In the Spanish Empire the cigar was the preferred means of smoking, but the Indigenous North Americans encountered by the English used pipes. Although it is unclear whether tobacco pipes made specifically from clay were an Indigenous or English

*I.*

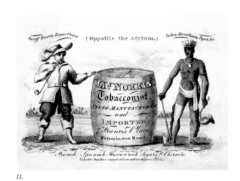

II.

III.

invention, a thriving domestic industry soon emerged. While visiting London in 1598, the German lawyer Paul Hentzner marvelled: 'the English are constantly smoking tobacco and in this manner: they have pipes on purpose, made of clay.'[87]

The most important consumption venue for the new smoking craze was the alehouse, where tobacco was said to be 'drunk' – its intoxicating effects lubricating conversation and intensifying male bonding. By 1610, the philosopher Francis Bacon had noted tobacco's habit-forming qualities: 'In our time the use of tobacco is growing greatly and conquers men with a certain secret pleasure, so that those who have once become accustomed thereto can later hardly be restrained therefrom.'[88] Four years later, smoking further expanded during an outbreak of plague, with smokers believed to be less prone to infection.

This rapid growth was soon met by voices of opposition. The first anti-smoking pamphlet, *Work for Chimny-Sweepers: or, a Warning for Tabacconists*, was published in 1602 and sought to tarnish tobacco by its association with 'Indian cannibals'. A second wave of criticism was headed by no less than King James I. In his *A Counterblaste to Tobacco*, published anonymously in 1604, the monarch condemned those who wanted to imitate 'the barbarous and beastly maners of the wilde, godlesse, and slavish Indians', likened the dependency smokers experienced to that of the heavy drinker, and saw the habit as unleashing a decadence that, if left unchecked, would undermine the very fabric of society.[89]

Such condemnations notwithstanding, the spread of smoking was initially limited by the high price of tobacco. This began to change when Virginia colonist (and husband of Pocahontas) John Rolfe cultivated a tobacco crop and shipped it to London in 1616. Soon a pipeful could be had for less than a farthing and pipe bowl sizes increased as tobacco became more affordable and consumption spread to all tiers of society. Barnaby Rich, a critic of smoking, duly complained that a Londoner might now have 'his pot of ale, his pipe of tobacco and his pocksy whore and all for his 3d'.[90] In 1640, Virginian tobacco exports had grown to around 1.5 million pounds. By the end of the century, the use of enslaved Africans predominated in the cultivation of tobacco, and the amount being shipped to England annually reached approximately 38 million pounds.

Smoking's dominance as the means to enjoy tobacco was challenged in the eighteenth century by 'snuffing' – inhaling powdered tobacco into the nasal cavity – but the use of pipes persisted among the lower orders. Tobacco smoking also retained some medical applications: in a case of drowning in 1746, it was suggested a pipe be inserted into the victim's rectum and smoke blown into her body to help revive her. The woman was indeed revived, and equipment for administering tobacco smoke enemas was later deployed along the Thames for use in such emergencies. The following century saw a revival in the popularity of the pipe across all classes, and also the emergence of the more convenient cigarette.

# Finds Relating to Smoking.

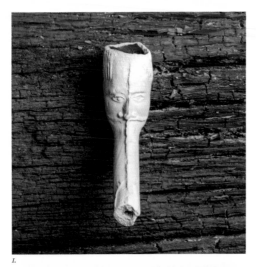

I.

II.

III.

IV.

**I.**
*Dutch 'Jonas' Clay Pipe.*
*c.* 1630–1670
*Found* at Southwark
by Claire Everitt.

The stem of this
Dutch-made pipe
features a fearsome,
open-mouthed creature,
while its bowl carries
the bearded face of
a man. It probably
represents the biblical
figure of Jonah being
swallowed by a whale
and thereby saved from
drowning, which may
explain the design's
popularity among
sailors.

**II.**
*'Chesapeake' Clay*
*Tobacco Pipe Bowl.*
17th century
*Found* at undisclosed
location by Anna
Borzello.

The foreshore
occasionally reveals
pipes made in the
American colonies,
combining Indigenous
and European motifs
– a reminder of the
Indigenous origins
of tobacco smoking.
These would have
been the discarded
personal possessions
of transatlantic sailors.

**III.**
*Pipe Bowl Bearing*
*the Arms of the House*
*of Hanover.*
*c.* 1740–1750
*Found* at City of
London by the Author.

Richly decorated
pipes bearing royal
arms were made
during the eighteenth
century amid a wave
of patriotism. These
have been associated
with Tom King's
Coffee House in Covent
Garden. Open from
the time the taverns
shut until dawn, Tom's
was primarily a place
for drunken patrons
to gamble and pick
up sex workers.

**IV.**
*Pipe Bowl Bearing the*
*Arms of the Company*
*of Watermen and*
*Lightermen.*
*c.* 1740–1760
*Found* at the City of
London by the Author.

Watermen piloted
the small ferries that
carried passengers
across and along
the Thames. Iconic
London figures, they
carried a reputation
for fierce rivalry
and overcharging.
Lightermen used
similar craft to convey
goods between ships
and riverside wharves.

*V.*

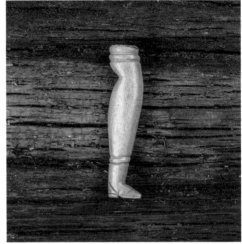

*VI.*

*VII.*

*VIII.*

V.
*Alderman Pipe.*
Late 18th to early
19th century
*Found* at Royal
Borough of Kensington
and Chelsea by Seán
O'Mara.

Designed for leisure
smoking, the
introduction of longer
pipes in the eighteenth
century was perhaps
influenced by the
fashion for 'Turquerie':
the imitation of aspects
of Ottoman culture.
A longer pipe also
helped cool the smoke
before it was inhaled.

VI.
*Pipe Tamper.*
19th century
*Found* at Westminster
by Seán O'Mara.

A useful tool for
smokers, a pipe tamper
was used for packing
a pipe's bowl with
tobacco and breaking
up ash to aid relighting.

VII.
*Clay Pipe Bowls.*
Late 19th to early
20th century
*Found* at Westminster
by Seán O'Mara.

Elaborate Victorian
and Edwardian pipes
depicted the celebrities
of their day: sportsmen,
military commanders,
explorers, monarchs
and entertainers. These
examples feature Major-
General Charles Gordon
(left), heroized after
meeting his death
fighting anti-colonial
forces in the Sudan in
1884 and Royal Navy
Commander John
Jellicoe (right).

VIII.
*'Cutty' Pipe.*
Early 20th century
*Found* at Westminster
by Seán O'Mara.

Short turn-of-the-
century pipes were
known as 'cuttys'.
This example features
the insignia of the
Irish regiment of the
British Army, the Royal
Inniskilling Fusiliers.
This includes a sphinx
commemorating the
regiment's posting
in Egypt. Why pipes
bearing this specific
regiment's insignia
were so popular is
something of a mystery.

# IN FOCUS—
## *Clay Tobacco Pipes.*

White, easy to spot and made in vast numbers for over three hundred years, the first find for many mudlarks is a fragment of clay tobacco pipe. Most common are pieces of stem: the tubular part through which smoke was inhaled. Bowls, the part in which tobacco was burnt, are also abundant, but complete pipes from any period are a rarity.

The earliest examples, from the late sixteenth century, feature the smallest bowl size (due to the then high price of tobacco). During the seventeenth century, pipe bowls grew larger as tobacco became cheaper. Some feature a maker's mark stamped on the underside of the protrusion underneath the bowl, referred to as the heel. Most seventeenth-century pipes are plain, however, save for a milled ring around the mouth of the bowl. A burnished bowl indicates the pipe was deemed to be of better quality and was perhaps enjoyed by a smoker higher up the social scale.

Eighteenth-century pipes are generally thinner and more brittle. Makers' marks, such as flowers, crowns or a set of initials are common on the outside edges of the heel or spur. Holding the pipe as if smoking it, the maker's Christian name is typically seen on the left and their surname on the right. Testament to the growing skill of mould makers, some pipes are also richly decorated with royal arms, tavern or trade-related imagery, which allowed the smoker to signal their interests and allegiances to others. During the mid-century, a fashion arose for extra-long pipes of 18 to 24 inches (45 to 61 centimetres) in length, known as 'aldermen' or 'straws'. Leaf or barley motifs along the seam of the bowl also emerged.

The early nineteenth century saw fluted decoration become popular, and in the 1850s pipes of up to 36 inches (91 centimetres) in length appeared, referred to as a 'yard of clay'. During the Victorian era, makers' names and addresses were sometimes featured along the pipe's stem and decorated pipes become ubiquitous. Bowls carried regimental insignia and Masonic symbolism; commemorated exhibitions and jubilees; celebrated new technologies such as steam trains and the bicycle; and depicted flora, fauna and sporting activities. This decorative urge culminated in bowls shaped to represent monarchs, generals, politicians and popular comedians. At the same time, short pipes known as 'cuttys' or 'nose warmers' were made for the working man, who could easily hold one between his teeth for long periods. This practice could, however, lead to the smoker's canines wearing down to form a 'V'-shaped notch.

When finding a pipe of any age, be sure to examine the contents of its bowl when cleaning it out – it is not uncommon to find the remnants of centuries-old tobacco still inside, preserved by the low-oxygen conditions of the Thames mud.

I.

II.

Jacobean.
1610–1640

Interregnum.
1640–1660

Restoration.
1660–1680

Restoration.
1680–1710

Georgian.
1740–1800

Victorian.
1830–1860

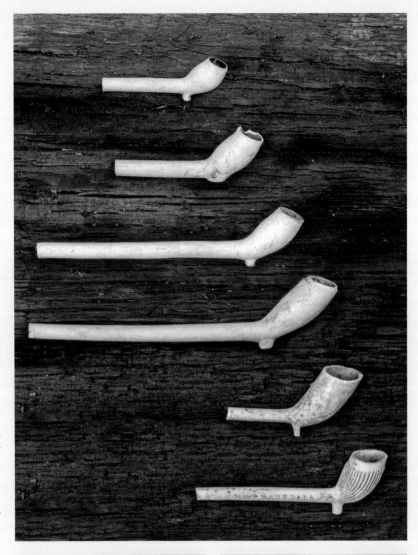

ABOVE.
The evolution of the clay tobacco pipe. The smaller size of the earliest bowls reflects the higher price of tobacco when they were made.

III.

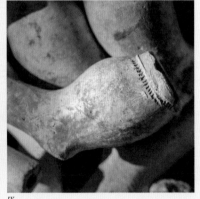

IV.

I.
Late nineteenth-century clay pipe, featuring a bearded figure reminiscent of a Green Man.

II.
Late nineteenth-century to early twentieth-century clay pipe with tree trunk decoration.

III.
The maker's identifying mark is stamped on to the underside of the heel of this seventeenth-century pipe.

IV.
Milled decoration has been applied around the rim of this seventeenth-century pipe bowl.

# Gamesters—

Gambling addicts of Georgian London, *revealed by a die*.

*OPPOSITE.*
*Bone Die.*
1600–1800
*Found* at City of London
by the Author.

*ABOVE.*
*A dispute breaks out*
*during a dice game in*
*Thomas Rowlandson's*
Kick Up at a Hazard
Table, *1787. Within six*
*years of producing this*
*print, the artist himself*
*would be destitute after*
*gambling away his fortune.*

*THE EIGHTEENTH CENTURY SAW* an increasingly wealthy upper-class take up gambling with unprecedented vigour. Such was its popularity, fears arose that the country was suffering a problem of epic proportions, caused by what the *Gentleman's Magazine* described in 1731 as 'the Mother of Many Vices'. One particular focus of critics was 'Hazard', the game of chance this die may well have been used to play. A more complex precursor to today's craps, Hazard saw large stakes wagered on each throw of the dice.

With winnings and losses flowing quickly,
habitual players were prone to addiction.
The gambling guide *The Compleat
Gamester* warned: 'when a man begins
to play, he knows not when to leave off;
and, having once accustomed himself
to play at Hazard, he hardly, ever after,
minds anything else.'[91]

A second peril was being cheated by
a rival player using a loaded die. These
were known as a 'low fulham' or a 'high
fulham', depending on which numbers
the die was biased towards. Such a die,
*The Compleat Gamester* revealed, could
be made by sticking a 'strong and short'
hog's hair into the corner of a regular die,
'so it will not lie of that side, but will be
tript over'.[92] Apart from examining a
die for such protrusions, in *The Whole
Art and Mystery of Modern Gaming Fully
Expos'd and Detected*, its anonymous
author recommended a loaded die could
also be detected by shaking it in a box
and listening for a noise 'as if the Box
was crack'd'.[93] Alternatively, a player
could utilize the newly discovered laws
of gravity by placing the die 'into a Pale
of Water about 14 or 15 inches deep, or
deeper' in order to 'know the Propension
or Inclination of the cube'.[94]

Even if a die were not loaded,
duplicitous methods of play could cheat
a gamester of their wager. 'Topping'
meant shaking one die in the box while
secretly holding the other against its
side in order to release it on the required
number, whereas 'knapping' was the
technique of throwing a die so it landed
exactly flat. London gamesters notorious
for practising such methods were said
to include shadowy figures such as 'The
Mathematician', 'Captain Whimper',
'The Black Dwarf' and 'The Calculator'.

The highest stakes gaming, known as
'deep play', occurred at London's private
clubs that catered to the aristocracy.
Members were notorious for placing
wagers on a constant stream of trivial
and ridiculous events. In 1785, the
betting book of White's club recorded
that Lord Cholmondeley gave 'two
guineas to Ld. Derby, to receive 500
guineas whenever his lordship fucks a
woman in a balloon one thousand yards
from the earth'.[95] Equally absurdly, Lord
Alvanley wagered £3,000 on which of
two raindrops would reach the bottom
of the club's bow window first. The
*Connoisseur Magazine* meanwhile, noted
'Many pounds have been lost upon the
colour of a coach-horse, an article in
the news, or the change of the weather.'[96]

Such behaviour inevitably often had
catastrophic consequences. In 1754 at
White's, Lord Montfort wagered Sir John
Bland one hundred guineas that a Mr

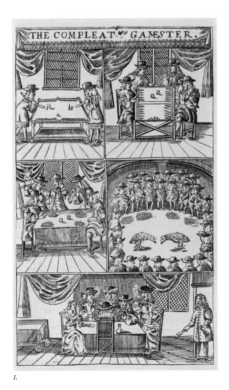

*I.*

11.

Cibber would die before a Mr Nash. The bet was never decided, as Montfort and Bland died first. Although repayment of gambling debts was not legally enforceable, loss of honour led Montfort to shoot himself, while Bland did the same after losing £32,000 on Hazard in one sitting.

An association with suicide was not the only criticism levelled at gambling. It was also attacked as the enemy of polite conversation and condemned for diverting the aristocracy from their public duties. The *London Magazine* even went so far as to blame gaming for the loss of the American colonies, lamenting: 'To this dreadful vice must every misfortune which has lately fallen on this country be attributed.'[97] The harshest criticism, however, was reserved for female gamesters. Excluded from the male-only clubs, women predominantly gambled in private homes, often under the pretext of a musical concert. Among the most notorious were Lady Archer and Lady Buckinghamshire who, after being caught running an illegal Faro bank, were pilloried and pelted with rotten vegetables by onlookers.

Critics of female gamesters often declared that gambling ruined their beauty as a result of the stresses of play and staying up late. John Hamilton Moore, author of an guide for the young and well-to-do, claimed he 'never knew a thorough-paced Female Gamester hold her Beauty two Winters together'.[98] Of even greater concern was that a gambling woman, especially if she became indebted to a male creditor, might lose her sexual honour.

Georgian London's mania for gaming was fuelled by growing wealth, increasingly generated from borrowed capital. Outrageous wagers at the Hazard table allowed this new money to be flaunted. Efforts at control included the Gaming Act of 1738, which specifically forbade the playing of Hazard as well as the card game Faro. However, gamesters simply switched to a form of roulette, which saw players roll a ball across the table rather than dice. A few raids took place on public venues such as coffee shops where gaming occurred, but it continued to thrive in private settings where the law could not reach. It was only towards the end of the eighteenth century, when a more sober outlook was ushered in by events in Revolutionary France, that gaming's status as a fashionable pastime among the elite diminished.

# Finds Relating to Gambling and Gaming.

I.

II.

III.

IV.

V.

VI.

I.
*Bone Dice.*
AD 43–410
*Found* at City of London
by Ed Bucknall.

The Romans officially
prohibited the wagering
of money on games of
chance, such as those
played with dice. The
only exception was
supposed to be during
the Saturnalia festival.

II.
*Bone Gaming Counters.*
AD 43–410
*Found* at City of
London by Ed Bucknall
and the Author.

Games involving
moving counters on a
board were popular in
Roman London. These
included *Duodecim
scripta* (similar to
backgammon) and the
strategy game *Ludus
latrunculorum.*

III.
*Bear Tooth.*
Date unknown
*Found* at Westminster
by Seán O'Mara.

Placing wagers on the
outcomes of blood
sports such as bear-
baiting, monkey-baiting,
rat-baiting and cock-
fighting was a popular
form of gambling in
Georgian London.

IV.
*Cufflink.*
Late 18th century
*Found* at Tower
Hamlets by Ed
Bucknall.

Featuring a fox and
the cry 'Tallio', this
cufflink reflects the
emergence of fox
hunting as a sport
during the eighteenth
century. Inevitably the
outcome of hunts was
the subject of wagers,

with the sport's critics
associating it with
drunkenness, excessive
gambling and profligacy.

V.
*Gaming Counter.*
19th century
*Found* at Southwark
by the Author.

In the nineteenth
century, thousands
of variations of copper-
alloy gaming counters
were made imitating
the official gold coins
of the previous century.
This enabled them to
assume a coin-like
appearance without
falling foul of
counterfeiting laws.

VI.
*Tobacco Pipe Featuring
Arthur Wellesley, 1st
Duke of Wellington.*
19th century
*Found* at City of
London by the Author.

As a young man,
Wellesley accumulated
gambling debts and
contemplated selling
his military commission
to pay his creditors.
He was bailed out by
the politician Lord
Camden, who was
saddened that such
a talented soldier
might have to leave
the army. As the Duke
of Wellington he later
led British forces to
victory at the Battle
of Waterloo.

*ABOVE.*
*In the eighteenth-century
painting* The Royal
Sport, Pit Ticket, *after
Hogarth, a crowd has
gathered to place wagers
on two fighting birds.
A shadow is cast across
the pit by a debtor
suspended in a basket
above it.*

# *Gin Drinkers—*

Imbibers of London's spirit,
*revealed by a bottleneck.*

OPPOSITE.
*'Pig Snout' Case Gin
Bottleneck.*
*c.* 1750–1850
*Found* at Tower Hamlets
by the Author.

ABOVE.
*Caricaturist and convert to
the temperance movement,
George Cruickshank, warns
of the social consequences
of gin consumption in* The
Drunkard's Children, *1848.
Neglected by their parents, the
children are shown drinking
in a gin shop, described as
'that fountain which nourishes
every species of crime'.*

*FROM THE MID-EIGHTEENTH* to mid-nineteenth century, Dutch *jenever,* or gin as it was known in England, was imported and smuggled into the country in tapered square bottles with a flared lip that earned them the nickname 'pig snout'. The shape enabled more bottles to be packed into each case as, unlike round bottles, they could sit flush together. Around the same time, *The Spectator* magazine railed that gin had produced in men 'incurable laziness, scottishness and fearful laxity of principle', while turning the 'lower female classes' into 'blear-eyed, half-clad wretches'.[99]

I.

*William Hogarth depicts the evils of gin drinking in* Gin Lane, *1751. In the foreground a woman drunk on gin with syphilitic sores lets her baby slip from her arms to fall into the stairwell of a gin cellar below.*

II.

*In this 1808 copy of Thomas Rowlandson's* Rum Characters in a Shrubbery, *three women stand at the counter of a gin shop, two with glasses of gin in hand, as the bartender pours a third.*

Such sentiments were the latest in response to a tempestuous relationship with gin in London that had lasted over a century. This had blossomed when the Dutch William of Orange assumed the British throne in 1688. Keen to bolster the support of his landowning promoters, the monarch championed legislation encouraging the distilling of gin. This provided his followers with an outlet for their surplus grain, while also raising tax revenue. Anyone could manufacture or sell spirits, and by the 1720s gin was being sold everywhere. A dram of the spirit could be bought at chandler's shops, from hawkers at public executions, in prisons, taverns, workhouses, coffee shops and even on the Thames itself, with at least twenty watermen peddling it as a sideline. Its most notorious outlet, however, was the gin shop. Usually no more than a simple wooden bar in a householder's spare room, gin shops proliferated in the city's slums. In 1736, it was claimed one fifth of all residences in Holborn harboured such an establishment.

Gin shops found a ready clientele among the young migrants flocking to London from the provinces seeking work as apprentices and servants. The gin shop provided them with a welcoming place in which to relax in an unfamiliar city, while gin provided an escape from the hardships of life, numbing its drinkers to tiredness, cold and hunger. Without gin, one market worker proclaimed, 'We should never be able to…keep body and soul together.'[100] Gin's potency, however, could also prove deadly. In 1741, George Wade was said to have 'drank a Pint of Gin off at a Draught' at a public house in Westminster and 'expired in a few minutes'.[101] The same year, a labourer in Newington Green was persuaded by a group of men to 'Drink three or four Pints of Gin…which he had no sooner done, but he fell down and died immediately'.[102]

With stories of fatalities circulating, gin inevitably began to attract the attention of moral reformers, who variously saw it as lowering economic productivity, reducing food consumption, increasing crime, loosening morals and making the poor less deferential. These concerns manifested themselves in the first Gin Act of 1729. This raised taxes on spirits, restricted gin sales to premises purchasing a licence costing £20 annually and introduced fines for selling gin in the streets.

These measures were widely ignored, however, and consumption continued to rise. Of particular concern to gin's critics were its female consumers. In 1736 it was reported that Jane Andrews, a maid, went to a gin shop where she met a guardsman, a chimneysweep and 'a Woman Traveller'. Having invited all three back to her employer's house, they

GIN LANE.

I.

drank all day before Andrews 'proposed to the Company...that they, and she, should go to Bed together', upon which all four 'stript, and...went into one Bed'.[103] Their fun was disturbed, however, when an unruly mob got wind of the tryst and noisily congregated outside.

Alongside concern over increased sexual deviance, reformers believed gin was undermining women's ability to care for their children. The most notorious instance highlighted was that of thirty-year-old Shoreditch silk weaver, Judith Dufour. In 1735, Dufour deposited her two-year-old child at a workhouse, where he was given a new set of clothes. A few days later she reclaimed the child, taking him with her on a gin binge during which she strangled him, left his naked body in a ditch and sold the clothes for sixteen pence which she spent on more gin. What most alarmed many leading anti-gin campaigners about such parental neglect was that it might result in a decline in the reserves of manpower available both to defend the nation and to toil in its economy.

The Gin Act of 1736 also proved ineffective at reducing consumption. Inventive sellers now simply peddled the drink under different names, such as 'King Theodore of Corsica', 'Tow-row' or 'Bob'. Another tactic for evasion was dreamt up by Irish soldier Captain Dudley Bradstreet, who purchased a wooden sign of a cat and fitted a pipe under its paw. A prospective buyer would put coins in the cat's mouth and whisper 'Puss', to which Bradstreet replied 'Mew'. Gin was then dispensed to the customer through the pipe, allowing the seller to operate unseen. With such ingenuity, and with the informers the Act relied on for its enforcement often beaten up by angry mobs, by 1740 gin consumption had reached an all-time high.

Learning from these shortcomings, the 1751 Gin Act proved more effective. Distillers were banned from selling gin at shops, the spirit was outlawed in workhouses and prisons, duty was increased and gin could no longer be bought on credit. Licence fees

II.

for retailers were raised and it was made harder for distillers to recover debts from small-time sellers. These measures, along with falling wages and a series of poor harvests reducing the supply of grain, led to a 75 per cent decline in gin consumption in 1757 from its peak in 1743.

Gin nevertheless remained part of the drinking repertoire of the urban poor, and in the early nineteenth century experienced a revival. Again, legislation provided the catalyst, with duty reduced on English spirits to make them more attractive than imported or smuggled ones. As a result, gin consumption doubled in a year, and drinkers were provided with a new venue in which to imbibe it. The gin palace was inspired by the new-style shopfronts of London's West End, featuring large windows, mirrors, gas lighting and ornate detailing, while still catering to working-class drinkers. Even with no seating or food, the fourteen largest gin palaces in London served more than half a million customers a week at their peak. Gin's renewed fortunes were to be short-lived, however. To control consumption, the government removed taxes on domestic beer and allowed it to be sold widely for a small licence fee. Beer once again came to dominate working-class drinking, and gin began its slow journey to respectability over the next century.

# Finds Relating to Alcohol Consumption.

I.

II.

III.

IV.

I.
*Drinking Beaker Base.*
AD 43–410
*Found* at City of
London by the Author.

As in the eighteenth
century, Romans
associated heavy
drinking by women
with immorality.
The custom of a
man kissing a female
relative upon meeting
her was claimed to have
originated as a way of
checking whether her
breath smelt of alcohol.

II.
*Token.*
1669
*Found* at Tower
Hamlets by Ed
Bucknall.

This token was issued
by tradesman John
Perry, who was located
near The King's Brew
House in St Katherine's,
a neighbourhood to
the east of the Tower
of London. The
brewery's proximity
to the Thames allowed
for its beer to be
easily exported for the
enjoyment of English
soldiers serving abroad.

III.
*Bottle Seal.*
1675
*Found* at City of
London by the Author.

This seal was attached
to a bottle owned by
the Crown Tavern,
Oxford, which was
popular with students
attending the city's
university. It features
the cipher of licensees
William and Anne
Morrell, reminding
those buying a bottle
from the tavern for
home consumption
to return it.

IV.
*'Onion' Bottle.*
c. 1690–1700
*Found* at Tower
Hamlets by Ed
Bucknall.

The seventeenth
century saw the
invention of the
modern wine bottle,
often attributed to
Sir Kenelm Digby,
philosopher, pirate,
alchemist and
antiquarian. Using
tunnels to funnel
oxygen into a coal-
fired furnace, Digby
discovered its
temperature could
be raised, producing
stronger and thicker
glass.

V.

VI.

VII.

VIII.

V.
*Bottle Seal.*
1700–1750
*Found* at Westminster
by Seán O'Mara.

Individuals would
have seals attached
to bottles they owned
as a marker of their
social standing, and to
ensure the bottles were
returned to them after
being sent for refilling.
Samuel Pepys recorded
in his diary in October
1663 that he 'saw some
of my new bottles
made, with my crest
upon them, filled with
wine, about five or six
dozen'.[104] This example
bears the name James
Scott.

VI.
*Cufflink Featuring
Queen Anne.*
c. 1702–1714
*Found* at Wandsworth
by the Author.

Sharing her
predecessor William
of Orange's enthusiasm
for gin, Queen Anne
was nicknamed
'dramshop' for her
alleged regular
consumption of
the spirit.

VII.
*Tankard Fragment
with Excise Mark.*
1702–1714
*Found* at Southwark
by the Author.

Excise marks were
applied to tankards
to indicate that they
contained the quantity
of liquid they should.
This was deemed
necessary as publicans
were known to short-
change customers
by using vessels with
raised bottoms. This
example is that of
Queen Anne – 'AR'
for 'Anna Regina'.

VIII.
*Puzzle Jug Spout.*
19th century
*Found* at Westminster
by the Author.

Popular in taverns,
puzzle jugs challenged
the drinker to consume
their contents without
spilling them. This was
testing, as the neck of
the jug was perforated,
making the task
impossible to complete
conventionally. The
solution lay in sucking
from one of the jug's
spouts and so drawing
the liquid though a
hidden tube, while
closing off others
with the fingers.

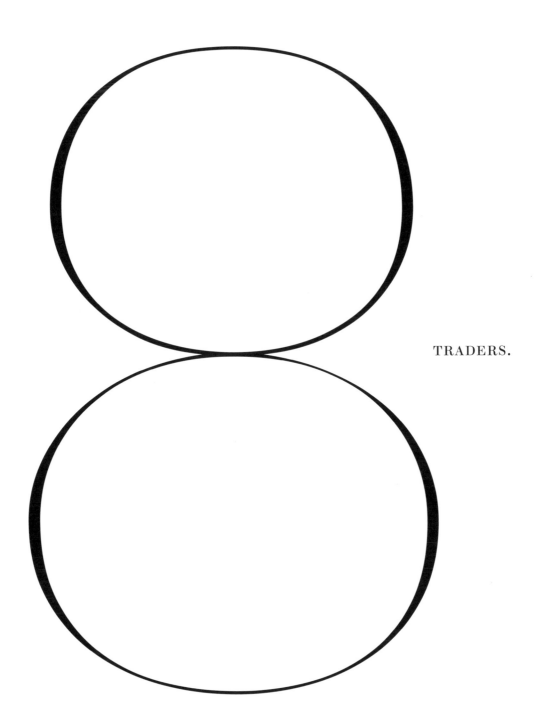

TRADERS.

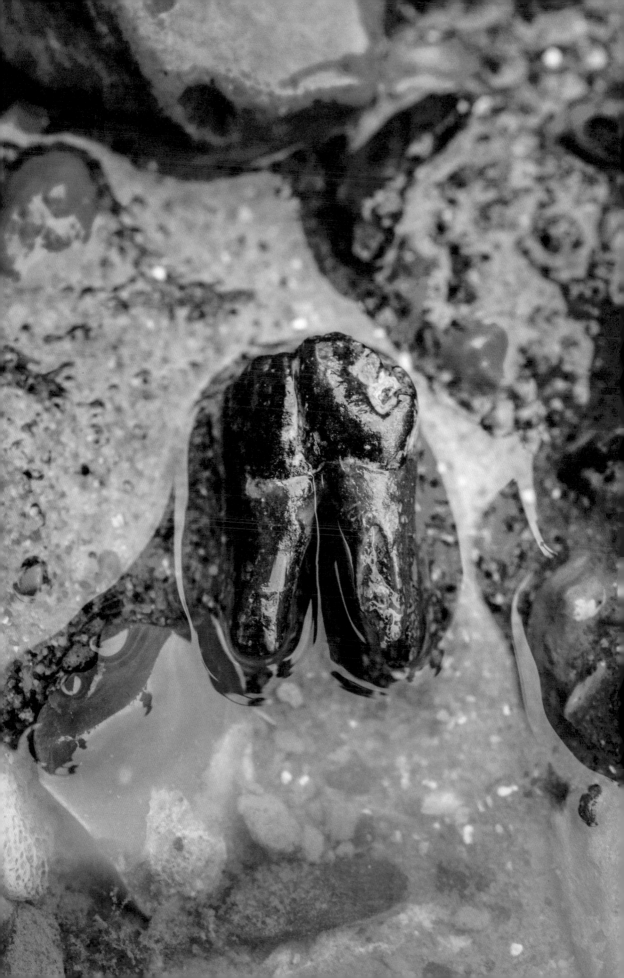

# Mountebanks & Dentists—

The evolution of oral care,
*revealed by a tooth.*

OPPOSITE.
Human Tooth.
Date unknown
*Found* at City of London
by the Author.

ABOVE.
*In* Hob and Stage Doctor *Edward Dighton depicts an itinerant tooth-drawer on a public stage at a country market or fair, extracting a patient's tooth, while his assistant in a clown's costume provides entertainment and distraction. William Davison published Dighton's print in* Some Alnwick caricatures, *c. 1812–1817.*

EDWARD DIGHTON'S EARLY nineteenth-century engraving, *Hob and Stage Doctor*, shows a wooden stage on which an itinerant tooth-drawer, sometimes referred to as a mountebank, is extracting a male patient's lower incisor using an instrument known as a tooth key. To provide distraction, the tooth-drawer's assistant is squatting in front of the patient dressed as a clown and holding aloft a clay pipe. The crowd around the stage looks on in amusement and horror. It is possible that this find – a human tooth – may have left its owner's mouth by such means.

In early modern London, tooth pain was still believed to be caused by worms burrowing into the teeth. When remedies such as *Pulvis Benedictus* – a worm extermination powder – inevitably failed to bring relief, extracting a tooth was often the only option. Barbers (who also offered bloodletting services), blacksmiths, cutlery makers, jewelers, wigmakers and apothecaries were all known to extract teeth as a sideline. It was itinerant tooth-drawers, however, who formed the core of what passed as oral care for most of the population.

Operating in public settings, tooth-drawers incorporated elements of showmanship to pull in crowds and help divert patients' minds from the inevitable pain. Clowning, juggling or the playing of musical instruments all figured in such displays. A member of one troupe was renowned for placing his head in a sack and extracting teeth with one hand while firing a pistol with the other. Other tooth-drawers captivated crowds by using a sword tip to flick out a tooth while on horseback. The eccentric Martin van Butchell was London's most colourful such practitioner. His taste for spectacle was such that he was known for riding around town on a pony painted with purple spots (or sometimes entirely purple) and for displaying the embalmed body of his wife in his home, drawing substantial crowds.

I.

II.

This fusion of tooth extraction and performance drew the disdain of physicians, who had long seen oral medicine as beneath them. The 1605 pamphlet *The Anatomies of the True Physician and Counterfeit Mountebank*, condemned all itinerant medical practitioners as 'the abject and sordidious scumme and refuse of the people, who having run away from their trades and occupations leane in a corner to get their livings by killing men'.[105]

During the following century, oral care finally began to benefit from the scientific revolution influencing other areas of medicine. The catalyst was the publication of Pierre Fauchard's *Le Chirurgien-Dentiste* – the first use of the word '*dentiste*'. Fauchard identified foodstuffs that were especially damaging to the teeth – particularly the sugar-rich foods that now formed a significant part of European diets. In response, he advocated a simple tooth-care regime consisting of rubbing, using a toothpick and rinsing the mouth with one's own urine. Fauchard also pioneered the use of artificial teeth, bound together with fine silk or gold wire into a block and then wired to adjacent natural teeth to hold them in place. He was also renowned for removing and cleaning a diseased tooth and reinserting it into the jaw. If replacements were required, they might be sourced from battlefield corpses or purchased from members of the public down on their luck.

Fauchard's reorientation of oral care from extraction to preservation was more apparent when compared with the practices of infamous Parisian tooth-drawers such as *Le Grand Thomas*. Also known as 'the terror of the human jaw', Thomas pulled teeth on a mobile cart with a huge tooth, dubbed 'Gargantua's awesome molar', hanging from it. Fauchard, in contrast, treated patients in a private consulting room where passers-by could no longer hear their cries of pain.

In Fauchard's wake came Nicolas Dubois de Chémant. De Chémant pioneered the manufacture of artificial teeth made of porcelain paste, hailed as more durable and less malodorous than materials previously used, such as hippopotamus jaw, ivory, walrus tusk and wood. Demand for his services was also heightened by the spread of Enlightenment values. As historian Colin Jones has demonstrated, in 1700 a tight-lipped smile was seen as the most appropriate for social elites, as it covered poor teeth and signified control over one's emotions.[106] Open-mouthed smiles were depicted in portraiture as plebeian or the preserve of the insane. By mid-century, however, the expression of emotion was regarded as a sign of a well-developed consciousness, and the white-toothed smile evolved into a desirable expression of progressive values.

The Great Terror that followed the French Revolution changed the meaning of the open-mouthed smile once again. Aristocrats about to be guillotined took to smiling to onlookers as an act of resistance, and *dentistes* servicing the wealthy now seemed dangerously out of step with the mood of the times. Fearing for his life, Dubois de Chémant fled to London in 1792 and began operating from premises on Frith Street in Soho, immediately elevating the standard of dental care available in the capital. Nevertheless, it would be more than a century before dentistry for the masses evolved beyond the practices of the mountebank to scientifically grounded preventative care.

*III.*

# Finds Relating to Oral Care.

I.

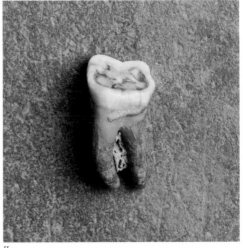

II.

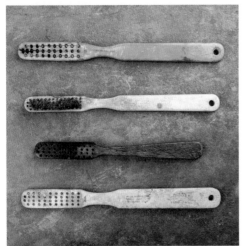

III.

IV.

I.
*Honey Pot.*
Late 17th to 18th century
*Found* at Southwark by the Author.

As sugar began to replace honey as England's preeminent sweetener, not everyone welcomed the change. The physician James Hart warned young people to 'beware how they meddle' with sugar, fearing it 'produceth dangerous effects in the body', including heating of the blood, a weakened constitution and rotten teeth.[107]

II.
*Human Tooth.*
Date unknown
*Found* at City of London by the Author.

In the seventeenth century, it was believed that teeth or hair clippings falling into the hands of a witch could make a person vulnerable to *maleficium*. This perhaps led some to see the Thames as a suitable place to dispose of any extracted teeth.

III.
*Toothbrush Handles.*
19th to early 20th century
*Found* at Westminster by Seán O'Mara.

One notable early manufacturer of toothbrushes in London was the company founded by William Addis. Addis's toothbrush handles were made from ox and bullock thigh bones, with bristles sourced from animals, including badgers, pigs and boar.

IV.
*Rimmel's Cherry Tooth Paste Pot Lid.*
*c.* 1900
*Found* at Wandsworth by Mark Iglesias.

Another oral care innovation of the nineteenth century was toothpaste. This eventually replaced abrasive tooth powders, with ingredients such as chalk, pulverized brick or salt.

*ABOVE.*
*A large, well-dressed gentleman*
*is portayed having a tooth drawn*
*by a dentist in this mezzotint*
*entitled* Teeth Drawn with a
Touch *by James Wilson,* 1773.

# *Quacks—*

Georgian medical entrepreneurs,
*revealed by a medicine bottle.*

*OPPOSITE.*
*Medicine Bottle.*
1700–1800
*Found* at City of London
by the Author.

*ABOVE.*
*Leading quack medicine*
*maker Isaac Swainson is*
*shown promoting his Velno's*
*Vegetable Syrup as a cure*
*for syphilis, in the face*
*of rival practitioners*
*advocating mercury, in*
*Thomas Rowlandson's print*
Mercury and his advocates
defeated, or vegetable
entrenchment, *1789.*

*OCCASIONALLY, COMPLETE* eighteenth-century glass medicine bottles miraculously wash up on the Thames foreshore. Some would have held medicines prepared by London's apothecaries, who mostly based their preparations on the official standard list of medicines published by the Royal College of Physicians. Others would have held 'nostrums'. These medicines, the formulas of which were kept secret, were made and sold by entrepreneurs operating outside the medical establishment, known pejoratively as 'quacks'.

A staggering array of such nostrums were created during this period, claiming to offer relief from everything from gout to scurvy to dropsy, worms and ulcers. Many, such as Spilsbury's Surprisingly Efficacious Drops, Dr Blenkensop's Bilious Specific and Dr Hooper's Female Pills, were named after their proprietor. Hooper's pills were marketed as an 'anti-hysteric' for women afflicted with 'The Irregularities', and as a cure-all for a host of ailments, such as 'giddiness, 'palpitations' and 'a dejected countenance'. The advice that they were not to be taken by pregnant customers was a veiled recommendation for their use in abortion. Other products evoked religious healing, such as Dr Trigg's Golden Vatican Pill, while self-proclaimed 'high doctor' Frederick van Neurenburg's trio of Persian Balsam, Chinese Antidote and Turkish Antidote promised to bring the sufferer the expertise of the Orient. Treatments

for venereal disease were multitudinous, with quacks offering alternatives to the painful treatment using mercury favoured by the medical establishment. G. Dean, billing himself as a 'chymical physican', offered a 'Speedy and Absolute Cure for the *French Pox*' without the use of any 'Poysonous Mercurial Remedies'; while John Case announced his new nostrum as 'A Most Infallible, and Sure, Cheap, Secret, Safe and Speedy Cure for a Clap.'

The success of such quacks was heightened by new opportunities for marketing and distributing their concoctions. Earlier nostrum-peddlers had sold their wares in person at markets and fairs, but their Georgian equivalents were able to reach a far wider audience through advertising in the growing medium of the newspaper. Between 1690 and 1780, the number of newspapers printed annually in England rose from less than a million to fourteen million, a growth far in excess of that of the population. Such was the preponderance of advertisements carried for nostrums that quacks were derisively dubbed 'advertising professors'.

The claims made in such publicity appealed to readers via a heady combination of fashion, vanity and fear. One common technique was to include the case of a supposedly cured patient. Dr John Moore, apothecary at the Pestle and Mortar off Upper Thames Street, placed an advertisement in the *Daily Post* in July 1736 for his worm powders. These, it was claimed, had successfully caused a 'worm or insect like a Hog-Louse with Legs and...a kind of Down all over it' to exit from the body of the son of Thames waterman Richard Sandford.[108] At the same time, Moore promoted smelling salts and a book which offered the reader

Come, Dilly, Dilly, Dilly, come and be killed!!!

A SHORT LIFE and a Merry one

A Receipt of my Grandmother's DECLINE ARRESTED Consumption prevented A Cure for all diseases BY THE SIMPLE process of SKINNING ALIVE protected by the NO-BILITY and a House-full of LADIES of the first Distinction Dr NEEDY HARLEY STREET NO QUACKERY

N.B. SHORT Accounts make LONG Friends.

A LONG WAY THROUGH A SHORT LIFE.

II.

'a natural history of tame pigeons' and advice on how to cure them of their distempers.[109] Another approach was the puff-piece, a seemingly impartial article reporting on a nostrum's brilliant effectiveness, but actually paid for by the maker of the drug. This technique was used by John Newbery, whose business activities combined those of being a newspaper proprietor, patent medicine wholesaler and a publisher of children's books. His most famous title, *The History of Little Goody Two-Shoes*, extolled the virtues of one of the most popular remedies he sold – Dr James's Powder – on its first page.

Such practices fuelled the condemnation of quacks by the medical establishment. Some objected to the lack of transparency, deeming it unethical to keep buyers in the dark about what they were taking. Others decried the quacks' lack of qualifications and the fact that they had undergone neither a university education nor an apprenticeship to an apothecary. To the dramatist Ben Jonson, quacks were 'turdy-facy-nasty-paty-lousy fartical' rogues.[110] For the physician Thomas Beddoes, they were the 'bastard brethren' of true healers. But the division between quacks and regular medical practitioners was not always clear-cut. Many orthodox physicians also developed their own nostrums: Dr Nehemiah Grew patented Epsom Salts; a physician at London's St George's Hospital sold Macleod's Bread Pills, which consisted only of bread; while Dr David Irish issued a pamphlet denouncing quacks, which also extolled the virtue of his own nostrums and his own private lunatic asylum. Furthermore, many quack remedies were in fact based on recipes outlined in the *Pharmacopoeia Londinensis*, the standard list of medicines and their ingredients issued by the Royal College of Physicians in 1618.

Popular accounts of quacks have tended to portray them as duplicitous charlatans preying on a naive public, in contrast with a virtuous medical establishment. In truth, however, they were simply one part of a medical system that failed in general to deliver effective treatments. Quacks could even be regarded in some instances as motors of medical innovation. Quack and botanist Isaac Swainson argued as much in the late eighteenth century, when he declared: 'In physic, all changes have been forced on the regulars by the quacks...and all the great and powerful medicines are the discoveries of quacks... The regulars adopted the discoveries and persecuted their benefactors.'[111]

You needs not be at all uneasy my dear Madam, if anything unpleasant should occur you have the satisfaction at least of knowing that your husband has been POISONED according to act of parliament, and I need not say what a pretty widow you'll make.

Here I am after a capital dose of STRYCHNINE !!!

III.

# Finds Relating to Quackery and Medicine.

*I.*

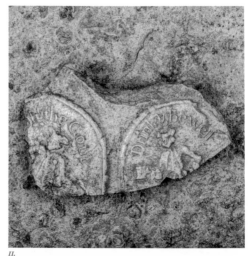

*II.*

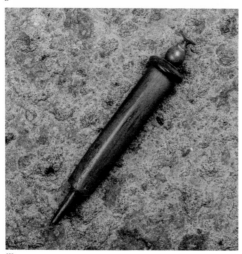

*III.*

*IV.*

*I.*
*Medicine Vial.*
17th century
*Found* at undisclosed
location by Florence
Evans.

Quacks flourished in
times of plague, with
the last major outbreak
in London occurring
in 1665. According
to the writer Daniel
Defoe, its nostrum
peddlers pasted up
signs offering sufferers
remedies, including
'Infallible preventive
pills, Sovereign cordials
against the corruption
of the air, and
Incomparable drink
against the plague'.[112]

*II.*
*Iron Pear Tree Gout
Water Bottle Fragment.*
*c.* 1752
*Found* at undisclosed
location by Anna
Borzello.

Iron Pear Tree gout
water was said to have
been discovered by
a publican who sank
a well near a pear tree
which grew small, iron-
hard pears. He believed
that the ale he brewed
using its water had
cured him of his gout,
and it was subsequently
sold in London for
twelve pence a gallon.

*III.*
*Syringe.*
Early 19th century
*Found* at Tower
Hamlets by Stuart
Wyatt.

One use of syringes
was to inject mercury
into the urethra as a
treatment for syphilis.
Mercury was effective
in burning away
syphilitic lesions, but
was also highly toxic,
causing neurological
problems as well as
swollen gums, rotting
teeth and hair loss.
This led to quacks
developing alternatives
such as Velnos'
Vegetable Syrup.

*IV.*
*Singleton's Eye
Ointment Pot.*
19th century
*Found* at Wandsworth
by Seán O'Mara.

Originating in a late
sixteenth-century
recipe, Singleton's Eye
Ointment was placed
on the eyelid or the
eye itself to reduce
inflammation. It was
apparently popular
among British troops
suffering from sand-
damaged eyes while
fighting the Napoleonic
forces in Egypt.

*V.*

*VI.*

*VII.*

*VIII.*

*V.*
*Dr Soule's Hop Bitters*
*Bottle.*
*c.* 1872–1900
*Found* at Westminster
by Seán O'Mara.

Asa Soule of Rochester,
New York, claimed his
Hop Bitters purified the
blood and regulated the
liver. Soule sponsored
a local baseball team,
giving each player
a tablespoon of his
product before the
game. After enjoying
initial success, the
team's performance
declined, and Soule
was ridiculed in the
press as the 'Medicated
Sportsman'.[113]

*VI.*
*A. J. White Bottle.*
*c.* 1884–1900
*Found* at Royal
Borough of Greenwich
by the Author.

New York quack
Andrew Judson White
sought to differentiate
his nostrums in the
public mind by buying
his ingredients from
the Shaker Christian
sect, which had
a reputation for
producing high-
quality medicines.
Shaker Extract of
Roots became one of
the company's most
popular products.

*VII.*
*Edwards' Harlene Bottle.*
*c.* 1890–1920
*Found* at Westminster
by Seán O'Mara.

Edwards' Harlene
promised to promote
hair growth. Each
bottle was accompanied
by a pamphlet detailing
how to apply Harlene to
the head. It instructed
that 'The manner in
which a cat moves
among shrubbery is
a good illustration as
to the way the fingers
should be moved
through the hair.' The
*British Medical Journal*
declared its chances
of restoring a balding
pate were minimal.

*VIII.*
*Coronavirus Survivor's*
*Medalet.*
2020
*Found* at undisclosed
location by Monika
Buttling-Smith.

More recently, the
coronavirus pandemic
prompted an upsurge
in quackery. One of
the most high-profile
examples saw US
President Donald
Trump endorsing an
injection of bleach
to treat Covid-19,
as promoted by the
Genesis II Church
of Health and Healing.

# *Costermongers—*

Victorian London's street sellers,
*revealed by a token.*

*IN VICTORIAN LONDON, THE PLACE TO GO* for wholesale fruit and vegetables was Spitalfields Market. Stallholders sold their produce in baskets, and to ensure these were returned they charged a deposit and issued the buyer with a token, such as this find. Many of Spitalfields's customers were costermongers: traders who purchased fruit, vegetables and fish wholesale at official markets and then sold it from barrows on the streets. In doing so, they played a crucial role in supplying the city's poor with cheap food and left a cultural imprint that still resonates today.

According to interviews conducted by the journalist Henry Mayhew, costermongers typically arrived at wholesale markets at around six or seven o'clock in the morning to pick up bargains among the stock not already purchased by shopkeepers. The aim was not to stock a full range of produce but to offer whatever was in season and could be purchased most cheaply. Sprats, apples, eels, turnips, oranges, strawberries and cherries could all be loaded on to a costermonger's barrow which was pushed through the streets. On his round, the costermonger was typically accompanied by a boy aged between six and sixteen (often his own son), who would call out for customers. This itineracy frequently brought costermongers into conflict with the police; one told Mayhew that 'To serve out [punch] a policeman is the bravest act by which a coster-monger can distinguish himself.'[114] An attempt was made to curb the roaming nature of the trade by opening the gargantuan Columbia Market in Bethnal Green in 1869, but it closed after a mere six months, its long list of regulations running contrary to the independence costermongers valued.

Many of London's estimated thirty thousand street sellers lived in identifiable residential clusters, in which, according to social campaigner Charles Booth,

II.

it was not uncommon to see a donkey entering or leaving by the front door. Some neighbourhoods consisted of traders drawn from London's immigrant communities. Mayhew believed there were ten thousand Irish street sellers active in London around 1850, their numbers swollen by the famine that forced one million Irish to emigrate. One trader reported that his neighbours back home had become so hungry they had resorted to foraging for wild greenery to eat. East London's Jewish population was also engaged in street selling, mostly of old clothes, having been supplanted by the Irish as hawkers of oranges around the city's coaching inns.

As working-class Londoners, costermongers made up a significant proportion of the audience at London's music halls. They were also a source of inspiration for the performers, some of whom were former costermongers themselves. The patter of street selling infused Bessie Bellwood's hit song, 'Wot Cheer, 'Ria', which opened with the singer declaring that the finery she was wearing was the result of her being a 'girl what's a-doing very well in the vegetable line'. Alfred Vance's 'Chickaleary Cove', meanwhile, saw him performing in the character of a street seller boasting of his sharp tailoring. Such acts reflected the reputation costermongers had for their showy style of dress. For males

I.

I.

*Cover of the sheet music for music hall song 'Costermonger Joe', 1866, written by C. H. Witt, and made famous by performer Alfred Vance, also known as 'The Great Vance'.*

II.

*Photograph of an ice-cream seller trading from a small cart on the street, featured in* Street Life in London, *1877, by John Thomson and Adolphe Smith.*

III.

*An early twentieth-century photograph of a Pearly King and Queen and their children waving at crowds from a cart pulled by a donkey, recalling the tradition's costermonger roots.*

this included a corduroy waistcoat, often featuring buttons made from mother of pearl. Hyram Travers, a music-hall performer with a costermonger act, was described in the press as the 'Pearly King' because of his elaborate pearl-buttoned stage costumes. Such music-hall performers influenced a street sweeper and charity worker named Henry Croft. To draw attention to his fundraising activities, Croft created a suit decorated with hundreds of mother-of-pearl buttons· His efforts evolved into the working-class charitable tradition of Pearly Kings and Queens in which a Pearly King and Queen is crowned for each borough of London.

Croft's activities and the Pearly tradition he founded, along with music-hall acts, changed how the costermonger was perceived. In the mid-nineteenth century, middle-class commenters denounced the costermonger as one of London's 'nomadic tribes'; an object of disgust who found regular labour repugnant, was crude, licentious, fond of inebriation and posed a danger to the more civilized members of society.[115] By the late 1930s, however, the costermonger was typically represented as a humorous, good-natured type with an attachment to working-class tradition. This transformation was due in no small part to the influence of the musical *Me and My Girl*, which captured the nation with its rags-to-riches story of Bill Snibson, a Lambeth costermonger who inherits an earldom but finds it difficult to adapt to life among the social elite. The high point of the show was Snibson leading a grand dinner party in a dance number called *The Lambeth Walk*, named after a south London street market. The dance, based on the costermonger's swagger, became a national phenomenon, performed everywhere from Mayfair ballrooms to suburban dance halls, Cockney parties and village hops. The image of the London costermonger had transitioned from vagabond to national treasure.

III.

# Finds Relating to Costermongers and Street Selling.

*I.*

*II.*

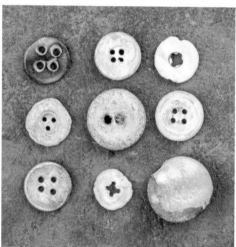

*III.*

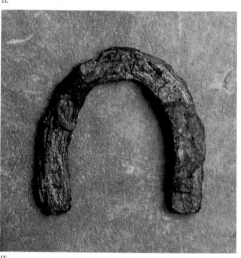

*IV.*

*I.*
*Queen Victoria Penny.*
1862
*Found* at Tower
Hamlets by the Author.

One penny bought
Victorian London's poor
entry to a 'Penny Gaff'
– a shop turned into a
temporary theatre in
which costermongers
often made up the bulk
of the audience. Comic
turns, smutty songs
and dancing could
be found on the bill.

*II.*
*Gatti's Palace of
Varieties Refreshments
Token.*
*c.* 1865–1910
*Found* at Westminster
by Seán O'Mara.

Costermonger-
inspired music-hall
acts could be found
performing at Gatti's
Palace of Varieties on
Westminster Bridge
Road. This token was
issued to customers
on entry for them
to exchange for
refreshments.

*III.*
*Mother-of-Pearl Buttons.*
19th to early 20th
century
*Found* at City of
London and Southwark
by the Author.

London's
costermongers were
known for their showy
style, including the
wearing of mother-
of-pearl buttons. This
influenced the stage
outfits of costermonger
music-hall acts and
the working-class
charitable tradition
of the Pearly Kings
and Queens.

*IV.*
*Boot Heel Reinforcer.*
19th to early 20th
century
*Found* at Tower
Hamlets by the Author.

Costermongers'
keen sense of style
also extended to
their footwear. 'The
costermonger's love
of a good strong boot
is a singular prejudice
that runs throughout
the whole class,'
wrote journalist
Henry Mayhew in
1851.[116] Among younger
men the fashion was
for leather uppers
ornamented with
hearts, thistles and
roses.

*V.*

*VI.*

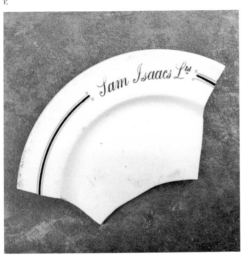

*VII.*

*VIII.*

*V.*
*Penny Lick.*
Mid-19th to early
20th century
*Found* at undisclosed
location by Florence
Evans.

Almost any commodity
could be purchased on
the streets in Victorian
and Edwardian London.
Ice cream was sold
in a glass known as a
penny lick; customers
would lick their treat
before handing it back
to be refilled for the
next purchaser. These
remained in use until
1926, when they were
banned due to concern
over the spread of
tuberculosis.

*VI.*
*Ring.*
Late 19th to early
20th century
*Found* at Tower
Hamlets by the Author.

Cheap jewelry, often
made in Birmingham
(known as 'Brummagen'
ware) was a staple of
London's working-class
street markets, sold by
sellers who were said
to be in the 'swag trade'.

*VII.*
*Sam Isaacs Ltd*
*Plate Fragment.*
Late 19th to early
20th century
*Found* at Westminster
by Seán O'Mara.

Many of east London's
street traders were
drawn from the Jewish
immigrants who had
fled persecution in the
Russian Empire. Other
Jewish emigres such
as Sam Isaacs created
culinary innovations.
In 1896, Isaacs opened
the first sit-down fish-
and-chip restaurant,
adding a touch
of glamour to the
working-class favourite.

*VIII.*
*Charlie Chaplin Brooch.*
Early 20th century
*Found* at Westminster
by Seán O'Mara.

Comic actor Charlie
Chaplin made his first
stage appearance aged
five performing the
costermonger song
*Jack Jones* at an
Aldershot music hall.
The lyrics told the story
of a street seller who
had inherited wealth
and begun to take
on airs and graces.

FIGHTERS.

PREVIOUS.
*The horrific scene depicted in* A House Collapsing On Two Firemen, Shoe Lane, EC4, *painted by Leonard Rosoman in 1940, was one the artist had witnessed first-hand while serving as a member of the Auxiliary Fire Service.*

# *Forgotten Heroes of the Crimea—*

War with Russia,
*revealed by a clay pipe.*

OPPOSITE.
*Turk's Head Clay Tobacco Pipe.*
*c. 1850*
*Found* at City of London by the Author.

ABOVE.
*Ottoman Field Marshal Omar Pasha, photographed on the Crimean Peninsula by Roger Fenton in 1855. As a commander in the Crimean War, he won several decisive victories against Russian enemy forces.*

THE MOTIF OF A 'TURK'S HEAD' had long been associated with London's coffee houses, and by the Victorian era had been incorporated into the designs of clay tobacco pipes. With the outbreak of the Crimean War, these enjoyed a wave of popularity – allowing smokers to show their affinity with Britain's ally in the fight against Russian imperial expansion: the ailing Ottoman Empire. Some bear the name of the Ottoman commander Omar Pasha. Born Mihajlo Latas, an Orthodox Christian in Austrian territory, he fled to the Ottoman Empire to escape embezzlement charges.

He converted to Islam, took the name Omar and went on to join the Ottoman military. Swiftly rising through the ranks, he led the empire's forces to a series of decisive victories against the Russians during the Crimean War. These actions marked him out as one of the more competent military leaders in a conflict that saw British command marred by bungled orders, poor planning and a shortfall of troops.

Another find from the Thames brings to light the stories of two of the war's less exalted heroes. With the press highlighting the many acts of bravery that were going unrewarded, a new award for soldiers displaying gallantry 'in the presence of the enemy' was created: the Victoria Cross. The medal remains the highest honour a British soldier can receive. In 2015, the mudlarker Tobias Neto plucked a Victoria Cross from the mud of the foreshore, immediately raising questions as to who it might have been awarded to and how such a prestigious object could have made its way into the Thames.

The back of the medal is inscribed with the date 5 November 1854: the date of the Battle of Inkerman. This commenced when a large number of Russian troops launched a surprise attack on British and French soldiers on a boulder-strewn ridge in thick fog. Poor visibility led to a confusing series of melees rather than a battle proper, with the damp rendering firearms unusable. Soldiers of both sides resorted to using bayonets, boots, swords, rifle butts and even stones as weapons. The fighting took a terrible toll on the minds of those who fought. Lieutenant Lleuellyn of the 46th Regiment arrived at the scene two days later, remarking of the soldiers' mental trauma in his diary: 'It is difficult to recognize in their haggard faces and ragged clothing the gay soldiers who left us the other day... the people who are left appear dazed and stupefied and unable to give us any idea of our position or chances.'[117]

Twenty Victoria Crosses were awarded to British soldiers who fought in these desperate conditions. When the medals

I.

were issued, their ribbons featured a bar inscribed with the recipient's name, but the ribbon was missing from the Victoria Cross found in the Thames. After Neto's find, eighteen of the twenty medals were accounted for, leaving two potential recipients: Privates John McDermond and John Byrne.

Infantryman John McDermond had run into a group of Russian soldiers to help rescue Lieutenant-Colonel William Haly, who had been dragged from his horse, surrounded and wounded. McDermond killed one of Haly's attackers and fought off several others. After receiving his medal, he is known to have visited London twice before his death from typhus in Scotland in 1868; first to be painted by French artist Louis Desanges, for a series celebrating Victoria Cross winners, and later to gain his military pension. Florence Nightingale wrote of how the 'ghosts of their troubles' haunted the soldiers she cared for in the Crimea. Perhaps, seeking to rid himself of such disturbing associations, McDermond cast his medal into the Thames on one of these visits.

Irishman John Byrne had travelled to England to seek work before joining the army. After a spell in a military prison, the volatile Byrne found himself on the battlefield at Inkerman. Risking his life, he had headed towards the enemy to rescue a wounded comrade-in-arms after his regiment had been ordered to retire. Later the same day he also killed a Russian soldier in hand-to-hand combat, preventing the enemy from storming his position. After the Crimean War, Byrne spent another fifteen years in the army, but failed to translate his bravery on the battlefield into advancement through the ranks. Upon being discharged, he re-enlisted within days, and eventually served for a total of twenty-one years.

Like many veterans with traumatic combat experience, Byrne struggled to reintegrate himself into civilian life, and spent some time in a lunatic asylum in the Straits Settlements, the British territories encompassing today's Malaysia and Singapore. By 1878, the former soldier was back in Britain looking for work, and secured a position as part of an Ordnance Survey mapping team in Newport. At some point his Victoria Cross had been retained for safekeeping by the army authorities. A request was sent to his superior at his new employment asking after Byrne's

state of mind, with a view to delivering his medal to him. The Lieutenant replied that Byrne seemed fine, and the medal was duly returned.

Byrne later fell into a conflict with an eighteen-year-old colleague named James Watts, whom he believed had insulted his Victoria Cross. Having disappeared for a period, during which he procured a gun, Byrne shot Watts in the arm at the Crown Inn, Newport, before taking refuge in one of the inn's rooms, saying he would only come out at three o'clock that afternoon. When a police sergeant approached him at that time, Byrne shot himself in the mouth, causing his own death. Whether he had visited London between the return of his medal and his death – during which time his medal ended up in the Thames – is unknown, and the mystery of the recipient of the Thames Victoria Cross remains unsolved.

II.

I.

II.

I.
*Australian Army Division
Commonwealth Military Forces
Cap Badge, c. 1914–1918. Found
at Westminster by Seán O'Mara.*

II.
*Duke of Cornwall's Light Infantry
Cap Badge, c. 1914–1918. Found
at Westminster by Seán O'Mara.*

*III.*

*IV.*

*III.*
*Machine Gun Corps Cap Badge,*
*1915–1922. Found at Westminster*
*by Seán O'Mara.*

*IV.*
*Grenadier Guards Cap Badge,*
*Late nineteenth century. Found*
*at Westminster by Seán O'Mara.*

# *Auxilary Firefighters—*

Extinguishing the Blitz,
*revealed by a button.*

*OPPOSITE.*
*Auxiliary Fire Service*
*Uniform Button.*
1938–1941
*Found* at City of London
by the Author.

*ABOVE.*
Members of London's
Auxiliary Fire Service
extinguishing a blaze in
a training exercise near
Greenwich, July 1939.

IN 1937, THERE WERE ONLY 5,000 full-
time regular firemen in Britain. As war
with Germany grew more likely, the
government ordered the creation of an
Auxiliary Fire Service (AFS) to meet
the possible threat of bombing. By the
end of 1940, 192,000 men and women
had joined, comprising over 80 per cent
of all the nation's firefighters. Whereas
regular firemen were overwhelmingly
ex-servicemen or policemen, many
auxiliaries were from clerical and
professional as well as working-class
backgrounds.

I.

Aerial view of a German Heinkel
He 111 bomber flying over Rotherhithe
on 7 September 1940 at the start
of a series of evening raids by
the Luftwaffe on London's docks.

II.

Firefighters tackle a burning
building after an evening bombing
raid on London by the Luftwaffe
during the Blitz.

III.

View of the City of London
taken from the roof of St Paul's
Cathedral, showing the devastation
caused by the bombing raids of
29–30 December 1940.

Dockers, lorry drivers, musicians, scientists, clerks and academics all found themselves serving together.

During the first year of the war the AFS saw little action. Their uniforms, one of which sported this button, remained unworn apart from occasional drills. Then, on the morning of 7 September 1940, everything changed. Several hundred German bombers suddenly appeared over London, their target the city's docks along the Thames. Warehouses, cargo vessels, sheds and yards stacked with foodstuffs and materials vital to the war effort were attacked, not only with high explosives but with thousands of incendiary bombs. These small devices, designed to start fires, accounted for the majority of the destruction during London's Blitz. West Ham firefighter Cyril Demarne recalled the scene that morning in his memoir: 'Flames erupted from the great warehouses and factories lining the River Thames on both banks, from North Woolwich to Tower Bridge. Massive warehouses and tiny houses alike came crashing down under the impact of high explosive, burying under the debris their occupants and any luckless passer-by.'[118]

Demarne ordered five hundred pumps to the scene. His commander thought this was excessive and sent someone else to assess the situation, who reported that one thousand engines were needed instead. One early casualty of the aerial onslaught was the West Ham ambulance depot. The crews of two fire pumps, one including Demarne's friend Wally Turley, ran into the blasted building to ensure no one was inside. They were about to leave when it collapsed on them. After arriving at the scene, Demarne found an arm protruding from underneath a concrete slab and identified it as Turley's by his malformed fingernail. By this time hundreds of fires were raging across London's docklands – in ships, sugar refineries, tar distilleries, chemical works, timber stacks and paint and varnish works.

Fire crews attempted to tackle the flames from boats on the Thames, but operations were imperilled by blazing barges being swept downstream. On the south bank of the river, huge stacks of imported timber were ablaze in Rotherhithe. A hastily requisitioned collection of taxicabs, cars and vans pulled pumps to the scene, but as soon as the fire had been extinguished in one stack, the heat from surrounding blazes ignited it again. Amidst this devastation, terrified families fled to the river seeking a means of escape. At North Woolwich they boarded small boats to be rowed to safety in scenes reminiscent of the Great Fire nearly three centuries earlier. By midnight, 430 men, women and children had been killed, and destruction was wrought along the Thames for three miles (five kilometres).

The attack on 7 September was the first of fifty-seven successive raids, many of which were at night. These followed

I.

*II.*

a grimly predictable pattern. Sirens forewarned the approach of the bombers as darkness fell. An initial attack commenced around five o'clock, followed by a lull. Another major wave of bombing then occurred, followed by the dropping of firebombs and high explosives until daybreak. While most of the civilian population took to air-raid shelters, firefighters operated out in the blazing streets with bombs still falling around them. The destruction of telephone lines meant calls for assistance relied on motorcyclists and teenage boys on bicycles, who sometimes arrived at their destination bloodied and bruised, having been blasted from their vehicles by a near miss.

During a huge raid on London's financial district on 29 December 1940, 100,000 bombs ignited 1,500 fires. Extinguishing them was made even more challenging by an especially low tide, which hampered efforts to pump water from the river. Fire service boats pulled as close to the bank as they could, but their crews were forced to wade ashore over a treacherously muddy foreshore at Blackfriars Bridge – near where this button was found eighty years later. Many were dragging hoses that were designed to fill inflatable swimming pools, repurposed to help compensate for ruptured water mains and destroyed hydrants. This was still not enough

to stem the water shortage; for some periods during the night all that could be done was to retreat and watch as blazes spread from building to building.

With the invasion of the Soviet Union, German resources were diverted, and the nightly raids ceased in mid-1941. At the time, it was not known whether bombing would be resumed, and review of the ongoing suitability of the AFS fell to the Home Office Chief of Fire Staff, the aptly named Sir Aylmer Firebrace. He judged the organization had reached the limit of its possibilities, and the AFS was disbanded and replaced with a more professional service. The country's 1,400 separate fire brigades were consolidated into one service with a common uniform, command and procedure. This new organization was never tried as ferociously as the AFS had been. In the four years between its creation and the end of the war 10,000 fires were fought, compared with the 50,000 during the eight months of the Blitz.

The 'Blitz spirit' of British folklore has been scrutinized by historians over the past few decades.[119] A darker side has been uncovered: one of rising anti-Semitism, fearful rumourmongering, psychological distress, rape and flourishing criminality. The fire service was not without its tensions, especially between regulars and auxiliaries. Once bombing commenced, however, the evidence suggests that the basic constituents of the Blitz story remain untainted: ordinary men and women from across different social classes overwhelmingly putting aside all conflict except for that against fire.

*III.*

# Finds Relating to Fire and the Blitz.

I.

II.

III.

IV.

I.
*Token.*
1666
*Found* at Tower
Hamlets by Seán
O'Mara.

This token was issued
by Thames-side trader
William Reade in
1666, the year in which
fire reduced most of
London to smoking
ruins. As the city
burned, the Thames
became a means of
escape for those fleeing
the conflagration.
Similar scenes were
repeated nearly three
centuries later in the
first days of the Blitz.

II.
*Sun Fire Office
Firefighter's
Uniform Button.*
c. 1800
*Found* at City of
London by the Author.

Prior to the Great Fire
of 1666, London had no
organized fire service.
Following the disaster,
insurance companies
such as the Sun Fire
Office, founded in
1710, formed private
fire brigades in a bid
to minimize payouts
to policyholders. Their
clients' property was
indicated by a plaque
known as a 'fire mark'.

III.
*Harden Star Fire
Grenade.*
Early 20th century
*Found* at Westminster
by Seán O'Mara.

Globular glass fire
extinguishers known
as 'fire grenades' were
designed to be thrown
into the base of a fire.
Their glass shattered
on impact, releasing
chemicals that
extinguished the flames.
This example still
contains its highly toxic
carbon tetrachloride,
the vapours of which
caused several deaths
when the Harden
Star was used in
a confined space.

IV.
*Dog Collar Tag, Bearing
the Name 'Bonzo'.*
20th century
*Found* at Royal Borough
of Greenwich by
Nicola White.

Fearing people would
split their wartime
rations with their pets,
the government advised
that such animals
should be euthanized
on the outbreak of war.
Some owners initially
resisted, but many
reluctantly had them
killed when the London
Blitz commenced a
year later. An estimated
750,000 animals were
euthanized during
the course of the war.

V.

VI.

VII.

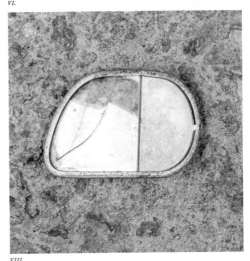

VIII.

V.
*Spitfire Fund Badge.*
1940–1941
*Found* at Westminster
by Seán O'Mara.

Badges were sold
during the Second
World War to
raise funds for the
manufacture of Spitfire
fighter planes. Despite
the aircraft's success
against German
fighters in the Battle
of Britain, it proved less
effective at destroying
enemy bombers. The
Royal Air Force Fighter
Command sometimes
failed to bring down
a single enemy aircraft
during a sortie.

VI.
*Anti-Aircraft Shell Case.*
1941
*Found* at Tower
Hamlets by Seán
O'Mara.

During the first week
of the London Blitz,
anti-aircraft gunners
attempting to fire
directly at German
bombers succeeded
in downing only a
handful of aircraft.
This prompted a switch
to a more successful
strategy: simply fire
as many rounds as
possible into the air to
loosen formations and
force attacking planes
to a higher altitude.

VII.
*Stonework, probably
from the Palace of
Westminster.*
19th century
*Found* at Westminster
by Seán O'Mara.

The Palace of
Westminster, commonly
known as the Houses
of Parliament, was
damaged by bombing
on fourteen occasions
during the Blitz. Pieces
of dislodged stonework
from the building were
sold off to raise funds
for the war effort. This
piece, found on the
adjacent foreshore,
perhaps sank unnoticed
into the mud.

VIII.
*Royal Air Force Goggle
Lens.*
*c.* 1939–1945
*Found* at Westminster
by Seán O'Mara.

Despite the extensive
damage London
suffered during the
Blitz, it was not as
severe as that inflicted
by the Royal Air Force
on the German city
of Hamburg. During
a single week in July
1943, a series of raids,
code-named Operation
Gomorrah, killed an
estimated thirty-seven
thousand civilians and
destroyed much of the
city in a fire storm.

# *The Red Army—*

Creating killers in the Second World War,
*revealed by a round of ammunition.*

*OPPOSITE.*
*Soviet Union, 7.62×54mmR*
*Cartridge Case.*
*1944–1945*
*Found* at Westminster
by the Author.

*ABOVE.*
*Red Army sniper Lyudmila*
*Pavlichenko, nicknamed*
*'Lady Death' for killing 309*
*German soldiers. Before*
*volunteering for military*
*service she was a history*
*student at Kyiv University.*

*THE 7.62×54R ROUND AND THE GUN* that
fired it – a heavy bolt action rifle named
the Mosin-Nagant – were the Red Army's
most ubiquitous weapons during the
Second World War. In 1942, however,
when the Soviet Union desperately
needed to push back the advancing
German forces, commanders were
concerned that most troops had not fired
a single shot since the war began. This
led to the development of propaganda
designed to help convert untrained and
fearful conscripts, restrained by the
powerful taboo surrounding the taking
of human life, into effective killers.

I.

*Soviet Union postage stamps, issued in 1943, commemorating the accomplishments of sniper Lyudmila Pavlichenko, who was given the Order of Lenin.*

II.

*Sniper Aleksandra Shliakhova, boasting of how many German soldiers she has killed, 1943.*

III.

*Soviet propaganda poster, 1942, depicting Hitler being strangled through combined Allied military might. The text above declares 'He can't slip out of his noose!'*

The results helped unleash the events that may account for a 7.62×54R casing travelling from a Soviet munitions facility known only as 'Factory 10' – where it was made in the last year of the conflict – across war-torn Europe, to eventually end its journey deposited in the River Thames.

An early method to encourage soldiers to pull the trigger was to give an individual weapon a name and to attach heroic stories to it, such as the rifle described as having belonged to 'Paramonov, who killed 114 and Savushkin 121.'[120] These details were recounted at special ceremonies in which the gun's new owner pledged to continue the work of their predecessor, while posters and military newspapers repeated the slogan: 'I have killed a German, and you?' Stories were also attached to specific types of weapons. The Mosin-Nagant was fifty years old when the Soviet Union was invaded, but what might have been seen as a deficiency was celebrated as proof of its superiority over more modern weapons. In particular, its deadliness in the hands of the Red Army's snipers was showcased to amplify the killing

II.

potential of this unsophisticated weapon. Many of these assassins were women, either self-taught or graduates of the Central Women's School of Sniper Training near Moscow. Sniper Lyudmila Pavlichenko was a figurehead for such campaigns. While some recruits struggled to fire, Pavlichenko, armed with her Mosin-Nagant, made two kills on her first day at the front. By the end of the war, she had taken 309 enemy lives and reported – officially at least – that killing Nazis aroused no complicated emotions in her. Male soldiers were invited to beat her impressive tally. To do this they were encouraged to keep a personal *schët* or 'body score', akin to a factory production quota. Alongside such challenges, battlefield tactics also evolved to encourage troops to shoot. The nineteenth-century practice of firing at the enemy in volleys was readopted, as it made failure to shoot more obvious. More drastically, special battalions were tasked with firing on their own troops if they failed to fulfil their combat duties.

As the front line finally approached Germany's eastern border, the Soviet propaganda machine shifted from encouraging killing in defence of the nation to doing it in the name of revenge. Red Army newspaper journalist Ilya Ehrenburg led the charge, declaring:

I.

'The Germans are not humans...
From now on, the word German causes
gunfire. We shall not speak. We shall
kill. If during a day you have not killed
a single German, you have wasted the
day.'[121] Such dehumanizing portrayals
of the enemy helped create the moral
vacuum that opened up as the Red
Army advanced into Germany. Enemy
troops were killed on an unprecedented
scale, alongside the murder and rape
of civilians and the looting of almost
every type of object imaginable, from
fine wines to entire factories.

This excess even extended to some
Soviet troops' first encounters with
their British counterparts, when the
two armies, advancing from opposite
directions, finally linked up in May 1945
in northern Germany. Private Denis
Edwards of the British Second Army
had been relishing the thought of the
moment when the two Allies would meet,
but the reality was more sobering. He
recorded in his diary that his division
was camped on the western bank of
a river looking across at the Soviets
camped on the other side. Drunkenly
crossing the river and entering the
British camp at night, Soviet soldiers
held the Quartermaster at gunpoint

and stole a tentful of rations. When
some British soldiers complained the
next morning to a Soviet officer, one of
the offenders was identified. Rather than
questioning him, the officer instead, as
Edwards recalled 'drew a revolver from
its holster, put the barrel against the
man's mouth and fired, blowing off half
of his head...grinning from ear to ear,
and indicating that, while the man may
have stolen our food, he would certainly
not be eating any more of it!'[122]

Edwards's experience notwithstanding,
war diaries and oral histories suggest
that most such encounters were more
good-natured. Accounts commonly
mention Western and Soviet troops
exchanging cigarettes, military insignia,
coins, hats, rings, watches, rations and
even weaponry as tokens by which to
celebrate and remember the momentous
events they found themselves part
of.[123] It is easy to imagine a round or a
spent casing functioning as a small gift
from a Soviet soldier to his British ally,
symbolizing in the last days of the war
not killing, but the end of killing. On his
return to London, with such souvenirs
officially frowned upon, the Thames
may have provided a convenient place
to dispose of it.

*III.*

# Finds Relating to the End of the Second World War.

I.

II.

III.

IV.

**I.**

*Hitler Youth Belt Buckle.*
*c.* 1939–1945
*Found* at Royal Borough
of Greenwich by Nicola
White.

Many British soldiers
fighting their way
across Europe returned
home with pieces of
Nazi paraphernalia
as souvenirs. Perhaps
this belt buckle of the
Hitler Youth – the
youth organization
of the Nazi Party –
arrived in Britain as
one such souvenir,
later to be thrown into
the Thames due to its
troubling associations.

**II.**

*United States Army,*
*Major's Badge.*
*c.* 1939–1945
*Found* at Westminster
by the Author.

Prior to D-Day, 1.5
million US troops were
stationed in Britain.
They were issued with
a copy of *Instructions*
*for American Servicemen*
*in Britain.* In a section
preparing Americans
for the more diminutive
scale of the landscape
in Britain. 'The
Thames,' it declared,
'is not even as big as
the Mississippi when
it leaves Minnesota.'[124]

**III.**

*'V for Victory' Lapel*
*Badge.*
*c.* 1941–1945
*Found* at Westminster
by Mark Igelsias.

The use of the letter
'V' as a symbol for
victory spread through
occupied Europe, with
Vs appearing chalked
on walls. From 1941, the
British Prime Minister
Winston Churchill
started using it as a
hand sign. Initially
he did this with palm
inwards, before being
advised that this
represented an insult
in working-class culture,
after which he switched
to palm outwards.

**IV.**

*Soviet Union Twenty*
*Kopek Coin.*
1961
*Found* at Westminster
by the Author.

The fraternization
between British and
Soviet troops at the
end of the Second
World War was short
lived. Foreign travel for
Soviet citizens became
highly regulated, and
those who were allowed
to visit the West had to
undergo pre-departure
instruction to reinforce
communism's superiority
over capitalism. Some
still visited forbidden
locations, such as
churches and strip clubs.

*ABOVE.*
*Photograph of part of the huge*
*crowd gathered in Parliament*
*Square, Westminster, on VE Day,*
*8 May 1945, to celebrate Germany's*
*unconditional surrender in Europe.*

# IN FOCUS—
## *Ammunition.*

Throughout its existence, London has been a centre of military activity. The city has been marched through, guarded and bombarded. The Thames has seen troops depart to the many corners of the world over which Britain has fought. Ammunition from all of these endeavours can be encountered on the foreshore.

During the seventeenth century, the musket was widely adopted for military use. The lead balls these weapons fired are among the oldest ammunition commonly recovered. Many examples are of the calibre fired by the 'Brown Bess', the nickname for the standard issue musket used by the British Army for over a century. While this weapon could cause horrific damage to the human body – with shot sometimes flattening and splintering inside it, making it hard for a surgeon to extract all the fragments – it was also inherently inaccurate and slow to load.

This spurred the development of the metallic cartridge: a brass case filled with powder with a bullet inserted at one end, and a primer – a small charge struck to ignite the powder – at the other. These were inserted not into the barrel, but into the breech at the back of the gun, significantly reducing loading time.

One early example was the .45 inch, designed for the Martini-Henry rifle: the British Army's weapon of choice for killing Indigenous people in the colonial wars of

the late nineteenth century. The suffering it wrought was writ large in the Battle of Rorke's Drift, during the Anglo-Zulu War in 1879. Several hundred Zulus, armed with spears and shields, were slaughtered with the loss of only seventeen British lives.

The Martini-Henry was replaced by rifles firing the .303 cartridge, which was also fired by the newly invented machine gun, with devastating effects on the battlefields of the First World War. In the interwar years, even more powerful machine guns were developed. These included the American .5 Browning M2, which was mounted into US Air Force planes conducting bombing raids on Nazi Germany from Britain. Returning crews were known to jettison spent cartridges from their aircraft, perhaps explaining their presence in the Thames.

The effectiveness of the machine gun inspired the development of the sub-machine gun as an antidote to the slower firing rate of the infantry rifle. These fired 9 millimetre cartridges typically used in pistols, and included the British Sten gun. Hastily conceived to replace weapons abandoned at Dunkirk, the Sten gun saw service from the beaches of Normandy to the jungles of south-east Asia.

Larger calibre ammunition used in the anti-aircraft weapons that defended London during the Second World War can be found in the form of shell casings and fragments of their detonating fuses. These often consist of pieces of the fuse's numbered ring, which a gunner would rotate to determine how much time would elapse after firing before the shell exploded.

Empty cases of any kind can be kept providing they contain no explosive charges. They can easily be identified by their headstamps: markings on their base, often indicating the date of manufacture, the maker and calibre (the internal diameter of the gun barrel for which it was designed).

*Musketball used in the Brown Bess rifle. c. 18th–mid-19th century.*

*.45-inch cartridge case used in the Martini-Henry rifle. 1880s.*

*8×56mmR cartridge case used in the Kropatschek rifle. 1896.*

*.303 cartridge case used in the Vickers machine gun. 1916.*

*9×19mm cartridge case used in the Sten sub-machine gun. 1942.*

*.5-inch cartridge case used in the M2 Browning heavy machine gun. 1942.*

*15mm projectile used in the Besa machine gun. 1939–1945.*

*Fragment of anti-aircraft gun shell fuse. 1939–1945.*

*OPPOSITE.*
Soldiers of the King's Royal Rifle Corps armed with Martini-Henry rifles, photographed in 1882 during the Anglo-Egyptian War, which saw Egypt fall under British influence.

*ABOVE.*
Cartridge casings and projectiles found on the foreshore illustrating the evolution of ammunition. All finds made by the Author except for the Besa projectile, found by Seán O'Mara.

*OVER.*
The author nightlarking by Southwark Bridge on the foreshore on the north bank of the Thames.

# A MUDLARKING PRIMER.

*Four centuries ago treasure hunting
had a strongly magical character.
The divining skills of folk healers were
enlisted to locate buried gold and deal
with the restless spirits thought to guard
it. One who sought the help of such spirits
was Goodwin Wharton, a politician,
alchemist and wreck investigator, who
spent twenty-five years treasure hunting
aided by 'George', an executed felon. For
those preferring a less ethereal approach,
here is a short mudlarking primer.*

STEP 1. — *Acquire a Permit.*
If you wish to search the Thames
foreshore anywhere between Teddington
Lock and the Thames Barrier, you must
first acquire a permit from the Port of
London Authority (PLA).

STEP 2. — *Know the Rules.*
A standard permit allows digging to a
depth of 7.5 centimetres in some areas.
In others disturbing the surface in any
way is forbidden. See the maps provided
by the Port of London Authority for
the search methods allowed on each
stretch of foreshore. They also detail
those locations where for archaeological
or security reasons all mudlarking is
forbidden.

STEP 3. — *Get Kitted Out.*
No equipment is essential for
mudlarking, but boots, waterproofs,
gloves, kneepads, a trowel and a
container in which to place your finds
are advisable. A head torch can also be
useful for illuminating the foreshore
while searching at night (often referred
to as 'nightlarking'), while leaving hands
free for scraping and picking up finds.

STEP 4. — *Choose a Spot.*
Use Port of London Authority tide tables
to find out what time low tide is at your
chosen spot, and plan to arrive an hour
or two prior. Always make sure you know

the location of your nearest exit from
the foreshore and beware of pinch points
– narrower sections of the foreshore –
which can leave the unwary cut off
as the tide comes in.

STEP 5. — *Search.*
Try to pick out shapes and textures that
do not occur naturally. If an object looks
interesting take it home to study and
research even if it is not immediately
apparent what it might be. You can
always return any unwanted finds
to the river on your next visit.

STEP 6. — *Identify Your Finds.*
A great place to start is sharing them
with the mudlarking community online.
Many people are only too happy to
share their expertise. Other invaluable
resources include the Portable
Antiquities Scheme database (see below).

STEP 7. — *Contextualize Your Finds.*
A find is what you make of it. Seemingly
mundane objects can yield remarkable
stories with a little research. Questions
you might ask include: How was
this object made, sold and used?
What spurred its creation and why
did it become obsolete? Whose lives
did it touch and what did it mean to
them? How might it have ended up
in the Thames?

STEP 8: *Report Your Finds.*
Any finds of archaeological interest
should be reported to a Finds Liaison
Officer for the Portable Antiquities
Scheme. The Portable Antiquities
Scheme is run by the British
Museum to encourage the recording
of archaeological objects found by
members of the public. Its Finds Liaison
Officers assess potential finds for entry
into its databases. Reporting your finds
makes an invaluable contribution to
our collective knowledge of the past.

KIT LIST.
i. *Headtorch.*
ii. *Trowel.*
iii. *Finds box.*
iv. *Waterproof jacket.*
v. *Kneepads.*
vi. *Wellington boots.*
vii. *Waterproof trousers.*

i.

ii.

iii.

iv.

v.

vi.

vii.

# *Endnotes.*

**INTRODUCTION**

1. Cited in https://www.jstor.org
   stable/1792806.
2. I. N. Hume, *Treasure in the
   Thames* (London: Frederick
   Muller, 1956), p. 14.

**CHAPTER 1**

3. Ovid, *Amores*, 1.4.45.
4. Ovid, *Ars* Amatoria, Book III,
   Part IV, 239–44.
5. Cornelius Tacitus, *The Annals*,
   Book XIV.
6. Cited in S. Hoss and A.
   Whitmore, eds., *Small Finds and
   Ancient Social Practices in the
   Northwest Provinces of the Roman
   Empire* (Oxford: Oxbow, 2016).
7. 'Venice: May 1517', in *Calendar
   of State Papers Relating To English
   Affairs in the Archives of Venice*,
   Volume 2: *1509–1519*, ed. R. Brown
   (London: HMSO, 1867), pp. 381–
   90; British History Online, www.
   british-history.ac.uk/cal-state-
   papers/venice/vol2/pp381–390
   [accessed 7 February 2020].
8. A. Duke, ed., *Private
   Correspondence between Flemish
   Strangers in England and their
   Families and Contacts in Flanders,
   1566–1573: Janssen Correspondence*,
   https://dutchrevolt.leiden.edu/
   english/sources/Pages/Janssen-
   correspondence.aspx [accessed
   8 February 2020].
9. *Ibid.*
10. Cited in L. H. Yungblut,
    *Strangers Settled Here Amongst
    Us: Policies, Perceptions and the
    Presence of Aliens in Elizabethan
    England* (London: Routledge,
    1996), p. 111.
11. Cited in L. B. Luu, *Immigrants
    and the Industries of London,
    1500–1700* (Abingdon and New
    York: Routledge, 2007), p. 111
12. Cited in *ibid.*, p. 59.
13. Cited in *ibid.*, p.154.
14. *Ibid.*
15. Yungblut, *Strangers Settled
    Here Amongst Us*, p. 104.
16. Cited in *ibid.*, p. 78.
17. Cited in P. Fryer, *Staying Power:
    The History of Black People in
    Britain* (London: Pluto Press,
    1984), p. 20.
18. I. Sancho, *Letters of the Late
    Ignatius Sancho, an African:
    To which are prefixed, Memoirs
    of His Life* (London, J. Nichols:
    1784), p. 292.
19. National Archives, *The Black
    Poor*, www.nationalarchives.gov.
    uk/pathways/blackhistory/
    work_community/poor.htm
    [accessed 14 July 2021].
20. J. Salter, *The Asiatic in England:
    Sketches of Sixteen Years' Work

Among Orientals* (London: Seeley,
Jackson and Halliday, 1873), p. 26.

**CHAPTER 2**

21. *East Anglia and the Hopkins
    Trials, 1645–1647: A County Guide*,
    University of Exeter [2014],
    http://practitioners.exeter.ac.uk/
    wp-content/uploads/2014/11/
    Eastanglianwitchtrial appendix2
    .pdf [accessed 11 May 2020].
22. J. Melton, *Astrologaster, or,
    The figure-caster. Rather the
    arraignment of artlesse astrologers
    and fortune-tellers* (London,
    1620), p. 21.
23. Cited in O. Davies, *Popular Magic:
    Cunning-Folk in English History*
    (London: Continuum, 2003), p. 70.
24. J. Glanvill, *Saducismus
    triumphatus: or, Full and plain
    evidence concerning witches
    and apparitions: In two parts...*
    (London, 1700), p. 109.
25. *Ibid.*
26. Cited in Davies, *Popular Magic*,
    p. 106.
27. Old Bailey Proceedings Online
    (www.oldbaileyonline.org, version
    8.0, 24 July 2021), January 1838,
    trial of John Hall (t18380129).
28. Cited in D. Oxley, *Convict Maids*
    (Cambridge: Cambridge
    University Press, 1996), p. 102.

**CHAPTER 3**

29. London Lives, 1690 to 1800,
    'Mary Knight, *c.* 1685–1716',
    www.londonlives.org/static/
    KnightMary.jsp [accessed 16 July
    2021].
30. J. Taylor, *A Bawd* (London, 1635).
31. Anon., *The Devil and the
    Strumpet: Or, The Old Bawd
    Tormented* (London, 1700).
32. *Ibid.*
33. S. Pepys, *The Diary of Samuel
    Pepys*, Wednesday, 25 March 1668,
    www.pepysdiary.com/diary/1668/
    03/25/ [accessed 25 July 2021].
34. R. Greene, *A disputation between
    a He-Cony-Catcher and a She-
    Cony Catcher* (London, 1592).
35. R. Ames, *The Female Fire-Ships:
    A Satyr Against Whoring*
    (London, 1691).
36. Anon., *The Wandering Whore*
    (London, 1660–3).
37. Pepys, *The Diary*, Saturday,
    23 August 1662, https://www.
    pepysdiary.com/diary/1662/08/23/
    [accessed 28 October 2020].
38. Cited in D. Cressy, *Birth,
    Marriage, and Death: Ritual,
    Religion, and the Life-Cycle in
    Tudor and Stuart England*
    (Oxford and New York: Oxford
    University Press, 2010), p. 255.
39. *Ibid.*, p. 243.

40. *Ibid.*, p. 240.
41. *Ibid.*, p. 241.
42. Cited in D. O'Hara, *Courtship
    and Constraint: Rethinking the
    Making of Marriage in Tudor
    England* (Manchester:
    Manchester University Press,
    2000), p. 85.
43. Cited in *ibid.*, p. 70.
44. J. Addison, 'The Adventures of a
    Shilling', *The Tatler*, no. 249 (1710).

**CHAPTER 4**

45. Cited in D. Webb, *Pilgrimage
    in Medieval England* (London
    and New York: Hambledon,
    2000), p. 48.
46. Cited in *ibid.*, p. 202.
47. Cited in Merrill Moore, Review
    of *Rats, Lice and History* by Hans
    Zinsser, *The Sewanee Review* 45,
    no. 2 (1937): 250–4, p. 250.
48. G. Potter, 'An Appreciation of
    Sir Emery Walker', *The Library
    Quarterly: Information,
    Community, Policy* 8, no. 3 (1938):
    400–14, p. 406.
49. *Manchester Guardian*, 10 March
    1904.
50. T. J. Cobden-Sanderson, *The
    Journals of Thomas James Cobden-
    Sanderson, 1879–1922*, 2 vols.
    (1926; New York: Burt Franklin,
    1969), vol. 2, p. 296.
51. *Ibid.*, vol. 2, p.181.
52. J. Gottlieb, *Feminine Fascism:
    Women in Britain's Fascism
    Movement, 1923–1945* (London:
    Bloomsbury, 2021), p. 20.
53. Cited in *ibid.*, p. 42.
54. Cited in *ibid.*, p. 19.

**CHAPTER 5**

55. Old Bailey Proceedings
    Online (www.oldbaileyonline.org,
    version 8.0, 28 July 2021),
    Ordinary of Newgate's Account,
    March 1729 (OA17290324).
56. Cited in C. Marsh, *Music and
    Society in Early Modern England*
    (Cambridge and New York:
    Cambridge University Press,
    2010), p. 64.
57. F. Furnivall, ed., *Philip Stubbes's
    Anatomy of the Abuses in England
    in Shakespeare's Youth, Part I*
    (1583; London: Trubner and Co.,
    1877–9), p. 171.
58. *The Actors Remonstrance, or
    Complaint: For the Silencing of
    their Profession* (1643), cited in
    Marsh, *Music and Society*, p. 108.
59. M. Bass, *Street Music in the
    Metropolis* (London: John
    Murray, 1864), p. 67.
60. *Ibid.*, p. 148.
61. *Great Britain's Wonder: Or,
    London's Admiration* (London,
    1684).

62. G. Catlin, *Adventures of the Ojibbeway and Ioway Indians in England, France and Belgium (Volume 1)*, (1852; New Delhi: Lector House, 2019), p. 105.

63. *Ibid.*, p. 99.

64. *Ibid.*

65. *Ibid.*

66. D. Shepherd, *When the 'Chute Went Up: The Adventures of an Edwardian Lady Parachutist* (London: Robert Hale, 1984), p. 66.

67. *Ibid.*, p. 137.

68. *Ibid.*, p. 161.

CHAPTER 6

69. Horace, *Satires*, 1.2.114–19, trans. C. Williams, in *Roman Homosexuality* (Oxford: Oxford University Press, 2010), p. 33.

70. Martial, 11.43.11–12, trans. Williams, in *Roman Homosexuality*, p. 25.

71. Cited in K. Olson, 'Masculinity, Appearance, and Sexuality: Dandies in Roman Antiquity', *Journal of the History of Sexuality* 23, no. 2 (2014): 182–205.

72. Martial, 7.62, trans. Williams, in *Roman Homosexuality*, p. 210.

73. E. Ward, *The History of the London Clubs, Or, The Citizens Pastime (London: J. Dutton, 1709), p. 28*; https://archive.org/details/cu31924028075293/cu31924028075293_djvu.txt. [accessed 4 August 2021].

74. Old Bailey Proceedings Online (www.oldbaileyonline.org, version 8.0, 25 September 2020), July 1726, trial of Margaret Clap (t17260711-54).

75. Cited in R. Norton, 'The Raid on Mother Clap's Molly House, 1726', www.rictornorton.co.uk/eighteen/mother.htm [accessed 25 September 2020].

76. Old Bailey Proceedings Online (www.oldbaileyonline.org, version 8.0, 25 September 2020), April 1726, trial of Gabriel Lawrence (t17260420-64).

77. *Ibid.*

78. *Ibid.*

79. Cited in R. Norton, 'Mother Clap's Molly House & Deputy Marshall Hitchin', www.rictornorton.co.uk/gu16.htm [accessed 25 September 2020].

80. *Daily Express*, 10 June 1918.

81. See L. Doan, *Fashioning Sapphism: The Origins of a Modern English Lesbian Culture* (New York: Columbia University Press, 2001), pp. 65–95.

82. *Eve: The Lady's Pictorial*, August 29, 1928.

83. *It's Not Unusual: A Lesbian and Gay History*, BBC Documentary, 1997; cited in Doan, *Fashioning Sapphism*, p. 123.

84. Doan, *Fashioning Sapphism*, p. 123.

85. J. Croft, ed., *Scrapeana: Fugitive Miscellany* (London, 1792)

CHAPTER 7

86. Cited in M. Norton, *Sacred Gifts, Profane Pleasures: A History of Tobacco and Chocolate in the Atlantic World* (Ithaca, New York, and London: Cornell University Press, 2010), p. 45.

87. F. W. Fairholt, *Tobacco: Its History and Associations* (London: Chatto & Windus, 1876), p. 58.

88. Cited in R. T. Ravenholt, 'Tobacco's Global Death March', *Population and Development Review* 16, no. 2 (1990): 213–40.

89. [King James I], *A Counterblaste to Tobacco* (London, 1604).

90. B. Rich, *The Irish hubbub, or, The English hue and crie briefly pursuing the base conditions, and most notorious offences of the vile, vaine, and wicked age, no lesse smarting then tickling* (London, 1618), p. 44.

91. Cited in J. Ashton, *The History of Gambling in England* (London: Duckworth, 1898).

92. C. Cotton, *The Compleat Gamester*, 5th ed. (London, 1725), p. 11.

93. Anon., *The Whole Art and Mystery of Modern Gaming Fully Expos'd and Detected* (London, 1726), p. 29.

94. *Ibid.*

95. Cited in L. G. Mitchell, *Charles James Fox* (Oxford and New York: Oxford University Press, 1992), p. 96.

96. Cited in C. Cock-Starkey, *The Georgian Art of Gambling* (London: British Library, 2013), p. 69.

97. Cited in *ibid*, p. 185.

98. J. H. Moore, *The Young Gentleman and Lady's Monitor, and, English Teacher's Assistant; Being a collection of select pieces from our best modern writers, calculated to... speaking the English language with elegance and propriety...* (London, 1780), p. 87.

99. Cited in O. Williams, *Gin Glorious Gin: How Mother's Ruin Became the Spirit of London* (London: Headline, 2014), p. 88.

100. Cited in P. Dillon, *The Much-Lamented Death of Madame Geneva* (London: Headline, 2002), p. 20.

101. *Read's Weekly Journal*, 21 July 1741, p. 4.

102. *The London Evening-Post*, 20–22 January 1741, p. 2.

103. *Read's Weekly Journal*, 3 April 1736, p. 2.

104. Pepys, *Diary*, Friday, 23 October 1663, www.pepysdiary.com/diary/1663/10/23/ [accessed 6 April, 2021].

CHAPTER 8

105. J. Oberndoerffer, *The Anatomies of the True Physician and Counterfeit Mountebank* (London, 1605).

106. See C. Jones, *The Smile Revolution in Eighteenth-Century Paris* (Oxford and New York: Oxford University Press, 2014).

107. J. Hart, *Klinike, or The diet of the diseased· Divided into three bookes. VVherein is set downe at length the whole matter and nature of diet for those in health, but especially for the sicke* (London, 1633), p. 98.

108. *Daily Post*, 14 July 1736.

109. J. Moore, *Columbarium of the Pigeon House* (London, 1735).

110. B. Jonson, *Volpone*, ed. B. Parker and D. Bevington (Manchester: Manchester University Press, 1999), p. 60.

111. I. Swainson, *Directions for the Use of Velnos' Vegetable Syrup* (London, 1790), p. 9.

112. D. Defoe, *A Journal of the Plague Year* (London, 1722), p. 46.

113. Cited in S. Adams, 'To the Greater Glory of Hop Bitters', *The New Yorker*, 16 August 1952.

114. H. Mayhew, *London Labour and the London Poor* (1851; Ware, Herts.: Wordsworth Editions, 2008), p. 19.

115. *Ibid.*, p. 3.

116. *Ibid.*, p. 71.

CHAPTER 9

117. Cited in E. Jones and S. Wessely, *Shell Shock to PTSD: Military Psychiatry from 1900 to the Gulf War* (Hove: Psychology Press, 2005), p. 3.

118. C. Demarne, *The London Blitz: A Fireman's Tale* (London: Battle of Britain Prints, 1991), p. 18.

119. See A. Calder, *The Myth of the Blitz* (London: Jonathan Cape, 1991), and R. Overy, *The Bombing War: Europe, 1939–45* (London: Penguin, 2014).

120. Cited in B. M. Schechter, *The Stuff of Soldiers: A History of the Red Army in World War II Through Objects* (Ithaca, New York, and London: Cornell University Press, 2019), p. 159.

121. Cited in A. Suppan, *Hitler – Beneš – Tito: National Conflicts, World Wars, Genocides, Expulsions, and Divided Remembrance in East-Central and Southeastern Europe, 1848–2018* (Vienna: Austrian Academy of Sciences Press, 2019), p. 739.

122. D. Edwards, *The Devil's Own Luck: Pegasus Bridge to the Baltic, 1944–45* (Barnsley: Pen & Sword, 2016), pp. 193–4.

123. See M. Scott and S. Krasilshchik, eds., *Yanks Meet Reds: Recollections of U.S. and Soviet Vets from the Linkup in World War II* (Santa Barbara, CA: Capra Press, 1989).

124. *Instructions for American Servicemen in Britain* (1942; Oxford: Bodleian Library, 2004).

# Further Reading.

Allason-Jones, L., *Women in Roman Britain* (York: Council for British Archaeology, 2005).

Andrew, D., *Aristocratic Vice: The Attack on Duelling, Suicide, Adultery, and Gambling in Eighteenth-Century England* (New Haven and London: Yale University Press, 2014).

Appadurai, A. (Ed), *The Social Life of Things: Commodities in Cultural Perspective* (Cambridge: Cambridge University Press, 1986)

Colvin, I. D., *The Germans in England, 1066–1598* (London: 'The National Review' Office, 1915).

Cressy, D., *Birth, Marriage, and Death: Ritual, Religion, and the Life-Cycle in Tudor and Stuart England* (Oxford and New York: Oxford University Press, 2010).

Davies, O., *Popular Magic: Cunning-Folk in English History* (London: Hambledon Continuum, 2003).

Doan, L., *Fashioning Sapphism: The Origins of a Modern English Lesbian Culture* (New York: Columbia University Press, 2001).

Findlen, P. (Ed.), *Early Modern Things: Objects and their Histories, 1500–1800* (London and New York: Routledge, 2013).

Fisher, M., *Counterflows to Colonialism: Indian Travellers and Settlers in Britain, 1600–1857* (Ranikhet: Permanent Black, 2004).

Gottlieb, J., *Feminine Fascism: Women in Britain's Fascism Movement, 1923–1945* (London: Bloomsbury, 2021).

Hume, I. N., *Treasure in the Thames* (London: Frederick Muller, 1956).

Jones, C., *The Smile Revolution in Eighteenth-Century Paris* (Oxford and New York: Oxford University Press, 2014).

Mayhew, H., *London Labour and the London Poor* (Ware, Herts.: Wordsworth Editions, 2008).

Marsh, C., *Music and Society in Early Modern England* (Cambridge and New York: Cambridge University Press, 2013).

McEnery A., and H. Baker, *Corpus Linguistics and 17th-Century Prostitution* (London and New York: Bloomsbury Academic, 2018).

Norton, M., *Sacred Gifts, Profane Pleasures: A History of Tobacco and Chocolate in the Atlantic World* (Ithaca, New York, and London: Cornell University Press, 2008).

Norton, R., *Mother Clap's Molly House: The Gay Subculture in England, 1700–1830* (London: Gay Men's Press, 1992).

Overy, R., *The Bombing War: Europe, 1939–1945* (London: Penguin, 2014).

Oxley, D., *Convict Maids: The Forced Migration of Women to Australia* (Cambridge and New York: Cambridge University Press, 1996).

Ponting, C., *The Crimean War: The Truth Behind the Myth* (London: Pimlico, 2004).

Porter, R., *Quacks: Fakers and Charlatans in English Medicine* (Stroud, Gloucs.: Tempus, 2001)

Sancho, I., *Letters of the late Ignatius Sancho, an African: To which are prefixed, Memoirs of His Life* (London: J. Nichols, 1784).

Schechter, B., *The Stuff of Soldiers: A History of the Red Army in World War II Through Objects* (Ithaca, New York, and London: Cornell University Press, 2019).

Shepherd, D., *When the 'Chute Went Up: The Adventures of an Edwardian Lady Parachutist* (London: Robert Hale, 1984).

Tidcombe, M., *The Doves Press* (London: British Library, 2002).

Warner, J., *Craze: Gin and Debauchery in an Age of Reason* (New York: Four Walls Eight Windows, 2002).

Weaver, J., *The Red Atlantic: American Indigenes and the Making of the Modern World, 1000–1927* (Chapel Hill: University of North Carolina Press, 2014).

Webb, D. *Pilgrimage in Medieval England* (London and New York: Hambledon, 2000).

Williams, C., *Roman Homosexuality* (New York: Oxford University Press, 2010).

Yungblut, L. H., *Strangers Settled Here Amongst Us: Policies, Perceptions and the Presence of Aliens in Elizabethan England* (London: Routledge, 1996).

# Sources of Illustrations.

Every effort has been made to locate and credit copyright holders of the material reproduced in this book. The author and publisher apologise for any omissions or errors, which can be corrected in future editions.

All commissioned photography by Matthew Williams-Ellis.

**a**=above, **b**=below, **c**=centre, **l**=left, **r**=right

**12–13** Museum of London/Heritage Images/Getty Images; **15l** *London Labour and the London Poor*, Henry Mayhew, 1862; **15r** Wellcome Library, London; **23** akg-images/Sotheby's; **25** Interfoto/Alamy Stock Photo; **26l** DeAgostini/Getty Images; **26r** Fabien Dany; **27** IanDagnall Computing/Alamy Stock Photo; **31** Fine Art Images/Heritage Images/Getty Images; **32** Van schiprechte, Hamburger Stadtrechts, 1497; **33l** Yale University Art Gallery; **33r** Allgemeiner Historischer Handatlas, Professor G. Droysens, 1886; **37, 38** Museum de Lakenhal, Leiden; **39** English Heritage/Heritage Images/Getty Images; **41** The Picture Art Collection/Alamy Stock Photo; **42** insidemystery.org; **43** Universal History Archive/Universal Images Group via Getty Images; **49** Art Collection 4/Alamy Stock Photo; **50** Werner Forman/Universal Images Group/Getty Images; **51** ©National Maritime Museum, Greenwich, London; **54** Mitchell Library, State Library of New South Wales; **57** The Picture Art Collection/Alamy Stock Photo; **58** *Saducismus Triumphatus*, Joseph Glanvil, 1689; **59** Fine Art Images/Heritage Images/Getty Images; **64** Oxford Science Archive/Print Collector/Getty Images; **67** The collections of the State Library of New South Wales; **68l** National Library of Australia; **68r** SSPL/Getty Images; **69** National Library of Australia; **72** ©Sir John Soane's Museum/Bridgeman Images; **75** ©Centraal Museum Utrecht/Ernst Moritz; **76** Wellcome Library, London; **77** The Metropolitan Museum of Art, New York; **79** Royal Collection Trust/©Her Majesty Queen Elizabeth II 2021; **81** ©The Trustees of the British Museum; **82** The Metropolitan Museum of Art, New York; **83l** Folger Shakespeare Library; **83r** ©Victoria and Albert Museum, London; **85–86** The Metropolitan Museum of Art, New York; **89** Interfoto/Alamy Stock Photo; **90l** The J. Paul Getty Museum, Los Angeles; **90r** Reproduced courtesy of the Chapter of Canterbury; **91** Bridgeman Images; **97** Bridwell Library Special Collections, SMU; **98** The William Morris Society; **99l** Cheltenham Borough Council and The Cheltenham Trust; **100** Digital Doves Type courtesy Robert Green; **101** Darling Archive/Alamy Stock Photo; **103** Topical Press Agency/Hulton Archive/Getty Images; **104** Mary Evans Picture Library; **105** Private Collection; **106** X3A Collection/Alamy Stock Photo; **109** Fine Art Images/Heritage Images/Getty Images; **110** Private Collection; **111** *Street life in London: with permanent photographic illustrations taken from life expressly for this publication*, J. Thomson and Adolphe Smith, 1876–1877; **113a** ©The Trustees of the British Museum; **113b** *The Frost Fair of 1814 on the River Thames in London*, Luke Clenell, 1814; **115** Album/Alamy Stock Photo; **116l** Sepia Times/Universal Images Group via Getty Images; **116r** Heritage Art/Heritage Images via Getty Images; **117** Buffalo Bill Wild West poster commemorating the company's 1887 performance before Queen Victoria, 1888. Calvin Printing Company, Hartford, Connecticut; **119** ©British Library Board. All Rights Reserved/Bridgeman Images;

**120** Artokoloro/Alamy Stock Photo; **121** Bruce Castle Museum (Haringey Archive and Museum Service); **123** Pictorial Press Ltd/Alamy Stock Photo; **124** Yale Center for British Art, Paul Mellon Collection; **127** Lupanar Brothel, Pompeii; **128l** ©The Trustees of the British Museum; **128r** ©Ad Meskens/Wikimedia Commons; **129l** Heritage Art/Heritage Images via Getty Images; **129r** Dea/A. De Gregorio/De Agostini via Getty Images; **131** Fotografica Foglia/Electa/Mondadori Portfolio via Getty Images; **133** *The Macaroni, a real character at the late masquerade*, Philip Dawe, 1773; **134** *The Women-Hater's Lamentation*, 1707; **135** Courtesy of The Lewis Walpole Library, Yale University; **139** The Metropolitan Museum of Art, New York; **141** The Women's Library, LSE Library; **142** ©Victoria and Albert Museum, London; **143l** The Women's Library, LSE Library; **143r** Fox Photos/Getty Images; **145** Hulton-Deutsch/Hulton-Deutsch Collection/Corbis via Getty Images; **146** Statens Museum for Kunst, Copenhagen; **148** The Metropolitan Museum of Art, New York; **151** Fine Art Images/Heritage Images/Getty Images; **152** *Panacea; or The universal medicine*, Gikes Everard, 1659; **153** ©The Trustees of the British Museum; **159** The Metropolitan Museum of Art, New York; **160** *The Compleat Gamester*, Charles Cotton, 1674; **161** The Metropolitan Museum of Art, New York; **163** Yale Center for British Art, Gift of Melville and Naomi Stone; **165** Wellcome Library, London; **166** Sepia Times/Universal Images Group via Getty Images; **167** The Metropolitan Museum of Art, New York; **170** Guildhall Library & Art Gallery/Heritage Images/Getty Images; **173** Provided by Harvard University; **174** Wellcome Library, London; **175** The Metropolitan Museum of Art, New York; **177, 179** Wellcome Library, London; **180** ©British Library Board. All Rights Reserved/Bridgeman Images; **181** Wellcome Library, London; **185** *Street life in London: with permanent photographic illustrations taken from life expressly for this publication*, J. Thomson and Adolphe Smith, 1876–1877; **186l** Chronicle/Alamy Stock Photo; **186r** *Street life in London: with permanent photographic illustrations taken from life expressly for this publication*, J. Thomson and Adolphe Smith, 1876–1877; **187** ©Hulton-Deutsch Collection/Corbis/Corbis via Getty Images; **190** ©Imperial War Museum (Art.IWM ART LD 1353); **193** GHI/Universal Images Group via Getty Images; **194–195** ©National Army Museum/Bridgeman Images; **199** World History Archive/Alamy Stock Photo; **200** German Air Force photographer/Imperial War Museums via Getty Images; **201l** Trinity Mirror/Mirrorpix/Alamy Stock Photo; **201r** Daily Mirror/Mirrorpix/Mirrorpix via Getty Images; **205** Sovfoto/Universal Images Group via Getty Images; **206l** Private Collection; **206r** Russian State Film and Photo Archives at Krasnogorsk, RussianArchives.com; **207** Shawshots/Alamy Stock Photo; **209** Nixon & Greaves/Mirrorpix/Getty Images; **210** Royal Collection Trust/©Her Majesty Queen Elizabeth II 2021.

# Index.

# Acknowledgments.

This book stands on the shoulders of the twenty-two mudlarks who entrusted me with their finds: Anna Borzello, Ed Bucknall, Monika Buttling-Smith, Florence Evans, Claire Everitt, Blain French, Robert Green, Mark Iglesias, Tobias Neto, Caroline Nunneley, Seán O'Mara, Łukasz Orliński, Guy Phillips, Nina Russell, Jason Sandy, Jay Sisu, Mark Sowden, Tony Thira, Mike Walker, Sarah Weston, Nicola White and Stuart Wyatt: thank you for so generously sharing your amazing artefacts, time and insight. My only regret is that it wasn't possible include every find you shared with me. I would also like to thank: the team at Thames & Hudson; my editors Jane Laing and Rose Bell for their expert guidance, associate editor Phoebe Lindsley for finding me and seeing the potential in my approach to social history; creative director Tristan de Lancey for his boundless enthusiasm and vision; production manager Sadie Butler for her work on the visuals; Matthew Williams-Ellis for his striking photography; my wife Liz Wade for tirelessly reviewing each draft and providing invaluable support in overcoming every challenge; London area Portable Antiquities Scheme Finds Liaison Officer, Stuart Wyatt for identifying many of the finds; Richard Hemery for his invaluable knowledge of pottery; David Higgins for his unrivalled expertise on clay tobacco pipes;

osteologist Julie Curl for identifying the Roman paw print; Tobias Neto, Museum of London curator Kate Sumnall and Gloria Winfield for their research on the Thames Victoria Cross; Bev Baker, Senior Curator at the National Justice Museum for identifying the prison warder's button; Dr Jenny Nex at the University of Edinburgh for her thoughts on the tuning peg and whistle; Professor Phil Withington and Dr James Brown at the University of Sheffield for allowing me to test some of my perspectives through the Intoxicating Spaces project and making me an Honorary Research Fellow of the history department; David Risley and Anna Borzello for encouraging me to write this book; my mother and my father for showing me objects from the past can be found all around us if we decide to go out and look for them.

## ABOUT THE AUTHOR.

Malcolm Russell has contributed to publications such as *Treasure Hunting, The Searcher* and *Beachcombing*. A lifelong mudlark, he studied history at the University of Sheffield, where he was also recently an Honorary Research Fellow in the Department of History. His remarkable finds were featured in the Thames Festival exhibition *Foragers of the Foreshore*.

Published in the United States and Canada in 2022 by Princeton University Press
41 William Street, Princeton, New Jersey 08540
press.princeton.edu

First published in the United Kingdom in 2022 by Thames & Hudson Ltd, 181A High Holborn, London WC1V 7QX

Published by arrangement with Thames & Hudson Ltd., London

*Mudlark'd* © 2022 Thames & Hudson Ltd, London
Text © 2022 Malcolm Russell
For image copyright information see p. 220

Designed by Daniel Streat, Visual Fields

*FRONT COVER.*
*The author searching the Thames foreshore at New Crane Stairs, Wapping, which were originally used to access the river by watermen and the passengers they ferried.*

*BACK COVER.*
*Eighteenth-century glass medicine bottle, found on the Thames foreshore at City of London by the author.*

ISBN 978-0-691-23578-3
Ebook ISBN 978-0-691-23597-4
Library of Congress Control Number 2021951136

Printed and bound in China by C&C Offset Printing Co. Ltd.

10 9 8 7 6 5 4 3 2 1

FSC www.fsc.org — MIX Paper from responsible sources — FSC® C008047